INDEX OF THE OFFICIAL REGISTER

OF THE OFFICERS AND MEN OF NEW JERSEY

IN THE REVOLUTIONARY WAR

Prepared by

THE NEW JERSEY HISTORICAL RECORDS SURVEY PROGRAM
Research and Records Section
Division of Community Service Programs
Work Projects Administration

Sponsored by

NEW JERSEY STATE PLANNING BOARD

CLEARFIELD

Originally Published
Newark, 1941

Reprinted for
Clearfield Company, Inc. by
Genealogical Publishing Co., Inc.
Baltimore, Maryland
1989, 1995

International Standard Book Number: 0-8063-0256-9

Made in the United States of America

PREFACE

The New Jersey Historical Records Survey Program was organized in February 1936 as a unit of the Work Progress Administration. It has operated since as a state-wide program associated with similar Historical Records Survey Programs throughout the nation, under the technical direction of Mr. Sargent B. Child, National Director. In New Jersey, this program is operated under the local sponsorship of the New Jersey State Planning Board, with State administrative supervision provided by Mrs. Elizabeth C. Denny Vann, State Director of Community Service Programs of the Work Projects Administration. The project, at present, is under the additional supervision of Mr. R. C. Branion, Regional Director of WPA.

The Survey has as its objective the preparation of complete inventories of the municipal, county, state, and federal archives in New Jersey, and the publication of these inventories as guides to the material of greatest historical interest. In addition to these inventories, work is proceeding in the cataloging and calendaring of manuscript collections, the inventorying of church archives, and the transcription of some of the earliest public records. In addition to these phases of work, the Survey has also conducted a state-wide inventory of early American portraits and early American imprints.

This publication, <u>Index of the Official Register of the Officers and Men of New Jersey in the Revolutionary War</u>, is not to be classified in any of the aforementioned categories of the Survey's editorial activities. Its purpose is strictly utilitarian, to serve as a key to the names of the New Jersey veterans of the War for Independence and to provide an aid to persons interested in genealogical research.

While this volume is a unique product of the Survey, it does nevertheless fit into several categories. Originally compiled under orders of His Excellency, Governor Theodore F. Randolph, by William S. Stryker, Adjutant General of the State of New Jersey, the Official Register was printed by authority of the State Legislature in 1872. The Official Register is, therefor, an official State document as well as an early New Jersey imprint, having been issued from the press of William T. Nicholson and Company, Trenton, N.J.

Practically every public library in New Jersey has its well-used reference copy of the Official Register, fondly known by genealogical researchers as "Stryker's". For many years, students of New Jersey history have been handicapped by the lack of a comprehensive and adequate index to the roster. In publishing this Index, the Survey is supplying an instrument of great usefulness to library patrons.

As indicated by the facsimile of the original commission by Governor Randolph to General Stryker, the work of compiling the record of Jerseymen who took part in the military service of this country in the Revolutionary War was as tedious as it was important. The same might be said of the index now supplied, almost seventy years later, by this publication.

The Survey is indebted to Miss Grace D. Rose, Librarian of the Morristown Library, Morristown, N.J., for proposing this publication and for preparing the Foreword. Preparations for publication were handled by the Morris County unit of the Survey, under the direction of John G. Mil The index was compiled by Mrs. Mabel Inslee, working under Miss Rose's direction, and was rechecked against the Official Register at the State Editorial Office of the Survey by Leon Gaynor and Joseph Clossick under the direction of Harry R. Fox, Supervisor of Publications.

The Survey is making a special free distribution of copies of this Index to insure its use in all public libraries in New Jersey as a companion volume to the Official Register. Copies are also being forwarded to the regular mailing list of universities, libraries, depositories and other research and reference centers throughout the United States.

The successful conclusion of any work of the Historical Records Survey, even in a single phase, would not be possible without the support of public officials, historical and legal specialists, and many other groups in the community. Their cooperation is gratefully acknowledged.

The entire personnel of the New Jersey Historical Records Survey Project wishes to express its gratitude to Robert W. Allan, State Administrator, for his personal service and assistance which have been and continue to be of inestimable aid to their sustained effort.

A complete list of Survey publications will be found at the end of this volume. Any inquiries or requests for technical data available from the Survey should be addressed to the undersigned at 1060 Broad Street, Newark, New Jersey.

                                                   Carl John Bostelmann
                                                   State Director

OFFICIAL REGISTER

OF THE

OFFICERS and MEN of NEW JERSEY

IN THE

REVOLUTIONARY WAR,

COMPILED UNDER ORDERS OF
HIS EXCELLENCY THEODORE F. RANDOLPH, GOVERNOR,

BY WILLIAM S. STRYKER,

ADJUTANT GENERAL.

PRINTED BY AUTHORITY OF THE LEGISLATURE.

TRENTON, N. J. :

WM. T. NICHOLSON & CO., PRINTERS

1872.

[Facsimile of original title page]

JOINT RESOLUTION NO. 5,

As to the Record of Soldiers of this State in the Revolutionary War, the War of One Thousand Eight Hundred and Twelve, and the Mexican War.

1. Be it resolved by the Senate and General Assembly of the State of New Jersey, That the Governor, the Treasurer, and the Comptroller be authorized to cause to be published such number of copies as they may deem proper, of the record of soldiers of this State in the Revolutionary War, which has been compiled in the Adjutant General's office, by order of the Governor; that they also be authorized to publish, if it can be prepared, a record of like character of the soldiers of this State in the War of One Thousand Eight Hundred and Twelve, and the Mexican War; that they be directed to make such disposition of the same, upon such plan and in such manner as shall appear to them most judicious and consistent with the public interests.

2. That the Treasurer be directed to pay, upon the warrant of the Comptroller, the expense incurred in carrying the foregoing resolution into effect.

Approved March 21st, 1871.

STATE OF NEW JERSEY)
)
)
EXECUTIVE DEPARTMENT,)
TRENTON, JUNE 1st, 1870)

GEN. WILLIAM S. STRYKER,
    Adjutant General of New Jersey,

                GENERAL:

                        A record of Jerseymen who took part in the military service of this country during the Revolutionary War has never been compiled. Having been informed that you have collected certain lists of the heroic men of that period, you are hereby directed to prosecute, as far as possible, your researches, with the clerical force of your office, and report the result to me. If successful, your labors will give new interest to the annals of this State, and perpetuate the names of the soldiers who fought in that early struggle.

                            THEODORE F. RANDOLPH,
                              Governor of New Jersey.

[Facsimile of original gubernatorial authorization]

STATE OF NEW JERSEY,
ADJUTANT GENERAL'S OFFICE,
Trenton, July 4th, 1871.

To His Excellency
   Theodore F. Randolph,
      Governor of New Jersey,

          Sir:

        When I first entered this office in April, 1867, I found few papers relating to the Revolutionary War. Constant inquiries from all parts of the Union for a certified copy of the records of soldiers of that war, brought the matter frequently to my attention, and I soon began to note such names and data as were verified in some way officially. These notations had already assumed considerable size and importance when your order of June 1st, 1870, was issued, and I immediately entered vigorously on such a research as I believe has hitherto been unattempted by this or any other State. The pension lists of the government, and the minutes of the Congress of the United States, and of the Legislature and Council of Safety of New Jersey, and all the records of the War Department, so far as they were found to relate to this State at that early period, were carefully examined. Original manuscripts, rolls of companies of Continental troops, diaries of officers, paymasters' memoranda, quartermasters' reports, treasurers' receipts, "returns" to the Commander-in-Chief, lists of soldiers paid at sundry times in Continental money, other lists of men who received notes for depreciation of said currency,—all these and various other kinds of vouchers have been most faithfully compared. The result of all this research I have now the honor to present you. After the lapse of nearly a century, and without the aid of any valuable documents preserved by the State, I cannot but be pleased with such success as I have met with. Not asserting that it is complete or without an error, I do affirm that no record has been made hastily or without what seemed to me to be well verified. I shall be thankful at any time to receive, from any one, well-authenticated proof of any omission or mistake, and make the same public.

    Before closing, I must acknowledge my indebtedness to Mrs. Dr. Jonathan E. McChesney, of Hightstown, for her kindness in allowing me an examination of the papers of the late Hon. Charles G. McChesney, for some years Secretary of State. They contained many invaluable records. To Miss Sarah S. Stafford, of this city, for permission to copy sundry lists of the Continental Line, in her possession. To the Hon. H. Van Aernam, Chief of the Pension Bureau, for the names and rank of certain officers, which I had tried in vain to discover. I am under great obligations to Mr. Jeremiah Dally, the efficient Librarian of the State, for a most hearty and zealous investigation of every volume or manuscript relating to the war, over which he has charge. To Col. Robert S. Swords, the Secretary of the Historical Society of New Jersey, the Hon. Whitfield S. Johnson, formerly Secretary of State, and others, for many courtesies. But I am greatly indebted to my assistants, Mr. William N. Nutt and James S. Kiger, who, with much experience in compiling the roster of New Jersey troops in the late war, entered upon, prosecuted, and finished the clerical part of this compilation with much zeal, great patience, and in a manner to me most satisfactory.

    If, sir, this work shall receive your sanction officially, and meet your personal approbation as a representative Jerseyman—connected as you are, paternally and maternally, with men who appear so distinguished in these pages—I shall account myself successful in the task of adding something to the history of my native State in that trying hour of her national birth.

                      WILLIAM S. STRYKER,
                      Adjutant General of New Jersey

[Facsimile of original transmittal letter]

Aaron, William	484	Adams, Joseph	485
Abbott, Caleb	140	Adams, Mathew	485
Abbott, Jacob	484	Adams, Matthew	140
Abbott, Jeptha	484	Adams, Paul	486
Abbott, John	484, 847	Adams, Richard	486
Abbott, Joseph	140	Adams, Samuel	486
Abbott, Richard	125, (2) 140, 484	Adams, Thomas	486, 872
		Adams, Uriah	448
Abbott, William	140	Adams, William	(2) 486
Abbott, William, Jr.	484	Addis, Simeon	486
Abbott, William, Sr.	484	Addis, Simon	380
Abeel, David	484, 872	Ader, Morris	140
Abeel, James	834	Aditon, Consider	140
Abel, John	484	Agar, Hugh	141
Abel, Jonathan	485	Ager, Archibold	141
Abel, Matthias	485	Aggings, Hugh	486
Abell, John	873	Agin, James	486
Abers, Abisha	485	Agness, John	486
Abers, Abner	485	Aher, John	486
Abers, Israel	485	Aikers, William	141, 486
Abers, Morris	485	Aim, Abram	486
Able, John	140	Aimes, John	141, 486
Able, William	140	Aitkins, -	110
Abner, Matthew	858	Aken, John	486
Abrams, James	485	Akers, Amos	141, (2) 486
Acans, John	485		
Ackens, Amos	140	Akers, Daniel	486
Acker, Thomas	850	Akers, John	486
Ackerly, Benjamin	448	Akers, Jonathan	486
Ackerman, Abraham	485	Akers, Obadiah	486
Ackerman, Johannes	485	Akers, Thomas	448
Ackerman, John	140, 485	Akers, William	474
Ackley, Bazaliel	140	Akin, John	486
Ackley, Daniel	485	Akors, Amos	141
Ackley, Hezekiah	485	Alberg, Jacob	858
Ackley, James	485	Albertson, Abraham	486
Ackley, John	485	Albertson, Albert	486
Ackley, Silas	485	Albertson, Garret	342, 362
Acy, Samuel	140	Albertson, Isaac	486
Adair, James	485	Albertson, Jacob, Jr.	486
Adams, Abel	140	Albertson, Jacob, Sr.	486
Adams, Andrew	485	Albright, Jacob	486
Adams, Asa	485	Alby, Jabez	141
Adams, Benjamin	858	Alden, Thomas	487
Adams, David	(3) 485	Aldhood, John	486
Adams, Elijah	485	Aldon, Thomas	141
Adams, Evi	485	Alexander, Joseph	843
Adams, Jacob	140, 485	Alexander, Quartus	487
Adams, James	485	Alexander, William	(2) 13, 63, 346,
Adams, Jediah	140		
Adams, Jeremiah	(2) 485	(Lord Stirling)	350
Adams, Jesse	485	Alger, Archibald	487
Adams, John	448, (3) 485	Alger, Joseph	858
Adams, Jonas	485	Aljou, John	487
Adams, Jonathan	485	All, Nathan	421

Allan, David	487	Alshouse, David	142
Allan, Joseph	487	Alston, Powell	142
Allcut, John	142, 487	Alward, Benjamin	488
Allen, see, also	142	Alward, Samuel	488
Alling end of Allens		Alwin, . . .	380
Allen, Aaron	141	Amam, John	142
Allen, Ananias	380	Ambler, John	483
Allen, Benjamin	141	Ammerman, Albert	488
Allen, Charles	329, 380, 871	Amerman, Daniel, Jr.	488
		Amerman, David	488
Allen, Cuff	487	Amerman, Jacobus	474
Allen, Daniel	(2) 487	Amerman, John	488
Allen, David	141, 487	Amerman, Powell	488
Allen, David, Jr.	487	Amerman, Powell J.	488
Allen, David, Sr.	487	Amey, David	488
Allen, Edward	487	Ammerman, Daniel	461
Allen, Enoch	487	Amos, John	142
Allen, George	110, 380, 441, 487, 847	Amy, David	110
		Anally, Patrick	142
		Anderson, Andrew	380
Allen, Gilbert	487	Anderson, Augustine	88
Allen, Henry	(2) 487	Anderson, Darias	142
Allen, Jacob	125, (2) 141, 461, 487	Anderson, David	328, (2) 380
Allen, Job	380	Anderson, Eli	488
Allen, John	(3) 141, (5) 487, 858	Anderson, Eliakim	488
		Anderson, Elijah	110, 488
Allen, Jonathan	487	Anderson, Enoch	488
Allen, Joseph	(3) 487	Anderson, Ephraim	16, (2) 17, 32, 33, 34, 77, 342, 362
Allen, Joshua	487		
Allen, Judah	487		
Allen, Moses	141, 487		
Allen, Nathan	(2) 488		
Allen, Nathan B.	488	Anderson, Ezekiel	142, 843
Allen, Peter	421, 488	Anderson, George	(2) 380
Allen, Richard	141	Anderson, Henry	142, 489
Allen, Robert	488	Anderson, Jacob	380, 489
Allen, Samuel	141, 448, (2) 488, 873	Anderson, James	58, 88, 142, (2) 380, (2) 48
Allen, Thomas	488		
Allen, William	(2) 488	Anderson, John	(2) 21, 38, 39, 77, 380, (5) 489
Allen, Zachariah	380		
Allent, John	488		
Alleor, Thomas	488		
Allerton, Jesse	142	Anderson, Joseph	142, 489
Allerton, John	488	Anderson, Joseph I.	22, (2) 36, 54, 55, 77 344, 371
Alleson, Seth	488		
Alling, (or Allen) John	142		
		Anderson, Kenneth	
Alling, Joseph	142, 380	Anderson, Lewis	489
Alling, Prudden	488	Anderson, Moses	489
Alling, Samuel	142	Anderson, Samuel	142, 489
Allington, John	488	Anderson, Thomas	142, 421, 489, 837
Allset, Jacob	488		
Allwin, Lawrence	488	Anderson, Tunis	489

Anderson, William	40, 51, 102, (2) 142, 489, 850, 858	Appleton, Peter	421
		Appleton, Samuel	491
		Archer, Benjamin	491
Andrew (Negro)	858	Archer, John	491
Andrews, Harbert	489	Archer, Peter	858
Andrews, Isaac	142	Archibald, Wm.	850
Andrews, James	142	Arents, Stephen	491
Andrews, John	376, (2) 489	Arey, Abner	491
Andrews, Malcolm	489	Armitage, Enoch	491
Andrews, Michael	489	Armstrong, Daniel	143
Andrews, Thomas	489	Armstrong, George	491, 858
Andrews, William	125, 142, 143, 474	Armstrong, Isaac	491
		Armstrong, James	491
Andries, Michael	489	Armstrong, Jas. F. (Rev)	75, 491
Andries, Robert	489	Armstrong, John	143, (2) 491
Angle, Jacob	489		
Angle, John	489	Armstrong, Robert	491, 858
Angle, Peter	489	Armstrong, Thomas	421, 491, 837, 850
Angle, William	489		
Angleman, Jacob	490	Armstrong, William	(2) 491
Angley, Peter	(2) 143	Arndt (or Arnet) Wm.-	491
Annely, Edward	839	Arnel, John	491
Annely, Thomas	839	Arnet, see, also Arndt	
Annin, Joseph	143	Arnet, Samuel	491
Annin, Samuel	421	Arnet, William	381
Annis, Abraham	858	Arney, David	143
Ansley, John P.	143	Arnold, Jacob	48, 374, 381
Ansley, Peter	143		
Anson, John	490	Arnold, James	491
Anthony, George	490	Arnold, John	491, 858
Apgar, Conrad, Sr.	490	Arnold, Lewis	492
Apperman, Garlin	143, 490	Arnold, Robert	347, 372, 858
Appleberry, Ambrose	490		
Appleby, Ambrose	490	Arnold, Robert, Jr.	492
Appleby, Amos	490	Arnold, Salvanus	143
Applegate, Andrew	(2) 490	Arnold, Stephen	143, 492, 858
Applegate, Asher	490		
Applegate, Barth	490	Arnold, William	474, 492
Applegate, Benjamin	143, 490	Arnold, Ziba	492
Applegate, Charles	490	Arrainson, Garret	492
Applegate, Daniel	135, 143, (2) 490	Arrainson, John	492
		Arrainson, Resolvent	492
Applegate, David	490	Array, James	143, 492
Applegate, James	143	Arrowsmith, Benjamin	492
Applegate, John	490	Arrowsmith, Edward	461
Applegate, Joseph	143, 490, 858	Arrowsmith, John	492
Applegate, Moses	126	Arrowsmith, Nicholas	492
Applegate, Nathaniel	490	Arrowsmith, Thomas	492
Applegate, Noah	490	Aruch, William	381
Applegate, Robert	143, (3) 490	Arvin, James	492
Applegate, Thomas	490, 850	Arvin, John	492
Applegate, William	143, (4) 491	Arvin, Peter	492
Applegate, Zebulon	491	Arvin, Robert	143
Appleman, David	491	Arwin, James	492
Appleton, Abraham	16, 33, 52, 53, 74, 88	Arwin, John	492
		Asbondon, William	492

Ash, James	492	Axford, Charles	(2) 31, 70, 480,
Ashcroft, Gibson	492		
Ashcroft, James	492		832
Ashman, James	16, 17, 99	Axford, James	493
Ashmore, Anthony	858	Axford, Samuel	14, 99
Ashmore, Jabez	492	Axtell, Ebenezer	29, 103
Ashton, George	143	Axtell, Henry	324, 362
Ashton, James	421	Ayers, Abijah	493.
Ashton, Robert	(2) 492	Ayers, Benjamin	493
Ashton, Thomas	492	Ayers, Daniel	859
Assit, Jacob	492	Ayers, David	493
Asten, John	492	Ayers, Ezekiel	448, 493,
Astim, Benoni	492		494
Astim, Edmund	493	Ayers, Isaac	494
Asy, Joseph	143	Ayers, Jacob	494
Atchley, Edward	847, 858	Ayers, James	494
Atchley, Thomas	143, 493	Ayers, Jediah	494
Atherton, Comiter	493	Ayers, John	494
Atherton, Joel	493	Ayers, Joseph	494
Atkinson, Isaac	493	Ayers, Levi	494
Atkinson, John	493	Ayers, Lewis	494
Atkinson, Joseph	850	Ayers, Moses	494
Atkinson, Samuel	493	Ayers, Nathan	494
Atkinson, William	143, 493	Ayers, Nathaniel	494
Atley, John	493	Ayers, Noah	494
Atol, John	493	Ayers, Reuben	494
Atten, Evert	493	Ayers, Samuel	494
Atten, Jacob	493	Ayers, Silas	494
Atten, Joseph	493	Ayers, Thomas	494
Atten, Zachariah	493	Ayres, Elice	494
Attenger, John	493	Ayres, Isaac	494
Atterman, ..	850	Ayres, Lewis	494
Auble, Andrew	493	Ayres, Obadiah	494
Augur, Hugh	143	Ayres, Phineas	(2) 494
Aulebat, Philip	143	Ayres, Reuben	144, 494
Aumoch (or Omock)		Ayres, Richard	494
Thomas	144	Ayres, Robert	144, 494
Aumock, Abraham	493	Ayres, Samuel B.	859
Aumock, John	(2) 493	Ayres, Silas	859
Aumock, Tunis	461		
Aumock, William	493		
Austin, ...	421	Babbet, Elkana	494
Austin, Cornelius	839	Babbet, Stephen	494
Austin, John A.	493	Babbit, Daniel	838
Austin, Joseph	493	Babbit, Isaac	461
Austin, Moses	493	Babcock, John	871
Auten, George	461	Babcock, William	494
Auten, John	(2) 493	Bachelor, William	144
Auten, Powell	493	Bachon, Benjamin	494
Auten, Thomas	(2) 493	Backoven, Jacob	494
Auter, Richard	441	Bacon, Aaron	144
Avert, J....	348, 376	Bacon, Abel	494
Avery, Jacob	858	Bacon, Andrew	494
Avins, Caleb	144	Badcock, Jonathan	855
Avis, Joseph	448	Badcock, Joseph	144, 381, 494, 495

Badeau, Elias	110	Baker, John	144, 381
Badgley, Asher	495		496
Badgley, Enoch	495	Baker, Jonathan	145, 496
Badgley, George	495	Baker, Joseph	496
Badgley, Ichabod	495	Baker, Lewis	496
Badgley, Isaac	495	Baker, Maline	145, 496
Badgley, James	495	Baker, Philip	496
Badgley, John	495	Baker, Samuel	496, 859
Badgley, Jonathan	(2) 495	Baker, Thomas	145, 496
Badgley, Joseph	(2) 495	Baker, Timothy	496
Badgley, Robert	495	Baker, William	145, (3)
Badley, William	144		496
Bagley, Asher	144	Baldwin, Aaron	496, 838
Bagley, Joseph	144	Baldwin, Annanias	496
Baham, Robert	495	Baldwin, Benjamin	135, 480
Baile, John	495	Baldwin, Caleb	(2) 496
Bailey, Aaron	144, 495	Baldwin, Cornelius	335, 348
Bailey, Abner	495		376, 497
Bailey, Asher	495	Baldwin, Daniel	13 (2) 30,
Bailey, Daniel	495		78, 145,
Bailey, H....	421		497
Bailey (or Baley) John	144	Baldwin, David	497
		Baldwin, Ebenezer	497
Bailey, Jonathan	144, 495	Baldwin, Eleazer	145, 497
Bailey, Richard	495	Baldwin, Elias	421, (2)
Bailey, Samuel	61, 144, 495		497
		Baldwin, Enos	497
Baily, see Baley		Baldwin, Ephraim	145, 497
Bainbridge, John	144, 495	Baldwin, Ethan	497
Bainbridge, Richard	495	Baldwin, Ezekiel	145, 497
Baird, Benjamin	347, 357	Baldwin, Ichabod	497
Baird, David	381	Baldwin, Israel	(2) 497
Baird, John	381, 495	Baldwin, Jabez	497
Baird, Joseph	495	Baldwin, Jeduthan	59
Baird, Obadiah	495	Baldwin, Jeremiah	497
Baird, Robert	495	Baldwin, Jesse	421, 497,
Baird, William	347, 362		835
Baisley, James	144	Baldwin, Job	497
Baits, James	144	Baldwin, John	145, (2)
Bake, George	495		497
Bake, Henry	495	Baldwin, John N.	497
Bake, John	496	Baldwin, John P.	497
Bake, Peter	496	Baldwin, John W.	497
Bakeman, Magness	496	Baldwin, Jonah	497
Baker, Cornelius	496	Baldwin, Jonathan	497
Baker, Daniel	126, 327, 448, (2) 496	Baldwin, Joseph	497
		Baldwin, Josiah	497, 838
		Baldwin, Levi	497
Baker, David	421, 496	Baldwin, Lewis	497
Baker, Elias	496	Baldwin, Linus	474
Baker, Ezekiel	496	Baldwin, Luther	498
Baker, Frederick	496	Baldwin, Martin	498, 859
Baker, George	496	Baldwin, Matthew	(2) 498
Baker, Henry	449	Baldwin, Moses	498
Baker, Isaac	144	Baldwin, Nathaniel	498

Baldwin, Samuel	(2) 498	Bamber, Jacob	421
Baldwin, Silas	(2) 498	Bandoine, John	871
Baldwin, Simeon	498	Banghart, Barney	145
Baldwin, Stephen	381, 498	Banker, Christopher	835
Baldwin, Thomas	(2) 498	Banks, David	835
Baldwin, Uzal	498	Banks, Jacob J.	499
Baldwin, Woolsey	498	Banks, Jacob T.	145, 499
Baldwin, Zachariah	498	Banks, Jameson	145
Baldwin, Zacheus	498	Banks, Josiah	499
Baldwin, Zadock	498	Bankson, Andrew	17, 32, 103
Baldwin, Zopher	498		
Baley, Daniel	498	Banta, Daniel	499, 500
Baley, James	(2) 498	Banta, Dirk	500
Baley, (or Baily)		Banta, Hendrick	500
John	(3) 498	Banta, John	146, (2) 500
Baley, Jonathan	498		
Baley, Joseph	498	Banta, Peter	500
Baley, Samuel	498	Banta, Samuel	500
Baley, William	499	Banta, Weirt	500
Baley, see also,		Baptist, John	146
Bailey		Barber, see also	
Balken, Benjamin	499	Barker at end	
Ball, Aaron	499	Barbers	
Ball, Abner	499	Barber, Francis	20, 35, 53, (2) 54, 65
Ball, Benjamin	850		
Ball, Bethuel	499		
Ball, Caleb	499	Barber, James	146, 500
Ball, Cornelius	145	Barber, Phineas	500
Ball, Daniel	499	Barber, Samuel	500
Ball, David	(2) 499	Barber, Thomas	344, 376, 500
Ball, Edward	110, 499		
Ball, Jacob	499	Barber, William	22, 35, 36, 67
Ball, John	449, (2) 499		
		Barcalow, Cornelius	146
Ball, Joseph	499, 835	Barcalow, S.A.	
Ball, Joshua	145	Barclay, Joseph	500
Ball, Justus	145	Barclay, Lewis	500
Ball, Nathan	449	Barclow, Gilbert	146, 500
Ball, Samuel	145, (2) 499	Barcly, Charles	855
		Bard, Jacob	500
Ball, Silas	499	Bard, John	500
Ball, Stephen	(2) 49, 74	Bardan, Henry	421
Ball, Thomas	499	Bardan, Isaac	500
Ball, Timothy	499	Barden, Haned	500
Ball, Uzal	499	Bardin, James	500
Ball, Valentine	145	Bardin, John	500
Ball, William	475, (3) 499, 843	Bareford, Lewis	449, 500
		Barger, John	500
Ballard, Alexander	145	Baris, John	500
Ballard, James	110	Barkelew, Runyan	461
Ballard, Jeremiah	22, 35, 36, 54, 55, 78	Barkelew, Runyon	481
		Barkelow, Coonrod	500
Ballard, John	499	Barkelow, Cornelius	500
Ballard, Nathaniel	499	Barkelow, David	500
Balor, Michael	499	Barkelow, Henry	500

Barkelow, Hunterdon	500	Barton, ...	421
Barkelow, James	500	Barton, Elisha	381
Barkelow, John	500	Barton, John	501, 850
Barkelow, S.A.		Barton, Jonathan	146, 501
Barkels, Farronton	501	Barton, William	38, 39,
Barkels, John	501		40, 49,
Barker, John	381		50, 51,
Barker, Peter	501		78, 146
Barker, Richard	501	Barton, Zebulon	441
Barker (or Barber), Robert	859	Bashit, Daniel	501
		Basset, Isaac	421
Barkley, George	501	Bastedo, George	501
Barkley, Hugh	501	Bastedo, James	501
Barkley, John	501	Bastedo, William	501, 859
Barkley, Joseph	501	Bateman, Daniel	501
Barksdale, Henry	501	Bateman, Manoah	501
Barnard, John	381	Bateman, Morris	502
Barnes, Andrew	381	Bateman, Moses	502, 146
Barnes, Daniel	381	Bateman, Peter	146
Barnes, David	146, 501	Bateman, William	146, 502
Barnes, John	501, 847	Bates, Benjamin	502
Barnes, Moses	501	Bates, Daniel	146, (2)
Barnes, Stephen	501		502
Barnet, George	501	Bates, David	381
Barnet, Oliver	343, 376	Bates, James	502
Barnet, William	362, 501	Bates, Joseph	502
Barnet, William M.	13, 28, 72	Bates, William	146, 502
		Batling, James	146, 502
Barr, ...	381	Battlow, Lifeless	502
Barr, Hugh	146	Baull, Matthias	146
Barr, William	108	Baxter, John	502
Barrel, Thomas	146	Baxter, William	147
Barrell, Thomas	501	Bayard, Joseph	502
Barrell, William	146, 501	Bayles, Augustine	381
Barrell, Zachariah	146	Bayles, Daniel	502
Barret, ...	501	Bayles, Platt	335, 362
Barret, Roger	501	Bayles, Richard	502
Barret, William	126	Bayles, Samuel	502
Barrett, Elijah	449	Bayles, Zopher	340
Barrett, James	146	Bayley, Barnet	147
Barrett, John	146	Bayley, James	502
Barricklo, Farrington	421	Bayley, John	502
Barrickle, John	501	Bayley, Jonathan	147, 502
Barron, Ellis	381	Bayley, William	382
Barry, Jacob	146	Baylor, George	62
Barry, John	146	Baylor, Michael	502
Barter, Robert	501	Beach, Abram	502
Barthoff, Jacobus	501	Beach, Asa	502
Bartholémew, Daniel	501	Beach, Daniel	502
Bartholf, Crynes	381	Beach, David	(3) 502
Bartholf, Cyrus	381	Beach, Elias	502
Bartlett, Hayes	146	Beach, Enoch	502
Bartley, James	847	Beach, Epinitus	502
Bartley, John	501	Beach, Gabriel	502
Bartlou, Cornelius	501	Beach, Isaac	502

Beach, Jabez	838	Beckerer, Abram	503
Beach, James	502	Beckhorn, Thomas	503
Beach, Jedediah	(2) 503, 838	Beckman, John	504
		Beckwith, Cyrus	382
Beach, John	461, 838	Becoman, Samuel	504
Beach, Joniah	147, 503	Becoman, Samuel	147
Beach, Joseph	382, 503	Bedel, Benjamin	110
Beach, Moses	503	Bedell, Abner	382
Beach, Nathan	503	Bedell, Benjamin	504
Beach, Nathaniel	503	Bedell, Isaac	461
Beach, Stephen	147, 503	Bedell, Jacob	147
Beach, Zopher	147, 503	Bedell, Joseph	147, 504
Beacher, Henry	835	Bedell, Moses	147
Beadle, Absalom	126	Bedford, Daniel	475
Beagle, William	147	Bedford, David	504
Beakes, Samuel	449	Bedford, Elias	475
Beam, Anthony	461	Bedford, John	504
Beam, Henry	503	Bedford, Joseph	147, 504
Beam, Henry, Jr.	503	Bedford, Stephen	504
Beam, James	503	Bedine, Nicholas	504
Beam, John	(3) 503	Bedlack, Benjamin	504
Beam, Lewis	503	Bedyne, John	504
Beam, Peter	503	Bee, Thomas	504
Beam, Samuel	147	Beedle, Abram	504
Beam, Yost	382	Beedle, Jacob	147, 504
Beamers, Josiah	850	Beedle, Joel	504
Beard, Bedent	503	Beedle, Nathan	832
Beard, Moses	503	Beedle, Thomas	147, 504
Beard, Robert	503	Beedle, Timothy	504
Bearmore, see Bevermore		Beedle, William	504
Bears, Henry	503	Beegle, Jacob	147
Beaster, William	503	Beehall, Casper	148
Beatson (or Beutson) Jacob	382	Beekman, John	504
		Beekman, Lawrence	504
Beatty, ...	39, 103	Beekman, William	461
Beatty, Daniel	859	Beekner, John	504
Beatty, David	147	Beekner, Michael	504
Beatty, Isaac	847	Beeman, Josiah	147
Beatty, Jacob	147	Beemer, Henry	504
Beatty, James	(2) 859	Beemer, John	504
Beatty, John	76	Beeseley, Jonathan	832
Beatty, Stewart	859	Beesley, Jonathan	382, 504
Beatty, William	147	Beesley, Walker	504
Beaty, John	503	Beetle, Josiah	148
Beauford, John	147, 503	Beigle, Thomas	504
Beavers, George	503, 841	Belange, James	504
Beavers, Joseph	342, 350	Balange, Nicholas	504
Beavers, Robert	382	Belange, Samuel	504
Beavin, Thomas	503	Belew, Daniel	504
Bebee, Thomas	503, 855	Bell, Henry G.	504
Bebout, John	503	Bell, Isaac	505
Bebout, Peter	(2) 503	Bell, Jabez	475
Beck, Robert	147	Bell, James	505
Beck, William	503	Bell, Jeremiah	505
Becker, Henry	835	Bell, John	148, 505

Bell, Joseph	505	Bennett, Samuel	(2) 148
Bell, Josiah	(2) 148	Bennett, Thomas	148, 506
Bell, Phineas	148	Bennett, William	506
Bell, Robert	505, 841	Bennington, Israel	506
Bell, William	460, (3) 505	Benscota, Cornelius	506
		Benson, John	506
Bellard, John	505	Bentley, William	148
Bellas (or Bellis), John	505	Benton, Zadoc	506
		Bents, John	506
Bellas, Philip	505	Bercan, Benjamin	506
Bellerjeau, Daniel	832	Bercan, John	506
Bellerjeau, John	832	Bercan, Peter	506
Bellis, see also, Bellas		Bercount, Daniel	506
		Berdan, Henry	421, 506
Bellis, John	148	Berdine, Walter	506
Belloes, Andrew	505	Bereger, Abraham	506
Bellos, Adam	505	Bereman, Thomas	148, 506
Bellows, George	859	Bergen, Christian	506
Bellyou, Cornelius	505	Bergen, Hendrich	506
Belton, Thomas	148, 505	Bergen, Jacob G.	422
Benham, Ephraim	148	Bergen, Jacobus	475
Benham, Joseph	111, 148	Bergen, John	855
Benham, Richard	505	Berham, Everet	506
Benham, Vinson	505	Berk, Richard	148
Benham, Zedekiah	505	Berkins, John	148
Benjamin, Daniel	505	Berkley, Hugh	506
Benjamin, Jonathan	838	Berkley, John	507
Benjamin, Nathan	505	Berksdeal, Henry	507
Benjamin, Samuel	505	Berlew, Abram	507
Benly, Joanthan	505	Berlew, Frederick, Jr.	526
Bennet, Abram	505	Bermit, Joseph	149
Bennet, Barnes	421	Berrion, John	507
Bennet, John	832	Berry, Daniel	507
Bennet, Joseph	126, 139	Berry, Ebenezer	343, 362
Bennet, William	506	Berry, Henry	507
Bennett, Aaron	148, 462	Berry, James D.	507
Bennett, Abraham	462	Berry, John	(2) 149, (2) 507
Bennett, Alexander	505		
Bennett, David	505	Berry, Peter	507
Bennett, Edward	505	Berry, Robert	(2) 149
Bennett, Ephraim	148	Berry, Sidney	323, 835
Bennett, Gershom	505	Berry, William	149
Bennett, Hendrick	505	Bertolf, James	507
Bennett, Isaac	462	Bertolf, John S.	507
Bennett, Jacob	505	Bertram, David	482
Bennett, Jeremiah	148, 382, (2) 505	Bertron, Abraham	475
		Besard, John	507
Bennett, John	148, 442, (4) 506	Bescherer, Abraham	347, 362
		Besson, John	449
Bennett, John L.	462	Best, John	507
Bennett, Jonathan	506	Bethe (or Birth), Archibald	149
Bennett, Joshua	382		
Bennett, Micajah	148	Bethuel, Gasper	149
Bennett, Michael	(2) 506	Betton, Thomas	507
Bennett, Nehemiah	148, 506	Betts, William	507

Beutson, see Beatson		Birth, see also Bethe	
Bevans, Matthew	475	Birth, (or Bethe), Archibald	508
Beven, Even	507		
Bevens, see also Bivens		Bishop, ...	871
		Bishop, Aaron	(2) 508
Bevens, see also Rivers		Bishop, Benjamin	508
		Bishop, Daniel	508
Bevens, David	507	Bishop, David	342, 343, 363
Bevermore (or Bearmore), Lewis	449		
		Bishop, James	150, 508
Bevin, Philip	475, 838, 859	Bishop, John	30, 50, 103, 435, 508
Bevins, David	149		
Bevins, Matthew	149	Bishop, Moses	508
Bezzard, John	507	Bishop, Richard	508
Bibble, George	832	Bishop, Shotwell	508
Bickner, John	859	Bishop, Vincent	150
Bickner, Michael	859	Bishop, William	(2) 150, 508
Bicknin, John	149, 507		
Biddle, Aaron	382	Bispham, Benjamin	508
Biddle, Jacob	149	Bissel, Samuel	150
Biddle, Moses	149	Bisset, Andrew	508
Bidlock, Benjamin	149	Bivens, see also Bevens	
Bier, Denice	422	Bivens, David	150
Begelow, Jabez	109, 481	Black, Alexander	508
Bigelow, Samuel	873	Black, Benjamin	508
Bigelow, Timothy	507	Black, Christopher	508
Biggs, John	507	Black, John	374
Biggs, Peter	507	Black, Simon	150, 508
Biggs, William	442	Blackford, Anthony	150, 329, 449, 508
Biglow, Aaron	422		
Bigner, Michael	507	Blackford, Benjamin	508
Bilberry, Woodrick	149	Blackford, Daniel	508
Bilderback, Jonathan	422	Blackford, David	508
Biles, James	449	Blackford, Ephraim	508
Billard, James	149	Blackford, Isaiah	508
Billings, John	507	Blackford, Jeremiah	508
Billington, Ezekiel	149	Blackford, John	508
Billington, Samuel	507	Blackford, Joseph	508
Billington, Thomas	507	Blackford, Manning	422
Bills, William	507	Blackford, Nathan	(2) 508
Bilson, William	149	Blackford, Phineas	508
Binge, William	507	Blackford, Samuel	508
Bingham, Osias	847	Blackledge, Ichabod	150, 509
Bingle, James	507	Blackledge, John	509
Birch, James	149	Blackman, Aaron	509
Bird, Henry	507	Blackman, Andrew	509
Bird, Isaac	149, 507	Blackman, David	509
Bird, James	507	Blackman, Godfrey	150
Bird, John	507	Blackman, John	509
Bird, Peter	507	Blackman, Nehemiah	509
Bird, William	111, 508	Blackman, Thomas	150
Birdsall, Burnet	508	Blackner, Godfrey	150
Birmingham, Daniel	149	Blackney, Godfrey	126, 509
Birney, Peter	149, 462	Blackstone, John	150

Name	Page
Blackwell, Beniami	509
Blackwell, Benjamin	509
Blackwell, Elijah	509, 841
Blackwell, Stephen	509
Blain, Thomas	422
Blain, William	382
Blaine, Benjamin	509
Blaine, John	509
Blair, Abraham	509
Blair, Benjamin	509
Blair, James	509
Blair, John	38, 39, 40, 54, 89, 449
Blair, Jonathan	509
Blair, Robert	61, 150, 509
Blair, Thomas	422
Blair, William	135, (2) 509
Blake, George	509
Blake, John	422
Blanch, Abram	509
Blanch, Isaac	509
Blanch, Thomas	327, 382
Blanchard, Clark	509
Blanchard, Cornelius	363
Blanchard, Isaac	150, 509
Blanchard, John	382
Blanchard, Laban	150
Blanchard, Labon	509
Blanchard, Rinear	20, 21, 94
Blandhard, William	150, 509
Blane, Benjamin	509
Blane, Jacob	509
Blane, John	509, 850
Blane, Robert	509
Blaney, Robert	509
Blany, Robert	150
Blaricum, Henry	150
Blauvelt, A...	382
Blauvelt, Abraham	510
Blauvelt, Abraham J.	382
Blauvelt, Abraham T.	510
Blauvelt, Abram	510
Blauvelt, Cornelius D.	435
Blauvelt, Frederick	150
Blauvelt, Harman	150
Blauvelt, Isaac	510
Blauvelt, Jacob	510
Blauvelt, Jacobus	510
Blauvelt, James J.	510
Blauvelt, James T.	510
Blauvelt, Johanas	510
Blauvelt, John	150, 510
Blauvelt, John A.	510
Blaw, William	510
Bleakman, James	510
Bleakman, Thomas	151
Blear, Robert	510
Blecker, John	510
Blew, Abram	510
Blew, Daniel	151
Blew, Frederick	510
Blew, Isaac	510
Blew, John	510
Blew, Sealey	510
Blew, William	(2) 510
Blinkerhoof, James	510
Blinkerhoof, Joris	510
Blizzard, Morgan	510
Bloodgood, John	151, 510
Bloodgood, Phineas	510
Bloodhead, Phenice	510
Blooks, James	510
Bloom, Abraham	510
Bloom, Frederick	510
Bloomfield, Aaron	510
Bloomfield, Captain	41
Bloomfield, Elias	510
Bloomfield, Ezekiel	510
Bloomfield, James	510
Bloomfield, Jarvis	37, (2) 55, 89
Bloomfield, Jervis	151
Bloomfield, John	511
Bloomfield, Jonathan	511
Bloomfield, Joseph	21, (2) 35, 67
Bloomfield, Moses	72, 511
Bloomfield, Nathan	511
Bloomfield, Robert	449
Bloomfield, Thomas	151, 850
Bloomfield, Thomas, Jr.	511
Bloomfield, Thomas, Sr.	511
Bloomfield, William	511
Blow, Michael	511
Blowers, John	511
Blowers, Robert	151
Blue, Cornelius	511
Blue, Daniel	511
Blue, Hendrick	511
Blue, Michael	511
Blue, Sealey	151
Boan, William	511
Board, Cornelius D.	511
Board, David	374
Board, John	511
Board, Joseph	382

Board, Philip	511	Bond, Jasper	152
Boayrd, Joseph	151, 511	Bond, John	512
Bockhover, George	422	Bond, Joseph	152
Bockhover, Jacob	382	Bond, Nathaniel	152, 512
Bockman, George	511	Bond, Samuel	512
Bockman, John	511	Bond, Thomas	512
Boden, James	151, 511	Bond, William	(2) 38, 78, 152, 347, 357, 512
Bodewine, Peter	151, 511		
Bodewine, William	511		
Bodine, ...	382		
Bodine, John	511	Boney, Michael	152
Bodine, Walter	511	Boney, Simon	152
Bodley, Nathan	151, 511	Bonger, John	512
Bogart, Abram	512	Bonham, Absalom	30, 40, 50, 51, 89
Bogart, Gilliam	442		
Bogart, Jacobus	327, 449		
Bogart, John	151	Bonham, Ephraim	152
Bogart, Peter	512	Bonham, John	513
Bogart, Samuel	512	Bonham, Levi	513
Boger, Samuel	512	Bonham, Malichi	843
Bogert, Casperus	512	Bonham, Zedekiah	513
Bogert, Cornelius	151	Bonia, William	513
Bogert, David R.	475	Bonnel, Aaron	152
Bogert, James N.	151	Bonnel, Abner	513
Bogert, Mathew	512	Bonnel, Benjamin	61, 152
Bogert, Nicholas	512	Bonnel, Gilbert	152, 513
Bogert, Samuel	512	Bonnel, Henry	152, 513
Boggs, Hezekiah	151	Bonnel, Jacob	513
Boggs, James	(2) 512	Bonnel, James	56, 57, 78, 328, 329, 383
Bohanin, John	512		
Bohanin, William	512		
Boice, George	512	Bonnel, John	513
Boice, (or Buyce) John	512	Bonnel, Nathaniel	513
		Bonnell, Abraham	336, 342, 357
Boice, William	512		
Boiles, Benjamin	512	Bonnell, James	152
Boiles, James	151, 512	Bonnell, Nathaniel	152, 513
Bolman, James	838	Bonnell, Samuel	152
Bolmer, Garret	512	Bonner, John	513
Bolmer, Robert	422	Bonnet, Aaron	152
Bolston, James	151	Bonny, James	383
Boltenhouse, Bedford	512	Bonny, Michawl	152
Bolterhouse, Joseph	151	Bonts, John	513
Bolton, John	151	Boon, Joseph	152
Bolton, Joseph	(2) 151	Boon, Moses	513
Bolton, William	151	Boorum, Hendrick	513
Boman, Benjamin	512	Boorum, Jacob	513
Boman, Coleman	512	Boorum, John	513
Bonam, Benjamin	382	Boorum, Nicholas	513
Bond, Abner	512	Boosey, Daniel	152
Bond, Benjamin	512, 859	Booth, William	513
Bond, Elihu	512	Booty, Joseph	513
Bond, Elisha	151	Boower, Henry	835
Bond, Jacklin	151, 512	Borden, Jesse	513
Bond, Jacob	512	Borden, Job	513

- 13 -

Name	Pages
Borden, John	513
Borden, Joseph	339, 350, 835
Borden, Joseph, Jr.	383, 835
Borden, Matthias	152
Borden, William	513
Bordet, Benjamin	513
Bordine, James	513
Boreford, John	152
Borhies, James	152, 513
Borton, Jonathan	513
Bosbourgh, John	152
Boss, Abram	513
Boss, Joseph	513
Bostick, William	513
Boston, John	152
Bostwick, William	36, 94
Bosworth, Daniel	513
Bott, William	339, 351
Boudinot, Elias	76
Boughner, Sebastian	514
Boulser, John	152, 514
Bound, Philip	514
Bound, William	152
Bours, James	514
Bowen, Charles	152
Bowen, Daniel	514
Bowen, Edward	514
Bowen, James	514
Bowen, John	152
Bowen, Joseph	153, 514
Bowen, Josiah	514
Bowen, Samuel	153, (2) 514
Bowen, Seth	17, (2) 32, 34, 94, 320, 420, 835
Bowen, Thomas	514
Bowen, Zadock	514
Bower, Elias	514
Bower, John	484
Bowers, James	109, 514
Bowers, John	135, 383, (2) 514
Bowers, Lemuel	(2) 514
Bowers, Levi	514
Bowers, Samuel	514
Bowers, Stephen	514
Bowers, William	514, 840
Bowing, Edward	514
Bowlsby, George	514
Bowlsby, Samuel	153, (2) 514
Bowlsby, Thomas	514
Bowman, Andrew	153, 514
Bowman, Coleman	153, 514
Bowman, Cornelius	514
Bowman, Edward	435
Bowman, John	514
Bowman, Nathaniel	16, 17, 32, 33, 34, 52, 54, 67
Bowman, Peter	514
Bowman, Thomas	153, 515
Bownd, Obadiah	515
Bowne, David	515
Bowne, Elias	515
Bowne, Henry	126
Bowne, James	515
Bowne, John	153, 515
Bowne, Joseph	475, 515
Bowne, Obadiah	859
Bowne, Peter	38, 39, 103, 515
Bowne, Samuel	515
Bowne, William	515
Bowyer, David	515
Bowyer, Henry	859
Bowyer, Jacob	859
Bowyer, John	859
Bowyer, Laban	126
Boyce, Adam	515
Boyce, William	153
Boyd, Alexander	153, 515
Boyd, George	515
Boyd, James	515
Boyd, John	126, 153, 515
Boyd, William	515, 847
Boylan, Aaron	153, 515
Boylan, James	475
Boylan, John	515
Boyle, Edward	153
Boyles, Edward	153
Boyles, James	153
Boyles, Jonathan	515
Boyles, Michael	515
Boys, John	515
Bozett, Robert	153
Brackenridge, Samuel	38, 99
Bracket, ..	449
Bracket, Nathaniel	515
Bradbury, Hezekiah	515
Bradbury, Hozea	515
Bradford, James	153, 515
Bradford, John	(2) 515
Bradrick, Daniel	153
Bradshaw, ...	462
Bradshaw, Thomas	153
Bradshaw, William	111

Brady, Barnabus	153	Breed, George	154
Brady, David	153	Brees, James	422
Brady, Dennis	153, 515	Brees, Samuel	154
Brady, Edward	153	Brees, Timothy	154
Brady, James	515	Breese, Garret	516, 848
Brady, Patrick	153, 515		859
Brag, see Bray		Breese, Henry	154, 516
Bragg, Henry	154	Breese, John	154, (2)
Braid, Joseph	516		516
Brailey, Robert	516	Breese, Samuel	345, 351
Bran, Joseph	154, 516	Breeze, Timothy	154
Brancroft, Solomon	516	Breis, Daniel	516
Brand, John	516	Breis, John	517
Brannan, Thomas	516	Brelson, William	154
Brannin, Isaac	461	Bresbey, William	449
Brannon, see also Bronnon		Bress, Cornelius	517
		Breton, Joseph	517
Brant, David	859	Brevoort, Elias	372
Brant, John	154, (2)	Brewbacker, Jacob	517
	516	Brewen, Barnabus	517
Brant, Lewis	383	Brewen, Elias	517
Brant, Mathias	462, 516	Brewen, Jonathan	517
Brant, Matthew	154, 516	Brewer, ..	383
Brant, Samuel	516	Brewer, Abram	517
Brant, Stephen	516	Brewer, Abram J.	517
Brant, William	516	Brewer, Eliezer	517
Brass, Herman	516	Brewer, George	(2) 517
Brass, Lucas	383	Brewer, Henry	517
Brass, Stephen	838	Brewer, Jacob	517
Brassington, Samuel	838	Brewer, John	154, (2)
Brasted, Isaac	516		517
Brawdwell, David	516	Brewer, John A.	517
Brawdwell, Ezra	516	Brewer, Jonathan	35, 99
Brawdwell, Simeon	516	Brewer, Paul	154
Bray, Andrew	154, 516	Brewer, Thomas	517 860
Bray, Daniel	383	Brewer, Timothy	517
Bray (or Brag), James	154, 847	Brewin, Joshua	154
		Brewster, Daniel	154
Bray, John	76, 836	Brewster, James	517
Bray, William	126	Briant, John	155
Brayman, Ezekiel	154	Briant, Samuel	517
Brearley, David	37, (2)	Brice, William	155
	49, 65,	Brickcount, Daniel	517
	334, 344,	Brickman, John	517
	351	Bridge, Benjamin	517
Brearley, John	516	Bridge, Ralph	155
Brearley, Joseph	16, 31	Bridge, Robert	517
	47, 78,	Briese, Henry	517
	342, 363	Briggs, John	517
Brearley, Solomon	850, 859	Bright, George	517
Breasted, Isaac	154	Bright, James	126
Breaty, David	154	Bright, John	517
Brecourt, Solomom	516	Bright, Philip	517
Bredan, Elias	111	Bright, Windham	517
Bredon, Sergeant	109	Brine, John	462

Brink, Aaron	155, 518	Brocaw, Adam	155, 519
Brink, Daniel	383	Brocaw, Benjamin	519
Brink, Emanuel	518	Brocaw, Burgum	462
Brink, Henry	155	Brocaw, Derrick	462
Brink, James	435	Brocaw, Evart	462
Brink, Peter	155, 475, 518	Brocaw, John	422, 519
		Brockover, Peter	519
Brink, Solomon	518	Broderick, Absalom	519
Brink, Thomas	450	Broderick, James	56, 78. 347, 363
Brink, Yorion	518		
Brinkerhoff, Cornelius	518	Broderick, John	519
Brinkerhoff, Garret	518	Broderick, William	111, 155, 462, 519
Brinkerhoff, George	435	Brokaw, Abraham	(2) 519
Brinkerhoff, Henry	518	Brokaw, Abram	519
Brinkerhoff, Jacobus	518	Brokaw, Corsparus	519
Brinkerhoff, James	518	Brokaw, George	155, 519
Brinkerhoff, Necause	518	Brokaw, Isaac	520
Brinley, George	518	Brokaw, Jasper	450
Brinley, Jacob	518	Brokaw, John	422
Brinley, John	422, 845	Brokaw, Peter	155, 475, 520
Brinley, William	518		
Brinson, John	518	Brokaw, Richard	520
Britt, Philip	518	Brokaw, Robert	520
Britt, Thomas	155	Brokaw, Solomon, Sr.	520
Brittain, Jacob	518	Bronnon, (or Brannon)	
Brittain, James	518	Thomas	155, 520
Brittain, Jeremiah	111, 518	Broockes, John	520
Brittain, John	518	Brookfield, Benjamin	520
Brittain, Joseph	518	Brookfield, Brown	520
Brittain, Samuel	475	Brookfield, Isaac	520
Brittain, William	(2) 518	Brookfield, Jacob	520
Britten, William	383	Brookfield, Job	383
Brittin, John	111	Brookhead, Benjamin	520
Britton, Abraham	(2) 518	Brooks, Almerin	34, 53, 103
Britton, Abram	518		
Britton, Daniel	155	Brooks, David	841
Britton, David	482	Brooks, Isaac	520
Britton, Israel	518	Brooks, James	155, 520
Britton, Jeremiah	(2) 519	Brooks, John	155, (2) 520
Britton, John	155, 519		
Britton, Joseph	155, (2) 519	Brooks, Jonathan	(2) 520
Britton, Nicholas	519, 860	Brooks, Oliver	520
Britton, William	155	Brooks, Seth	855
Broadhead, Garret	462	Brooks, Thomas	155
Broadhurst, Joseph	519, 848, 860	Brooks, Timothy	520
		Broon, William	155
Broadtrees, William	519	Brotherton, David	520
Broadwell, David	462	Brotherton, James	838
Broadwell, Jacob	155, 519	Brotherton, William	520
Broadwell, Moses	155, (2) 519	Brower, Abraham	375
		Brower, Abraham J.	482
Broadwell, Samuel	519	Brower, Abram	(2) 520
Broadwell, William	519	Brower, David	520
Brocaw, Abraham	519	Brower, Jacob	520

Brower, John	435, 520	Brown, Thomas	(3) 156, 435, (3) 522
Brower, Thomas	520		
Brower, William	520		
Browmen, Joseph	520	Brown, Timothy	156, 522
Brown, Aaron	462	Brown, Walter	422
Brown, Adam	155, 521	Brown, William	156, (5) 522
Brown, Andrew	383		
Brown, Anthony	327, 435, 521	Brown, Zebulon	157, (2) 523
Brown, Asa	155, 521	Browne, George	523
Brown, Asher	521	Browning, Jacob	(2) 383
Brown, Benjamin	422, 521	Brownson, Asbel	523
Brown, Benjamin A.	155	Bruce, Timothy	157
Brown, Charles	156	Bruen, Abraham	523
Brown, Daniel	13, 99, 345, 363, 521	Bruen, Caleb	442
		Bruen, Elijah	523
		Bruen, Jabez	523
Brown, David	34, 103, 156, (2) 521, 873	Bruen, Jeremiah	59, 67
		Bruer, John	523
		Bruer, Thomas	523
Brown, Ezra	156, 383	Bruere, James	383
Brown, George	156, (2) 521	Bruker, Abraham	157
		Brundage, Isaac	460
Brown, Gilliam	521	Brundage, Israel	383
Brown, Henry	156, (2) 521	Brundage, Solomon	523
		Bruner, Jacob	157, (2) 523
Brown, Isaac	521		
Brown, Jabez	521	Brush, David	157
Brown, Jacob	156, 521	Brush, Israel	523
Brown, James	(2) 156, (3) 521	Brush, Timothy, Jr.	450
		Brust, Israwl	157, 523
Brown, Jeremiah	156	Bryan, Jacob	157
Brown, Jesse	521	Bryan, John O.	157
Brown, Job	(2) 156, (2) 521	Bryant, Benjamin	157
		Bryant, David	523
Brown, John	89, (2) 156, 462, (6) 521, 522	Bryant, Jacob	157, 523
		Bryant, James	157
		Bryant, John	157, (2) 523, 850
Brown, John, Jr.	459	Bryant, Randolph	157
Brown, Joseph	383, (6) 522	Bryant, Thomas	157, 523
		Bryant, William	157, 523
Brown, Josiah	522	Buchal, Casper	523
Brown, Lewis	522	Buchanan, Alexander	523
Brown, Mathew	522	Buchanan, Robert	157
Brown, Nathan	522, 871	Buchanan, Walter	838
Brown, Obadiah	422	Buck, Elijah	523
Brown, Peter	135, 522	Buck, Ephraim	423
Brown, Phineas	522	Buck, Henry	523
Brown, Robert	325, 341, 357	Buck, Jeremiah	523, 874
		Buck, John	157
Brown, Rynear	522	Buck, Joseph	53, 89, 523
Brown, Samuel	(2) 156, 462, (2) 522	Buckalew, Abram	523
		Buckalew, Alexander	523
Brown, Stephen	156, 522	Buckalew, Cornelius	523

Buckalew, Edward	524	Burch, Joseph	525
Buckalew, Frederick	524	Burch, Richard	158
Buckalew, Gilbert	524	Burchan, Robert	525
Buckalew, Isaac	524	Burcrunt, David	525
Buckalew, John	383, 450, 524	Burd, Joseph	158, 525
Buckalew, Josiah	462	Burd, Richard	158, 525
Buckalew, Peter	157, 524	Burdan, Henry	525
Buckalew Runyon	524	Burden, Abram	158
Buckalew, Samuel	524	Burden, William	525
Buckalew, William	524	Burdine, James	525
Buckley, Cornelius	157, 524	Burdine, Wilson	525
Buckley, Reuben	524	Burding, Abel	158, 525
Buckleyou, William	524	Buren, James	158
Buckman, William	524	Burge, Jonathan	158
Budd, Barnabas	376	Burger, Henry	158
Budd, Conklin	157	Burges, Benjamin	158
Budd, John	524	Burgess, James	109
Budd, Joseph	339, 363	Burgher, Gerardus	158, 525
Budd, Josiah	524	Burgie, Thomas	525
Budd, Nathaniel	524	Burgin, John	442
Budd, William	524	Burk, Elijah	525
Budey, John	524	Burk, Henry	158
Budin, Abraham	158	Burk, Hubert	158
Budow, Hendrick	442	Burk, Samuel	525
Buffe, David	423	Burk, Thomas	525
Bugle, Benjamin	524	Burke, Herbert	111
Bulangey, James	524	Burkfield, Thomas	525
Bulangey, Joshua	524	Burlew, Abraham	525
Bull, William	56, 79	Burlew, Alexander	525
Bullas, Adam	524	Burlew, Edward	526
Bullin, James	524	Burlew, Frederick	526
Bullock, John	524	Burlew, Gilbert	526
Bump, Joseph	524	Burlew, Isaac	526
Bunn, Barnes	158	Burlew, John	475, 526
Bunn, Edward	375	Burlew, Josiah	462
Bunn, John	524	Burlew, Samuel	526
Bunn, Jonathan	524	Burlew, Thomas	159, 526
Bunn, Joseph	525	Burlew, William	526
Bunn, Thomas	435	Burlin, Peter	159, 526
Bunnel, Abner	158	Burnet, Aaron	(2) 526
Bunnel, Benjamin	158	Burnet, Andrew	526
Bunnell, Abner	525	Burnet, Daniel	526
Bunnell, Abram	525	Burnet, David	526
Bunnell, Daniel	158, (2) 525	Burnet, Ichabod	67
		Burnet, J.	850
Bunnell, James	525	Burnet, James	526
Bunnell, John	525	Burnet, James H.	526
Bunnell, Joseph	525	Burnet, John	327, 423, 450, 526
Bunnell, Samuel	158	Burnet, Josiah	450
Bunting, Abel	158, 525	Burnet, Mathew	526
Bunting, Ramoth	158, 525	Burnet, Mathias	526
Bunton, Robin	525	Burnet, Moses	526
Bunton, Samuel	525	Burnet, Ralph	838
Burch, James	111	Burnet, Rolf	526

Burnet, Samuel	526	Burt, John	527
Burnet, Squire	(2) 526	Burtes, John	527
Burnet, William	72, 341, 376, 526	Burtless, William	109
		Burtless, William, Jr.	159
Burnet, William, Jr.	72	Burton, John	160
Burnett, David	838	Burton, Samuel	527
Burnett, Edward	159	Burwell, Jedehiah	160
Burnett, Ichabod	159	Burwell, Joseph	527
Burnett, John	(2) 159	Burwell, Robert	527
Burnett, Joseph	159	Burwell, Thomas	527, 160
Burnett, Squire	159	Busbin, William	527
Burnett, William	159, 838	Bush, George	160
Burney, James	159	Bush, John	160, 527
Burney, James M.	159	Bushfield, Thomas	527
Burney, Peter	159	Busk, Joseph	160
Burnhart, John	159	Buskhart, John	527
Burnie, Peter	126	Bussingburg, William	528
Burns, Daniel	(2),159, (2) 526	Bust, Aric	528
		Butlar, John	528
Burns, Elijah	159	Butler, James	160, (2) 528
Burns, James	159		
Burns, Thomas	159	Butler, John	528
Burnside, James	379, 836	Butler, Richard	160
Burnside, Patrick	527	Butler, Stephen	528
Burr, Aaron	65	Butler, William	160
Burrel, Zachariah	159	Butterfoss, Andrew	160, 528
Burrell, Joseph	527	Buttersop, Jacob	160
Burrill, Robert	527	Butterworth, Moses	528
Burrill, Zachariah	527	Button, Daniel	160
Burris, John	159	Button, John	160
Burroughs, Anthony	527	Butts, Alexander	160, 528
Burroughs, Benjamin	527	Buyce, see Boice	
Burroughs, Edon	527	Buys, Jacob	528
Burroughs, James	159	Buzzy, Mathew	160
Burroughs, John	159, 462, 527	Buzzy, Mathews	528
		Byard, John	528
Burroughs, Jonathan	527	Byce, William	160
Burroughs, Stephen	527	Byn, Denice	423
Burroughs, Zebulon	423	Byram, Japhet	528
Burrowes, Eden	50, 89	Byram, Naphtali	528
Burrowes, Israel	848		
Burrowes, James	137		
Burrowes, John	56, 57, 67, 383	Cade, Aaron F.	160, 528
		Cade, John	160
Burrowes, John, Jr.	384	Cadmas, Andreas	528
Burrowes, Stephen	442	Cadmus, Henry	528
Burrows, David	527	Cadmus, Isaac	528
Burrows, Edward	527	Cadmus, John	528
Burrows, Henry	475	Cadmus, Peter	528
Burrows, Israel	527	Cadmus, Thomas	358
Burrows, James	527	Cadoser, Isaac L.	160
Burrows, John	159, 527	Cady, Daniel	160
Burrows, Joseph	527	Cagan, Solomon	160, 528
Burrows, Walter	527	Cahill, James	528, 860
Burt, Benjamin	159	Cahill, John	(2) 161, 860

Cahill, William	848	Campbell, Hugh	161
Cahoon, Jacob	161, 528	Campbell, Jacob	530
Cain, Dennis	161	Campbell, James	530
Cain, John	528, 873	Campbell, John	76, 161, 344, 373, 475, (4) 530
Cain, Joseph	528		
Cain, Samuel	528		
Caldar, Nineon	161, 528		
Caldwell, James	20, 75, 835	Campbell, Jonathan	161
		Campbell, Joseph	162, (2) 530
Caldwell, John	529		
Caldwell, William	529, 848	Campbell, Lewis	61, 162, 530
Callaghan, Daniel	161		
Callaghan, Noah	161	Campbell, McDonald	137, 482
Callihan, Daniel	161	Campbell, Moses	530
Calwall, Hugh	529	Campbell, Nathaniel	530
Calwall, John	529	Campbell, Peter	384
Camburn, Joseph	529	Campbell, Phineas	530
Camburn, Nathan	161, 529	Campbell, Richard	162
Cameron, Allen	850	Campbell, Robert	(2) 162, (3) 530
Camp, Aaron	529		
Camp, David	111, 529	Campbell, Samuel	530
Camp, Ephraim	529	Campbell, Simeon	162
Camp, Ezekiel, Jr.	529	Campbell, Spencer	530
Camp, Isaac	529	Campbell, William	(3) 162, 461, (2) 462, (2) 530
Camp, Jacob	529		
Camp, James	(2) 529		
Camp, James D	529		
Camp, Job	529	Campen, William	531
Camp, John	161, (2) 529	Campfield, Jabez	56, 73
		Campfield, John	531
Camp, Joseph	529	Campfield, William	384
Camp, Joseph, Jr.	529	Camson, Alexander	531
Camp, Joseph, Sr.	529	Candon, James	162
Camp, Nathaniel	(2) 384, 529	Canfield, Abiel	836
		Canfield, Abraham	832
Camp, Robert	529	Canfield, Benjamin	162
Camp, Samuel	529	Canfield, David	531
Campbell, Alexander	529	Canfield, Ebenezer	531
Campbell, Andrew	161	Canfield, Israel	531
Campbell, Archibald	(3) 529	Canfield, John	162, (2) 531
Campbell, Benajah	529		
Campbell, Christian	529	Canfield, Joseph	531
Campbell, Christopher	529	Canfield, Nathan	162
Campbell, Daniel	530	Canfield, Nathaniel	531
Campbell, David	(2) 530	Canfield, Timothy	531
Campbell, Dugel	530	Canfield, William	531
Campbell, Edward	161	Canington, Jacob	531
Campbell, Eleazer	530	Cann, John	111 531
Campbell, Eliscus	530	Cannion, William	462
Campbell, Ellis R.	530	Cannon, Thomas	162
Campbell, Enos	161	Canter, Jacob	860
Campbell, Frederick	161, 530	Cape, John	423
Campbell, George	(2) 161	Capon, Levi	531
Campbell, George W.	73	Capon, Robert	531

Name	Page
Cappel, Richard	531
Caranna, George	531
Carbon, Christopher	531
Carbury, Francis	112
Carby, Francis	162
Careck, James	531
Carens, John	531
Carey, Ezekiel	164
Carey, James	162
Carey, John	12
Carey, William	162
Carhart, Cornelius	342, 363
Carhart, Jacob	384
Carhart, John	531
Carhart, Richard	(2) 531
Carhart, Robert	(2) 531
Carhart, Samuel	328, 384
Carhart, Thomas	126, 531
Caries, Peter	531
Carill, David	162
Carl, Uriah	531
Carle, Aaron	531
Carle, Abram	531
Carle, Adrain	532
Carle, David	532
Carle, Elijah	532
Carle, Ephraim T.	162, 532
Carle, Israel	384, 532
Carle, John	162
Carle, Jonas	532
Carlisle, Ebenezer	163, 532
Carlisle, John	532
Carlisle, Langston	384
Carlisle, Longstreet	840
Carlisle, William	532
Carll, David	532
Carll, Loudon	532
Carlton, Francis	532
Carman, Daniel	163, 532
Carman, Elijah	532
Carman, John	(2) 532
Carman, Moses	163
Carman, Nathan	163
Carman, Nathaniel	532
Carman, Richard	532
Carman, Samuel	532
Carman, Stephen	450
Carman, Thomas	163, 532
Carmer, Abraham	163
Carmer, Isaac	532
Carmer, John	532
Carmichael, Alexander	423
Carmichael, Ichabod	532
Carmin, John	532
Carmon, Stephen	532
Carnes, Ephraim	532
Carnes, John	163
Carnes, Matthew	163
Carnes, Matthias	163
Carnes, Zophar	38, 39, 95, 384
Carney see also, Kearney	
Carney, Lawrence	163, 532
Carnine, Peter	112
Carnot, William	532
Carns, John	532
Carpenter, Ashman	532
Carpenter, Henry	532
Carpenter, Hope	533
Carpenter, Jacob	533
Carpenter, John	533
Carpenter, Philip	533
Carpenter, Powell	533
Carpenter, Richard	533
Carpenter, Thomas	346, 373, 375
Carpenter, William	533
Carperson, John	163
Carr, see also, Karr	
Carr, Ebenezer	533
Carr, James	533
Carr (or Kerr), John	163, 384
Carr, Paul	850
Carr, Peter	533
Carr, Samuel	533
Carr, Thomas	533
Carr, William	(2) 163, 533
Carragen, William	163, 533
Carrigan, Henry	163, 533
Carrington, Benjamin	533
Carrington, Jonathan	163
Carrington, Joseph	163
Carroll, Adrain	163, 533
Carroll, David	163
Carroll, Jeremiah	163, 533
Carroll, William	163
Carrunder, George	164
Carson, Charles	533
Carson, Joseph	533
Carson, Robert	533
Carter, Aaron	533
Carter, Abner	533
Carter, Barnabas	533
Carter, Benjamin	112, 384, 534
Carter, David	126
Carter, George	127, (2) 534
Carter, James	164
Carter, Job	164
Carter, John	423

Carter, Moses	534	Castner, James	535
Carter, Peter	534	Casto, see Castro	
Carter, Richard	164, 534	Casto (or Castro), Azariah	535
Carter, Samuel	164, 384, (2) 534	Casto, David	165, 535
Carter, Spencer	836	Castolin, James	535
Carter, Stephen	164, 847	Castor, Isaac	165
Carter, Thomas	423	Castro (or Casto), Azariah	165
Carter, Uzal	534		
Carter, William	32, 103	Catacunch, William	328, 423
Cartright, Aaron	534	Catalyou, Henry	535
Cartright, Solomon	534	Catarich, William	36, 103
Cartwright, Aaron	164	Caterline, Ebenezer	165, 535
Cartwright, James	850	Catherland, Joseph	436
Cartwright, Thomas	164	Cato, John	165
Carty, Daniel	164	Catolin, Joseph	535
Carty, Isaac	112, 164	Caton, Thomas	165
Carty, John	164	Catou, John	535
Carty, William	164, 534	Catrell, William	165, 535
Caruthers, James	534	Cattell, Elijah	384
Caruthers, Obadiah	534	Cattell, Jonas	535
Caruthers, Richard	371	Cattell, William	535
Case, Daniel	534, 860	Catterlin, Jonathan	535
Case, Elijah	534	Catterlin, Joseph	436
Case, Henry	850	Catterline, Jacob	535
Case, John	534	Catterline, John	535
Case, Joshua	534	Catterline, Joseph	327, 328
Case, Samuel	(2) 534	Cavaleer, David	535
Case, Thomas	164, 534	Cavaleer, John	535
Case, Tunis	534	Cavana, John	165, 535
Case, William	534	Cavance, Joseph	165, 535
Casey, Adam	534	Caveleer, John	535
Casey, Henry	112, 164	Cavendire, George	165
Casey, James	164	Cavener, George	535
Casey, John	164, 534	Cavener, John	165
Casey, William	112, 535	Caveny, Edward	535
Casgrove, Charles	164	Cavileer, John	165
Cashart, Robert	535	Cawood, David	165
Casker, Benjamin	535	Caywood, John	536
Casker, Simeon	535	Caywood, Thomas	536
Cason (or Casor), John	164	Caywood, William	536
		Cazan, Solomon	165
Casor, see Cason		Ceasar, James	165, 536
Casperson, John	164	Ceasar, John	165
Casperson, Tobias	535	Ceaser, John	536
Cass, Christopher	860	Ceaser (Negro)	860
Cassade, John	535	Ceers, Samuel	165
Casterline, Abraham	164, 535	Celes, David	165, 536
Casterline, Amariah	535	Celly, Jesse	536
Casterline, Benjamin	535	Chadwick, Caleb	536
Casterline, Hiram	165	Chadwick, Elihu	423
Casterline, Jacob	462	Chadwick, Jeremiah	436
Casterline, Joseph	535	Chadwick, John	165
Casterline, Silas	535	Chadwick, Levi	165
Castle, John	165	Chadwick, Thomas	384

Name	Page(s)
Chaffey, Thomas	536
Chaffy, Thomas	165
Chamard, James	166
Chamberlain, Aaron	536
Chamberlain, Clayton	536
Chamberlain, David	166, 536
Chamberlain, Godfrey	536
Chamberlain, Henry	536
Chamberlain, James	536
Chamberlain, John	(3) 536
Chamberlain, Joseph	536
Chamberlain, Lewis	166, (2) 536
Chamberlain, Niean	850
Chamberlain, Seth	166, 536
Chamberlain, Thomas	(2) 536
Chamberlain, William	342, 358, 536
Chamberlain, Zephaniah	536
Chamberlain, Uriah	112
Chamberline, John	536
Chambers, Alexander	379, 536
Chambers, David	324, 343, 351, 384, 450
Chambers, Henry	463
Chambers, James	(3) 166, 450, (4) 537
Chambers, John	166, (3) 537, 860
Chambers, Robert	537
Chambers, Roland	537
Chambers, William	384, 537
Chambers, Zebulon	537
Chamor, William	166
Champion, Daniel	537
Champion, John	537
Champion, Thomas	537
Chandler, Daniel	537
Chandler, Ichabod	537
Chandler, James	537
Chandler, James, Jr.	166, 537
Chandler, John	537
Chandler, Jonathan	537
Chandler, Martin	166
Chandler, Peter	537
Chandler, Samuel	(2) 166, 537
Chandler, Stephen	384
Chapin, Leonidas	13, 71
Chapman, Daniel	166, 537, 841
Chapman, James	537, 860
Chapman, John	537
Chapman, Joseph	166, 860
Chapman, William	(2) 537
Chappel, James	537
Chappel, John	537
Chappel, Thomas	537
Chappin, Leonard	166
Chappin, Leonidas	(2) 28
Chardewine, Anthony	537
Charis, Peter	537
Charles, Peter	538
Charlton, John	538
Charters, Joseph	127, 538
Chase, Daniel	166
Chasey, John	112, 463
Chasey, Thomas	166
Chatfield, Elthan	538
Chatham, John	423
Chattan, John	538
Chatterton, see also Shatterton	
Chatterton, John	166
Chattin, James	850
Cheesborough, ...	841
Cheeseman, John	538
Cheeseman, Joseph	538, 850
Cheeseman, Richard	385
Cheeseman, Samuel	538
Cheeseman, Thomas	538
Cheeseman, William	463, (2) 538
Cheeseman, Zachariah	538
Cherol, James	166, 538
Cherry, Henry	166
Chester, Hiram	166, 538
Chester, John	538
Chesters, Edmund	167
Chesters, Edward	167
Chesters, Jacob	167
Chesters, John	167
Cheston, John	167
Chew, Aaron	442
Chew, Richard	(2) 167, 538
Chew, Robert	538
Chidester, Holdridge	167
Chidester, Phineas	538
Chilcoat, Isaac	538
Childerhouse, John	167, 538
Childs, John	(2) 538
Chips, John, Jr.	538
Chips, Morris	538
Chishound, George	167, 538
Chose, Losey	538
Christey, James	(2) 167
Christian, Alexander	538

Christian, Charles P.	463		Clark, Michael	168, 540
Christie, Daniel	538		Clark, Morris	168
Christie, James	385		Clark, Nicholas	540
Christie, John	539		Clark, Noah	(2) 540
Christie, John W.	539		Clark, Norris	168
Christie, Peter D.	539		Clark, Parker	540
Christion, Michael	167		Clark, Peter	540
Christopher, Daniel	539		Clark, Reuben	(2) 540
Christopher, Jesse	167, 539, 860		Clark, Richard	168
Christopher, John	539		Clark, Robert	385, (2) 860
Christy, William	842, 845		Clark, Samuel	(2) 112, (2) 540
Chubb, John	167			
Chumard, Thomas	167		Clark, Thomas	(2) 320, (2) 385, (3) 540, 871
Churchward, William	167, 539			
Churles, John	539			
Claiborne, Richard	834			
Clark, Aaron	167, 320, 385		Clark, William	22, 35, 36, 95, (2) 168, 463, 540, (3) 541
Clark, Abner	539			
Clark, Abraham	26			
Clark, Adrial	539			
Clark, Alexander	(3) 539		Clarke, Arthur	168
Clark, Ambrose	539		Clarke, Robert	168
Clark, Andrew	167, 539		Clarke, William	541
Clark, Annanias	167, 539		Clarkson, Jeremiah	541
Clark, Azariah	832		Clarkson, John	450
Clark, Benjamin	(2) 539		Clarkson, Randolph	168, (2) 541
Clark, Bird	167, 539			
Clark, Charles	329, 450		Class, Frederick	541
Clark, Daniel	539		Clawson, Anthony	541
Clark, David	(2) 539		Clawson, Iraker	541
Clark, Edward	167, 539		Clawson, James	541
Clark, Eli	168, 539		Clawson, John	168, 450, 541
Clark, Elias	539			
Clark, Elijah	341, 358		Clayton, Asher	(2) 541
Clark, Ely	168, 539		Clayton, Elijah	541
Clark, Ezekiel	540		Clayton, Henry	168
Clark, Ezra	168, 540		Clayton, Jehu	168
Clark, Francis	540		Clayton, Job D.	541
Clark, Henry	540		Clayton, John	541
Clark, Ichabod	540		Clayton, Jonathan	450, (2) 541
Clark, Jacob	540			
Clark, James	168, (2) 540		Clayton, Joseph	541, 845
			Clayton, Noah	541
Clark, Japnet	450		Clayton, Robert	541
Clark, Jeremiah	423, 850		Clayton, Zebulon	541
Clark, Jesse	840, 850		Cleare, Godfrey	541
Clark, John	168, (2) 540, 832		Clemans, Richard	168
			Clemens, David	850
Clark, Jonathan	540		Clemens, John	168, 542
Clark, Joseph	71, 168, (4) 540, 850		Clemens, Richard	542
			Clement, David	542
			Clement, Victor	542
Clark, Joshua	540		Clemins, Henry	168

Clendennin, Isaac	542			Cochran, Jacob	169	
Clerkson, Lewis	542			Cochran, John	73	
Cleveland, Ichabod	481,	542		Cochran, Squire	169	
Clevenger, Thomas	168			Cock, David	543	
Clevenger, Zachariah	385			Cock, Henry	543,	850
Clevinger, Isaiah	168			Cock, Jacob	543	
Clifford, James	450			Cock, Jacob W.	543	
Clifford, John	436			Cock, John	543	
Clifton, George	112,	542		Cock, William	543	
Clifton, William	542			Cocke, William	543	
Cline, ...	385			Cocker, Samuel	169,	543
Cline, Hermanus	436			Cocker, William	543	
Clinton, Benjamin	542			Cockran, Tobias	543	
Clinton, George	542			Cockrum, Squire	543	
Clinton, James	542			Cockrum, William	543	
Clinton, Peter	169,	542		Codar, George	543	
Clisby, James	542			Coddington, Benjamin	169	
Clisby, Jonathan	542			Coddington, David	543	
Clisby, Joseph	542			Coddington, Enoch	543	
Clisby, Samuel	542			Coddington, James	544	
Cloason, Ebenezer	542			Coddington, John	(2) 544	
Clough, Alexander	13, 14, 15, (2) 28, 70			Coddington, Joseph	544	
				Coddington, Robert	137,	482
				Coe, Ebenezer	463	
Clough, Jacob	542			Coe, Enos	544	
Clover, Peter	542			Coe, Halsted	544	
Cloward, Abram	542			Coe, Jacob	544	
Clunn, John	385,	850		Coe, Peter	169	
Clunn, Joseph	385			Coe, Uzal	544	
Clunn, Matthew	33,	103		Coerser, John	169	
Cluson, Josiah	542			Coevert, Burgun	482	
Clutch, John	542			Coevert, Janis	169	
Clutch, Obadiah	169			Coevert, Thomas	475	
Clutten, John	542			Coevert, Tunis	169	
Clutter, Daniel	169			Coffey, Michael	169,	544
Clutter, Paul	169,	542		Coggswell, James	169	
Coach, Jacob	542			Coggswell, Joseph	135,	169
Coachey, Thomas	21, 22, 104			Cogh, Casperus	544	
				Cogh, Elias	544	
Coal, Barent	542			Coghran, Tobias	544	
Coal, Henry	169,	542		Cogswell, Joseph	544	
Coal, Jacob	542			Colas, ...	385	
Coalman, Samuel	543			Colbaugh, John	544	
Coalton, John	385			Colbaugh, Peter	544	
Coats, Charles	543			Colbert, Ezekiel	544	
Coats, Joseph	543			Colburn, Robert	544	
Cobb, Amos	543			Colby, Henry	544	
Cobb, Clisby	543			Cole, Aaron	169,	544
Cobb, John	543			Cole, Abraham	169,	544
Cobb, Mathew	543			Cole, Abram	169	
Cobb, Mathias	112,	543		Cole, Andrew	169	
Cobb, Morris	543			Cole, Benjamin	170	
Cobb, Samuel	543			Cole, Daniel	544	
Cobb, Thomas	113,	543		Cole, Henry	170, (3) 544	
Cobb, William	543					

Cole, James	544		Colyer, Thomas	89, 546
Cole, John	170, 544		Combs, Charles	546
Cole, Joseph	544		Combs, Gilbert	170
Cole, Josiah	385		Combs, Isaac	546
Cole, Richard	170		Combs, James	546
Cole, Samuel	463, (2) 544		Combs, John	546
			Combs, Jonathan	385, 546
Cole, William	544		Combs, Joseph	463, 546
Colegrove, ...	860		Combs, Lawrence	170
Coleman, Daniel	544		Combs, Moses	170, 546
Coleman, David	544, 545		Combs, Moses, Jr.	546
Coleman, Jacob	170, 545		Combs, Moses N. see also Combs, Moses W.	
Coleman, Joab	545			
Coleman, Job	170, 545		Combs, Moses W. (or N)	463
Coleman, John	(2) 170, 545		Combs, Samuel	(2) 546
Coleman, Joseph	545		Combs, Stephen	546
Coleman, Samuel	545		Combs, Thomas	385, 546, 838
Coleman, William	(3) 545			
Colerton, James	170		Combs, William	546
Coley, Nathan	463		Commens, John	170
Colfax, William	60, 61, 79		Commins, John	546
			Commins, Robert	546
Collard, Reuben	545		Conner, John	546
Collater, Jacob	170		Compton, see also Cumpton	
Colleger, Joseph	545			
Colley, Henry	170		Compton, Ephriam	546
Collier, James	855		Compton, Gabriel	546
Collier, Richard	170		Compton, George	127, 546
Collings, John	545		Compton, Jacob	170, (2) 546
Collings, William	545			
Collins, Abraham	545		Compton, James	546, 547
Collins, Albermarle	385		Compton, Job	423, 547
Collins, Anthony	545		Compton, John	(2) 171, (6) 547
Collins, George	463			
Collins, James	170		Compton, Joseph	(3) 547
Collins, John	(2) 170, (2) 545, 843		Compton, Lewis	547
			Compton, Richard	547
			Compton, Samuel	547
Collins, Joseph	385, 545		Comstock, Caleb	547
Collins, Richard	170		Con, Elisha	547
Collins, Stephen	(2) 170		Conally, James	171
Collins, William	(2) 170, 545		Conaway, John	547
			Concklin, Benjamin	547
Collough, Peter	545		Concklin, Joseph	171
Colt, Peter	837		Conckling, John	171
Colter, Alexander	545		Conden, James	171
Colter, John	545		Condict, Benjamin	547
Colvin, Caleb	545		Condict, Daniel	547
Colvin, James	(2) 545		Condict, David	341, 358
Colwall, Hugh	385		Condict, Nathaniel	547
Colwell, John	545		Condict, Zenas	547
Colwell, Robert	546		Condit, Abner	171
Colwell, William	546		Condit, Amos	547
Colyer, John	546		Condit, Benjamin	547
Colyer, Moses	546		Condit, Daniel	171, 547

Condit, Ebenezer	547	Conkling, Josiah	549
Condit, Enoch	547	Conkling, Nicholas	549
Condit, Isaac	547	Conkling, William	461, 549
Condit, Japhia	547	Conley, Neal	171
Condit, Japhsah	547	Conn, Samuel	39, 52, 89, 423
Condit, Japtha	548		
Condit, Joel	548	Connard, Andrew	549
Condit, John	334, 376, 450	Connel, Charles	171
		Connel, Michael	171, 549
Condit, Jonathan	386	Connelly, Bryant	549
Condit, Moses	548	Connelly, John	(2) 171 (2) 549
Condit, Philip	548		
Condit, Samuel	548	Connelly, Neal	549
Condit, Simon	548	Conner, Benjamin	549
Condit, Timothy	(2), 548	Conner, Edward	171, 549
Condon, James	171	Conner, Mathew	172, 549
Condon, John	171, 548	Conner, Timothy	(2) 172 549
Condon, Michael	171		
Conelyou, John	548	Connet, Anthony	549, 860
Conelyou, William	548	Connet, Mathew	549
Coner, Thomas	548	Connet, William	549
Conerd, James	171	Connil, George	549
Conger, Alfred	171	Connolly, James	172
Conger, Daniel	171, 548	Connolly, Thomas	172
Conger, David	548	Connolly, William	549
Conger, John	(2) 548	Connor, Benjamin	549
Conger, Jonas	548	Connor, Edward	172
Conger, Jonathan	(2) 548	Connor, George	549
Conger, Samuel	423	Connor, Isaac	549
Conger, Stephen W.	548	Connor, Patrick	549
Conger, Zenas	548	Conover, David	549, (2) 550
Congleton, Allen	386		
Congleton, Andrew	842	Conover, Elias	(2) 550
Congleton, Henry	476, 548	Conover, Jesse	550
Congleton, James	171	Conover, John	368, 550, 846
Congleton, John	450		
Coningham, John	548	Conover, John M.	550
Conk, Hendrick	548	Conover, John N.	550
Conk, John	548	Conover, Levi	172
Conkilton, David	548	Conover, Mecajah	550
Conklin, ...	860	Conover, Peter	550
Conklin, Elias	548	Conover, Peter B.	550
Conklin, Isaac	548	Conover, Ruleif	423
Conklin, John	171, 548	Conover, Samuel	550
Conklin, Jonathan	548	Conover, William	386, 550
Conklin, Joseph	548	Conrad, Adam	550
Conklin, Seth	548	Conro, Levi	550
Conklin, William	451	Conrow, Casper	172
Conkling, Benjamin	549	Consauly, John	550
Conkling, Daniel	549	Consdoffer, Nicholas	851
Conkling, Henry	549	Conselyea, Aaron	550
Conkling, John	549	Conselyea, Andrew	172, 550
Conkling, Jonathan	171	Conselyea, Ariel	172, 550
Conkling, Joseph	549	Conselyea, Ariel, Jr.	172, 550
Conkling, Joshua	549	Contraman, John	550

Convey, Peter	442	Coon, Daniel	172, 552
Convey, Thomas	550	Coon, Ebenezer	552
Conway, John	14, 28,	Coon, Felty	552
	29, 37,	Coon, Israel	127
	49, 53,	Coon, Jeremiah	480
	65, 172	Coon, Levi	552
Cook, ...	460	Coon, Peter	552
Cook, Benjamin	(2), 550	Coon, Runy	552
Cook, Charles	172	Cooper, ...	386
Cook, Daniel	346, 363,	Cooper, Abraham	552
	838	Cooper, Alexander	173, 552
Cook, David	550, 838	Cooper, Annanias	552
Cook, Elisha	550	Cooper, Benjamin	386
Cook, Ellis	172, 336,	Cooper, Constant	843
	345, 351,	Cooper, Cornelius	552
	851	Cooper, David	173, 552
Cook, Epaphras	551	Cooper, Derrick	552
Cook, Ezra	551	Cooper, Dickinson	552
Cook, George	38, 40,	Cooper, Gasper	173
	99, 172,	Cooper, Henry	552, 851
	371, 424,	Cooper, Ichabod	552
	(4).551	Cooper, Jacob	329, 386,
Cook, Henry	(2) 551		552
Cook, Jabez	551	Cooper, James	552
Cook, Jacob	172, (2)	Cooper, James B.	173
	551	Cooper, James W.	552
Cook, James	551	Cooper, John	173, (2)
Cook, Joel	551		552, (2)
Cook, John	172, 345,		553
	363, (2)	Cooper, Michael	553
	551	Cooper, Reuben	553
Cook, Jonathan	551	Cooper, Thomas	553
Cook, Joshua	551	Cooper, William	173, (3)
Cook, Patterson	551		553
Cook, Peter	(2) 551	Coosard, Valentine	553
Cook, Richard	551	Coovert, Daniel	173
Cook, S....	386	Coperat, Joseph	553
Cook, Samuel	551	Coperit, Edward	553
Cook, Silas	551	Copton, Richard	553
Cook, Stephen	172, 551	Cordry, William	553
Cook, Thomas	424, (2)	Corey, Abner	553
	551	Corey, Abraham	860
Cook, William	172, (2)	Corey, Benjamin	386
	551, (2)	Corey, Ezekiel	553
	552, 860	Corey, Isaac	553
Cook, Zebedee	373	Corey, Peter	553
Cooke, William, Jr.	552	Corey, William	553
Cool, David	552	Corflin, John	173, 553
Cool, Isaac	463	Corhart, Cornelius	553
Coolbagh, Peter	851	Coriell, Michael	553
Coolbaugh, William	552	Corigan, Henry	(2) 173,
Coole, Peter	552		553
Cooms, ...	463	Corin, see Covin	
Coon, Aaron	552	Corle, Samuel	553
Coon, Abijah	552	Corley, John	127

Corlies, Benjamin	386	Cortright, John	348, 363
Corlow, Benjamin	553	Cortright, Jonas	555
Cornelison, Garrett	553	Cortwright, Henry W.	386
Cornelison, John	(2) 553	Cortwright, Solomon	555
Cornelison, Michael	554	Corwell, Cornelius	555
Cornelius, ...	386	Corwin, Benjamin	838
Cornelius, John	173, (2) 554	Corwine, Bartholemew	555
		Corwine, George	127, 476
Cornelius, Peter	554	Corwine, John	173, 555
Cornell, Cornelius	(2) 554	Corwine, Joseph	555
Cornell, John	554	Corwine, Richard	424
Cornell, Joseph	554	Corwine, Samuel	555
Cornell, Nathaniel	554	Cory, Abraham	555
Cornell, Peter	554	Cory, Daniel	555
Cornell, Roeliff	554	Cory, David	173, 555
Cornell, Wesel	554	Cory, Elnathan	555
Cornell, William	554	Cory, Ezekiel	838
Cornine, Edward	173	Cory, Gabriel	555
Cornwell, William	173	Cory, John	555
Correl, Joseph	173	Cory, Joseph	555
Correll, Elisha	554	Cory, Peter	173
Correll, John	173	Cory, Samuel	555
Correll, Joseph	554	Cory, Stephen	555
Corriell, Abram	554	Cory, Timothy	173, 555
Corriell, David	554	Coryell, Abram	556
Corrington, Archibald	554	Coryell, David A.	173
Corrington, Benjamin	554	Coryell, Emanuel	843
Corrington, John	554	Coryell, George	386
Corrington, Jonathan	554	Coryell, John	173, 556
Corrington, Robert	173	Cosar, James	173
Corsat, Anthony	554	Cosar, John	173
Corsen, John	451	Cosart, John	173
Corshon, Joseph	386, 554	Cosgrove, Charles	173
Corshon, Joshua	386, 554	Cosgrove, Joseph	442
Corson, Abel	138, 554	Coshier, John	556
Corson, Abraham	554	Coshier, Simon	556
Corson, Cornelius	554	Coshow, Abraham	556
Corson, Darius	554, 873	Coshow, Cornelius	476
Corson, David	554	Coshow, George	556
Corson, Jacob	554, 872	Coshow, Jacob	556
Corson, Jesse	554	Cosier, Benjamin	556
Corson, John	463, (3) 555	Cosier, Simon	536
		Coslick, David	556
Corson, Levi	555	Cosner, Joseph	556
Corson, Nicholas	555	Cosort, John	556
Corson, Parmenas	555	Coss, George	556
Corson, Rem	555	Cosselman, William	556
Corter, Elias	555	Costard, Henry	556
Cortland, John	555	Costigin, Francis	14, 29, 99
Cortleyou, Harm	555		
Cortleyou, Hendrick	555	Costigin, Lewis J.	14, 15, 30, 95
Cortleyou, Henry	555		
Cortleyou, John	555	Cotheal, Alexander	556
Cortleyou, Ruliff	555	Cotheal, Isaac	174, 556
Cortright, Jacob	555	Cotman, Warrel	108

Cottnam, George	22, 104	Covert, Ben	558
Cottrell, Eleazer	556	Covert, Bunyan	558
Cottrell, James	556	Covert, Burgum	174, 558
Cottrell, Nicholas	556	Covert, Daniel	558
Cottrell, Thomas	556	Covert, Eder	558
Cottrell, William	556	Covert, Elison	558
Couch, John	556	Covert, Isaac	174
Coudrick, John	451	Covert, Jacob	(2) 558
Coulson, James	174	Covert, John	(2) 558
Coults, James	556	Covert, Luke	558
Couperthwaite, Joseph	386	Covert, Peter	174, 559
Coupland, Joshua	386	Covert, Thomas	(2) 559
Course, Isaac	556	Covert, Tunis	559, 838
Course, William	556	Covert, William	(2) 559
Courter, Peter	556	Covin, (or Corin) Edward	559
Courter, William	557		
Courtfellow, Tosan	557	Coward, John	442
Courtney, Luke	174, 557	Coward, Joseph	174, 559
Couterman, ...	424	Coward, Samuel	559
Covenhoven, Albert	174, (2) 557	Cowell, John	377
		Cowell, Isaac	559
Covenhoven, Benjamin	442, 557	Cowgill, John	559
Covenhoven, Cornelius	(4) 557	Cowper, Alexander	559
Covenhoven, David	557	Cox, ...	28, 75
Covenhoven, Denice	557	Cox, Abraham	873
Covenhoven, Dominicus	557	Cox, Andrew	174, 559
Covenhoven, Francis	557	Cox, Asher	559
Covenhoven, Garret	557	Cox, Jacob	559
Covenhoven, Garrett	557	Cox, James	174, 424, 559, 848, 860
Covenhoven, Isaac	(2) 557		
Covenhoven, Jacob	386, 557		
Covenhoven, Job	557	Cox, John	174, 559
Covenhoven, John	351, (3) 557, 558, 845	Cox, Jonathan	559
		Cox, Joseph	(2) 174, 559
Covenhoven, Joseph	(4) 558	Cox, Richard	21, 22, 35, 36, 52, 54, 55, 68
Covenhoven, Levi	558		
Covenhoven, Lewis	463		
Covenhoven, Luke	558		
Covenhoven, Lukus	558	Cox, Tunis	463
Covenhoven, Mathias	558	Cox, William	174, 559
Covenhoven, Peter	375, 442, 463	Coxe, Isaac	463
		Coykindall, Benjamin	387
Covenhoven, Ralph	424	Coykindall, Cornelius	559
Covenhoven, Ruleif	424	Coykindall, Samuel	559
Covenhoven, Ruliff	860	Coykindall, William	559
Covenhoven, Ruliff	558	Coyne, Dominie	174
Covenhoven, Rutes	558	Cozens, John	174, 387, 559
Covenhoven, Theodorus	463		
Covenhoven, Theodosius	558	Cozens, Samuel	174
Covenhoven, William	386, (3) 558	Cozier, Benjamin	559
		Crab, James	559
Covenover, Joseph	387	Crabb, James	174
Covert, Abraham	451	Craft, Robert	559
Covert, Adrian	558	Crafton, John	174, 560

Crager, Samuel	560	Crane, Israel	460
Craig, Daniel	127, 174	Crane, Israel, Jr.	561
Craig, Daniel T.	560	Crane, Jacob	325, 341, 358, 387
Craig, David	463, 560		
Craig, Elias	560	Crane, James	175, (2) 561
Craig, Frazee	560		
Craig, James	33, 34, 104, 387, 451, 560	Crane, Jesse	175, 561
		Crane, John	175, 436, 442, (4) 561
Craig, John	59, 79, 327, 329, 375, (2) 387, 436, (3) 560, 860	Crane, Jonas	561
		Crane, Jonathan	175, 451
		Crane, Jonathan E.	561
		Crane, Joseph	(2) 175, 442, 561
Craig, Moses	560	Crane, Joshua	(2) 175, 387
Craig, Samuel	560		
Craig, Thomas	175, 560	Crane, Josiah	387
Craig, William	860	Crane, Mathias	561
Craige, John	113	Crane, Moses	(2) 561
Craley, Hugh	175	Crane, Nathan	371, 561
Cramer, Andrew	175	Crane, Nathaniel	(2) 561
Cramer, Frederick	387	Crane, Obadiah	463
Cramer, John	860	Crane, Obed.	561
Cramer, Josiah	175	Crane, Phineas	561
Cramer, Noadiah	860	Crane, Rufus	561
Crammer, David	560	Crane, Samuel	561
Crammer, Isaac	560	Crane, Sayres	562
Crammer, Israel	560	Crane, Seth	562
Crammer, Peter	560	Crane, Silas	175, 562
Crammer, Seymour	560	Crane, Stephen	175, 562
Cramner, William	175	Crane, Sutphen	562
Crampton, William	560	Crane, Timothy	562
Crandell, Levi	560	Crane, William	56, 79, 363, 562
Crandle, Elihu	560		
Crane, ...	848	Cranmer, John	851
Crane, Aaron	(2) 175, (2) 560	Cranmore, William	562
		Craven, ...	342, 379
Crane, Abraham	560	Craven, Joseph	175
Crane, Amos	175, (2) 560	Craven, Stophel	175
		Craven, William	176, 562
Crane, Asa	175, (2) 560	Craw, Thomas	562
		Crawford, Eleazer	873
Crane, Benjamin	480	Crawford, James	424, 562
Crane, Caleb	424	Crawford, Joseph	176
Crane, Daniel	561	Crawford, Richard	562
Crane, David	(2) 561	Crawford, Stephen	562
Crane, David D.	480	Crawford, William G	562
Crane, Eliakim	135	Cray, Jacob	562
Crane, Eliakum	561	Cray, James	562
Crane, Elias	561	Crealy, Hugh	176, 562
Crane, Elijah	(2) 561	Creasey, Alexander	562
Crane, Ezekiel	175, 387	Creasey, William	562
Crane, Ichabod	561	Creeley, Nicholas	860
Crane, Isaac	561	Creesey, Andrew	562

- 31 -

Name	Pages	Name	Pages
Creesey, James	(2) 562	Crowell, Samuel	563, 851
Cregar, William	443	Crowell, Sylvanus	563
Creike, Andrew	176	Crowfoot, Joseph	177
Cremer, William	138, 176	Crowfoot, Stephen	177
Cremn, Godfrey	851	Crozer, John	563
Cresse, Amos	48, 443	Cruger, John	563
Cresse, Jacob	451	Cruly, John	177
Cresse, John	47, 176, 387	Crum, Henry	563
		Crum, Richard	177, 563
Cresse, Matthias	139	Crumb, George	177
Creyser, Frederick	176	Crunel, Henry	563
Crill, John	127, 176	Cruser, Cornelius	851
Crill, Joseph	562	Crutch, Isaiah	861
Crill, Martin	176	Cryer, John	563
Crilly, John	562	Cryier, Frederick	177
Crineshea, John D.	375, 843	Cubberson, James	563
Cripps, Whitton	324, 337, 346, 351	Cuffee, Amos	564
		Cuffey, William (Indian)	177, 564
Crisman, George	562		
Critser, Leonard	176, 562	Cugle, Peter	564
Crittenden, Nathaniel	424	Cugo, John	177
Critter, Leonard	860	Cugo, Thomas	177
Croel, Jacob	563	Cullom, Cornelius	564
Croel, Joel	563	Cullum, William	564
Croel, Joseph	563	Cully, John	177
Croes, John	460, 563	Cully, William	177, 564
Croft, William	176	Culpit, Andrew	177
Croine, George	176	Culver, Abraham	564
Crolus, John	563	Culver, Nathaniel	564
Crolus, William	563	Culver, Samuel	(2) 564
Cromwell, Oliver (Indian)	176, 563	Culvert, Azariah	564
		Cumberford, James	564
Cronk, Mathew	563	Cumming, John N.	17, 31, 33, 49, 51, 52, 54, 66
Crook, John	843		
Crook, Martin	176		
Crookshanks, William	176		
Cross, Samuel	563	Cummings, John	851
Crossman, Amos	176	Cummings, Richard	564, 861
Crossman, Joshua	176, 563	Cummings, William	463
Crouce, Adam	176, 563	Cummins, Asa	177
Crow, Abram	563	Cummins, Jacob	564
Crow, David	443	Cummins, John	564
Crow, Eleseus	563	Cummins, Richard	564
Crow, Garret	176, 476, 563	Cummins, Robert	347, 377, 564
Crow, Jeremiah	177	Cummins, Theophilus	177
Crow, Samuel	343, 358	Cummins, William	443
Crowell, Aaron	563	Cummon, Minard	564
Crowell, Daniel	563	Cumpton, Aaron	177
Crowell, David	177, (2) 563	Cumpton, Ezekiel	564
		Cumpton, (or Compton) George	177
Crowell, Edward	563		
Crowell, John	563	Cumpton, (or Compton) James	177
Crowell, Joseph	177, 463, 563		
		Cumpton, John	564

Cuney, George	178	Dallas, Archibald.	14, 29, 30, 40, 56, 79, 387
Cunningham, Daniel	178		
Cunningham, John	(2) 178, 460, 564		
Cunningham, Matthew	564	Dalleman, Robert	178, 565
Cunningham, Richard	178	Dalley, Gifford	387
Cunningham, Thomas	564	Dallis, Samuel	565
Cunter, Jacob	861	Dally (or Dalby), Gifford	836
Cuntryman, Conrad	564		
Curly, John	178	Dally, Jeremiah	565
Curren, Richard	564	Dally, Samuel	565
Currington, Jonathan	861	Dalrymple, Edmund	565
Curry, James	851	Dalrymple, William	565
Curry, John	(3) 178, 564	Dalton, James	(2) 178
		Dalton, William	178
Curry, Joseph	76	Dan, William	565
Curry, Samuel	(2) 564	Dana, Daniel	178
Curtis, ...	387	Danburry, William	565
Curtis, Benjamin	564	Dane, James	565
Curtis, John	113, 564	Dane, Joseph	179, 565
Curtis, Joseph	838	Danelson, John	565
Curtis, Marmaduke	36, 47, 95, 387, 845	Danfield, John	565
		Dangwell, John	565
		Daniels, Jeremiah	179 (2) 566
Curtis, Thomas	564		
Curwin, Isaac	564	Daniels, John	387
Curwin, Joseph	565	Daniels, Jonathan	566
Curwin, Samuel	565	Daniels, Kidd	566
Custart, John	565	Daniels, Randolph	566
Custord, Isaac	178, 565	Daniels, Richard	566
Cuthright, Aaron	565	Daniels, Thomas	179, 566
Cutlar, Benjamin	565	Daniels, William	566
Cutlar, Jesse	565	Daniely, Daniel	179
Cutler, James	178	Danigin, John	179, 566
Cutler, John	178	Danolson, William	566
Cuttance, William	424	Dansee, Ebenezer	566
Cutter, Ebenezer	178	Danser, Joshua	851
Cutter, James	565	Daran, Peter	851
Cutter, John	565	Darby, Ephraim	37, 53, 54, 71, 388
Cutter, Kelsey	565		
Cutter, Samuel	565		
Cutter, Stephen	565	Darby, John	566
Cuyger, Frederick	178	Darby, Philip	566
		Darby, Samuel	566
		Darby, William	135
Dailey, Darius	565	Dare, Benoni	832
Dailey, John	178, 464	Dare, David	36, 104
Dailey, Michael	(2) 178	Dare, Philip	179, 484
Dair, Cain	565	Darey, John	179
Dair, John	565	Darwin, John	138
Dalby, see Dally		Daston, James	179, 566
Daley, Dennis	464	Daven, Joel	179, 566
Daley, Nicholas	565	Davenport, Franklin	388
Dalglaish, David	861	David, Israel	874

Name	Page	Name	Page
Davids, David	566	Davis, William	180, (3) 567
Davidson, George	566	Davison, David	851
Davidson, Jacob	179	Davison, James	180, (2) 567
Davidson, John	179, (2) 566		
Davidson, Nathaniel	451	Davison, Jediah	567, 848
Davies, Daniel	179	Davison, Jeptha	567
Davies, Edward	873	Davison, Jesse	851
Davies, John	179	Davison, John	(2) 568
Davis, Abisha	855	Davison, Joseph	832
Davis, Abraham	179	Davison, Thomas	568
Davis, Andrew	(2) 566	Davison, William	363, 464, 476, (3) 568, 848, 861
Davis, Benjamin	566		
Davis, Cain	566		
Davis, Caleb	179		
Davis, Conrad	861	Dawn, Aaron	180
Davis, Curtis	566	Dawson, John	568
Davis, Daniel	(2) 179, 861	Day, Aaron	37, 99, 845
Davis, David	179, 464 566, 848	Day, Amos	180, 568
		Day, Artemas	388
Davis, David Rhay	566	Day, Charles	568
Davis, Earl	566	Day, Daniel	851
Davis, Edmond	566	Day, David	180
Davis, Elijah	179, (2) 388, 566	Day, Elias	568
		Day, George	568
Davis, George	(2) 179, 566	Day, Isaac	127
		Day, Jehiel	568
Davis, Henry	566	Day, Jeremiah	180
Davis, Isaac	566, 855	Day, John	568
Davis, Jacob	566	Day, Joseph	568
Davis, James	179, 180, (2) 567	Day, Moses	180, (2) 568
Davis, Job	443	Day, Nehemiah	464
Davis, John	47, (2) 180, 328, 388, 424, (5) 567, 861	Day, Peter	464
		Day, Samuel	568, 851
		Day, Stephen	388
		Day, Thomas	(2) 180, (4) 568
Davis, Jonathan	180, 567	Dayley, Joseph	(2) 568
Davis, Joseph	(2) 567, 851	Dayton, Colonel	23, 41
		Dayton, Daniel	568
Davis, Joshua	567	Dayton, Elias	11, 20, 35, 53, 54, 55, 63, 341, 351
Davis, Josiah	373		
Davis, Lewis	567		
Davis, Moore	861		
Davis, Moses	424, 861		
Davis, Nathan	180, 567	Dayton, Ephraim	113
Davis, Patrick	180	Dayton, Ive	568
Davis, Peter	(2) 567	Dayton, Jonathan	20, 35, 53, 54, (2) 55, 79
Davis, Richard	476, (2) 567		
Davis, Robert	567, 855	Dayton, Joseph	(2) 320, 388, 443
Davis, Samuel	180, 567		
Davis, Thomas	(2) 180, 388, 567	D'Camp, Morris	113
		Deacon, Aaron	127, 180

Deacon, George	568	DeCou, John	570
Deal, Elias	568	Deemer, Joseph	570
Deal, George	569	DeForrest, Abraham	451
Deal, James	569	Defresh, Abram	476
Deal, John	569	Defresh, Isaac	570
Deal, Samuel	569	Degraw, Walter	570
Deamell, Patrick	569	DeGroat, Jacob	388
Dean, Abraham	569	Degroft, Walter	570
Dean, Benjamin	180	DeGroot, David	388
Dean, Daniel	569	DeGroot, William	424
Dean, David	569	Deharmond, James	181
Dean, Jacob	(2) 569	DeHart, Abram	570
Dean, John	(2) 569	DeHart, Cornelius	570
Dean, Jonathan	569	DeHart, Hendrick	570
Dean, Joseph	127, 181	DeHart, Henry	(2) 570
Dean, Matthew	569	DeHart, James	570
Dean, Micajah	569	DeHart, John	(2) 570
Dean, Nathaniel	569	DeHart, Morris	451
Dean, Nehemiah	569	DeHart, Peter	570
Dean, Nicholas	181	DeHart, William	464
Dean, Osgood	181	DeHart, Winant	570
Dean, Reuben	181	Deifel, Edward	570
Dean, Stephen	424	Deits, Peter	570
Dean, Thomas	569	Deitz, John	570
Dean, William	(2) 181	DeKay, Thomas	570
Deare, James	181, 569	Delamater, Abram	570
Deare, Jonathan	343, 358	Delancy, Cornelius	181
Deaskey, Leman	181	Delatush, Henry	436
Deat, Henry	569	Delfer, John	181, 570
Debow, Isaac	569	Dellimore, Robert	181
Debow, Jacob	855	Delop, James	570
Debow, James	388	Delop, Jeremiah	570
Debow, John	388, 569	Demans, Adam	181
Debow, William	569	Demarest, Adam	570
DeCamp, Abraham	181, 569	Demarest, Benjamin	570
DeCamp, Enoch	569	Demarest, Cornelius N.	570
DeCamp, Ezekiel	569	Demarest, Daniel N.	570
DeCamp, James	(2) 55, 104	Demarest, David	327, 388
		Demarest, David C.	570
DeCamp, Joab	569	Demarest, Gilliam	570
DeCamp, John	569	Demarest, Hendrick	571
DeCamp, Morris	569	Demarest, Henry	571
Deck, John	843	Demarest, Jacob D.	571
Decker, Abraham	464	Demarest, Jacob P.	571
Decker, Brewer	569	Demarest, James	571
Decker, Jacob	476	Demarest, John	571
Decker, Jeremiah	569	Demarest, Joseph	571
Decker, John	(2) 569	Demarest, Peter	571
Decker, Moses	569	Demarest, Peter B.D.	571
Decker, Peter	570	Demarest, Peter D.	571
Decker, Samuel	181	Demarest, Peter J.	571
Decker, Thomas	181	Demarest, Peter P.	571
Deckler, John	181	Demarest, Philip	571
Deckley, James	570	Demarest, Roelif S.	571
DeCou, Isaac	342, 363	Demarest, Samuel	388

- 35 -

Name	Page	Name	Page
Demarest, Simon	571	Denny, Thomas	323, 572
Demarest, William	571	Denton, Isaac	572
Dembery, Patrick	181	Deny, John	182
Demelt, Barnet	464	Denyer, Michael	182
Demer, Joseph	181	Depew, David	464
Demit, Derrick	464	Deposite, Augustine	182
Demont, Abraham	424	Depue, Daniel	436
Demont, John	832	Derby, John	572
Demot, Peter	181	Derrick, James	182, 572
Demott, Jacob	571	Derrick, John	843
Demott, Peter	571	Derrickson, Andrew	572
Demund, Edward	347, 363	Derry, John	182
Demund, Tenes	571	Desilvey, Joseph	572
Demund, William	571	Detmore, see Elinore	
Deneen, James	571	Deurt, Aaron	572
Denian, William	181	Devall, Thomas	572
Deniante, John	571	Devenport, Cornelius	572
Denice, Dennis	345, 364	Devenport, Franklin	364, 835
Denick, Jeremiah	571	Devenport, Jacob	572
Denick, Samuel	571	Devenport, Leonard	572
Denick, Samuel, Jr.	571	Devenport, William	572
Denight, James	181, 571	Devian, William	138
Denight, John	181, 571	Devins, John	182
Denike, Davis	481	Devit, Peter	855
Denise, Daniel	571	Devoe, John	572
Denise, Jacques	329, 420	Devoir, Luke	182
Deniston, William	571	Devons, Leonard	182
Denman, Andrew	571	Devorce, John	572
Denman, Isaac	571	Devore, Cornelius	572
Denman, John	182 (2) 571	Devore, John	182, 573
		Devorer, David	573
Denman, Matthias	571	Devour, David	573
Denman, Philip	572	Devour, Jacob	573
Denman, Samuel	572	DeVow, John	573
Denman, Stephen	572	Dewans, John	182
Denmark, Bernardus	572	DeWeelen, Samuel	573
Dennie, John	572	DeWitt, Barnett	573
Denning, William	182	DeWitt, Daniel	573
Dennis, Benjamin	388	DeWitt, John	573
Dennis, David	572	Dewlap, Samuel	573
Dennis, Enos	182, 572	Dey, Benjamin	573
Dennis, Ezekiel	36, 104	Dey, Cyrus	573
Dennis, John	388, 572	Dey, Daniel	573
Dennis, Joseph	572	Dey, David	573
Dennis, Matthew	572	Dey, Ezekiel	573
Dennis, Philip	572	Dey, James	573
Dennis, Reuben	572	Dey, Jeremiah	182
Dennis, Robert	572	Dey, John	389, (2) 573
Dennis, Samuel	388		
Dennison, John	182	Dey, Josiah	(2) 573
Denniston, John	182	Dey, Lewis	573
Denniston, William	424	Dey, Peter	(2) 573
Denny, Gideon	572	Dey, Richard	323, 324, 334, 339, 364
Denny, Henry	572		
Denny, Jonas	572		

Dey, Theunis	26, 47, 339, 351	Dillap, James (Indian)	183, 574
Dey, William	573	Dillen, Peter	574
D'Hart, Cyrus	14, 15, 49, (2) 50, 51, 53, 79	Dillmore, Robert	183
		Dillon, Isaac	837
		Dillon, James	16, 17, 32, 33, 79, 836
D'Hart, Maurice	68		
D'Hart, William	13, (2) 28, (2) 51, 66, 389	Dillon, Joseph	836
		Dilly, Ephraim, Sr.	574
		Dilly, John	574
		Dilly, Joseph	574
Diamond, James	484	Dils, Peter	574
Dick (Negro)	861	Dilts, Jacob	574
Dick, Samuel	346, 351	Dimon, John	183, 574
Dickerson, Abram	573	Dine, Andrew	574
Dickerson, Benjamin	182, 573	Dingman, Andrew	574
Dickerson, Daniel	573	Dingman, John	574
Dickerson, Isaac	182	Dingman, Peter	574
Dickerson, Moses	573	Dingwell, John	(2) 574
Dickerson, Nathaniel	573	Direck, James	574
Dickerson, Peter	21, 35, 79, 573	Disbrow, Daniel	464
		Disbrow, Elijah	574
Dickerson, Thomas	389	Disbrow, John	574, 861
Dickerson, Walter	573	Disbrow, John D.	575
Dickey, Alexander	871	Disbrow, Joseph	575, 848
Dickinson, Ashbrook	182, 573	Disbrow, Samuel	575, 855
Dickinson, Brigadier General	354, 366	Diskill, Nathaniel	183
		Disney, John	113
Dickinson, John	573	Ditmars, Johannas	575
Dickinson, Joseph	443, 832	Ditmars, John	575
Dickinson, Major General	351, 354, 365, 379, 384, 836	Ditmars, Peter	575
		Ditmos, Frederick	575
		Ditmos, John	575
Dickinson, Peter	389	Ditmos, Peter	575
Dickinson, Philemon	42, 338, 349	Ditres, Frederick	464
		Ditts, William	575
Dickinson, Samuel	183, 574	Dixon, Ashbrook	183
Dickinson, Walter	574	Dixon, Daniel	575
Dickinson, William	574	Dixon, Isaac	183
Dickison, Bernard	574	Dixon, John	575, 842
Dickison, David	574	Dixon (or Dickson), Thomas	113
Dickison, Isaac	574		
Dickson, see Dixon		Doaran, Joseph	575
Dickson, Alexander	574	Dobbin, Lodowick	183
Dickson, Christopher	861	Dobbins, David	575
Dickson, John	861	Dobbins, Seth	389
Dickson, William	183, 574	Dobbins, William	436
Dildine, John	574	Docherty, John	183
Dilkes, John	451	Dockrell, Richard	183
Dilkes, Samuel	183, 574	Dodd, Abiel	575
Dill, Frampton	574	Dodd, Abijah	575
Dill, Nicholas	183	Dodd, Abitha	575
Dill, Philip	843	Dodd, Amos	389

Dodd, Caleb	364		Doren Cornelius	(2) 576
Dodd, David	575		Dorey, Isaac	184
Dodd, Dekoda	575		Dorharty, John	576
Dood, Ebenezer	575		Dorland, Peter	482
Dodd, Eleizer	575		Dormant, Jesse	576
Dodd, Elias	183, 575		Dorn, Nicholas	576
Dodd, Isaac	575		Dorrey, James	184
Dodd, Israel	575		Dorrington, Jacob	576
Dodd, James	575		Dorrington, Thomas	576
Dodd, Jesse	183, 575		Dorsett, Benjamin	576
Dodd, John	575		Dorsett, John	576
Dodd, Joseph	575		Dorsett, Joseph	576
Dodd, Joshua	575		Dorsett, Samuel	577
Dodd, Matthew	575		Dorsey, John	56, 74
Dodd, Matthias	575		Dortan, William	577
Dodd, Moses	575		Dorton, Francis	184
Dodd, Permenus	575		Dorvill, John	464
Dodd, Robert	576, 836		Dossett, James	577
Dodd, Samuel N.	576		Dotey, Isaac	184
Dodd, Thomas	576		Dotey, Jacob	851
Dodd, Timothy	(2) 183		Dotey, Samuel Jr.	184
	(2) 576		Dotey, Samuel Sr.	184
Dodd, Uzal	576		Dotworth, George	184
Dodd, William	183		Doty, Ephraim	577
Dodders, Philip	389		Doty, George	577
Dodge, David	576		Doty, James	577
Dogerty, Charles	576		Doty, Jeremiah	577
Doherda, John	183, 576		Doty, John	(2) 577
Doherda, William	184		Doty, John Jr.	577
Doke, Robert	851		Doty, Joseph	577
Dolbier, Jesse	576		Doty, Nathaniel	577
Dolbier, John	576		Doty, Peter	184, 577,
Dolbur, Jasper	576			851
Doll, William	576		Doty, Skillman	577
Dolland, Peter	576		Doty, William	577
Dolles, William	851		Doty, Zebulon	577
Dollis, Samuel	576		Doud, Ebenezer	577
Dolton, James	184		Doud, James	184, 577
Dolton, William	184		Douers, Edward	577
Donaldson, James	184		Dougherty, Anthony	184, 185,
Donaldson, John	184, 576			832
Donaldson, Thomas	184		Dougherty, Charles	185
Donaldson, William	184		Dougherty, Edward	577
Donavan, John	184		Dougherty, Henry	185
Dones, Jonas	184		Dougherty, James	185.
Dones, Samuel	576		Dougherty, John	(2) 185,
Donnelly, Daniel	184			464, (2)
Doram, John	576			577
Doran, Cornelius	576			
Doran, Stacy	576		Dougherty, Peter	135
Dorcar, Silas	576		Doughty, Abel	577
Dorchester, Abram	184		Doughty, Abige	577
Doremus, ...	389		Doughty, Abner	577
Doremus, David	424		Doughty, Absalom	577
Doremus, George	576		Doughty, Christopher	185
Doremus, Thomas	576		Doughty, Daniel	861

Doughty, Francis	577	Drake, Ephraim	578
Doughty, Isaac	185	Drake, Francis	578
Doughty, Jeremiah	577	Drake, George	579
Doughty, John	(2) 35, 68, 320, 345, 371, 420, 577	Drake, Isaac	579
		Drake, Jacob	345, 351, 579
Doughty, Jonathan	577, 861	Drake, James	(2) 185, (2) 579
Doughty, Josiah	577	Drake, John	425, 443, (2) 579, 832
Doughty, Levi	577		
Doughty, Linton	577		
Doughty, Michael	851	Drake, John Z.	579
Doughty, Skillman	838	Drake, Joseph	579
Doughty, Thomas	578	Drake, Nicholas	185, (2) 579
Douglas, ...	389		
Douglass, Alexander	373	Drake, Peter	(2) 186, 579
Douglass, David	185		
Douglass, Ephraim	71	Drake, Philip	579
Douglass, James	578, 851	Drake, Samuel	579
Douglass, John	185, 425, 461, (2) 578	Drake, Simeon	579
		Drake, Stephen	579
		Drake, William	186, 579
Douglass, Moses	185	Draper, George	377
Douglass, Nathan	578	Drew, Thomas	579
Douglass, Samuel	578	Drew, Timothy	579
Douglass, Thomas	851	Drewer, John	186, 579
Dow, Andrew	436	Drewer, Timothy	186, 579
Dow, Derrick	464	Drigus, Jacob	579
Dow, Fulkert	185, 464	Driskell, John	579
Dow, Henry	185	Driskey, Cornelius	579
Dow, James	578	Driskey, John	579
Dow, John	578	Drullinger, Frederick	579
Dow, John, Jr.	578	Drum, Christopher	186
Dowan, Edward	578	Drumm, Andrew	579
Dowdney, John	340, 373	Drumm, Christian	580
Dowdney, Samuel	113	Drummond, Benjamin	580
Dowelson, John	578	Drummond, John	580
Dowens, Griffin	185, 578	Drummond, Robert	389
Dower, John	578	Dubois, Abraham	389
Dowit, Moses	578	Dubois, Benjamin	580
Downer, James	185	Dubois, Cornelius	580
Downer, Samuel	(2) 578	Dubois, David	580
Downey, William	185, 578	Dubois, Jacob	389
Downie, John	389	Dubois, Jerediah	580
Downs, Robert	185, 578	DuBois, Minne	464
Doyle, Henry	113	Dubois, Nicholas	580
Doyle, Hugh	185, 578	Dubois, Peter	389
Drake, Abram	578	Duboys, Manicus	464
Drake, Alexander	578	Ducker, Peter	580
Drake, Benjamin	578	Duckworth, John	481
Drake, Cheeseman	578	Duclos, Francis	17, 22, 34, 95
Drake, Chesur	578		
Drake, Cornelius	127, 185	Dudder, Jacob	580
Drake, Elisha	578	Dudderer, Abram	580
Drake, Enoch	578, 861	Dudley, John	580

Duff, William	186, 580		Dunham, John	186, (3) 581, 582, 843, 855
Duffe, John	580			
Duffe, Randolph	580			
Duffell, Edward	580		Dunham, Jonathan	582
Duffey, Archibald	186		Dunham, Joseph	582
Duffie, John	186		Dunham, Joshua	582
Duffy, Francis	186		Dunham, Lewis F.	20, 35, 53, 54, 73
Dugan, Daniel	580			
Dugan, Samuel	580			
Dugan, William	186		Dunham, Manasah	582
Dulaney, Samuel	580		Dunham, Nathaniel	187
Dumar, Justin	580		Dunham, Samuel	582
Dumaris, Adam	186		Dunham, Stephen	21, 22, 30, 95, 425, 844
Dummer, John	186, 580			
Dummon, John	186			
Dumon, Hendrick	580		Duning, John	582
Dumon, Peter	580		Dunlap, Andrew	848, 851, 861
Dumon, Peter P.	580			
Dumont, Abram	436		Dunlap, Edward	375, 842
Dumont, Albert	580		Dunlap, James	582
Dumont, Elbert	580		Dunlap, Nenian	582
Dumont, John	581		Dunlap, Robert	855
Dumont, John B.	581		Dunlevy, Patrick	187
Dumont, John, Jr.	476		Dunlop, Samuel	187, 582
Dumont, Peter	389, 581		Dunn, ...	848
Dumont, Peter J.B.	581		Dunn, Aaron	582
Dumott, Abraham	581		Dunn, Benjamin	582
Dumott, Barent	581		Dunn, Clawson	582
Dumott, Benjamin	581		Dunn, Daniel	582
Dumott, Dirch	581		Dunn, Enoch	582
Dumott, Lawrence	581		Dunn, Ephraim	451, 582
Dunaway, Thomas	581		Dunn, Gershom	582
Dunbar, Alexander	186, 581		Dunn, Hugh	389
Dunbar, David	186		Dunn, Ichabod	582
Dunbar, Lott	581		Dunn, Isaac	582
Dunbury, Patrick	581		Dunn, Jacob	389, 844
Duncan, ...	113		Dunn, James	327, 389, 582, 861
Duncan, Alexander	186			
Duncan, John	581		Dunn, James F.	582
Duncan, Joseph	186		Dunn, Jeremiah	436, 582, 832
Duncan, William	186			
Dunfield, Henry	186		Dunn, Joel	582, 851
Dungan, Samuel	581		Dunn, John	333, 337, 343, 364, 476, 851
Dunham, Asher	581			
Dunham, Azariah	11, 19, 343, 358, 379			
			Dunn, Jonathan	582
			Dunn, Joseph	861
Dunham, Darius	581		Dunn, Lewis	832
Dunham, David	(3) 581		Dunn, Micajah	343, 358
Dunham, Elijah	581		Dunn, Moses	582
Dunham, Enoch	186, 581		Dunn, Nahum	464
Dunham, Frazee	581		Dunn, Philip	582
Dunham, Jacob	581		Dunn, Reuben	(2) 582
Dunham, James	186		Dunn, Richard	861
Dunham, Jehu	581		Dunn, Robert	483

- 40 -

Name	Pages
Dunn, Samuel	582
Dunn, Thomas	(2) 582, 851.
Dunn, Thomas P.	582
Dunn, William	(2) 187, 582, 851
Dunner, John	187
Dunny, Lodawick	582
Dunovan, John	187
Dunster, James	583
Dunster, John	583
Dunvier, Thomas	583
Durand, John	425
Duren, Briant	583
Duren, Elijah	583
Duren, John	583
Durham, Enoch	187
Durham, Nathaniel	583
Durland, Linus	583
Durling, Samuel	583
Dury, John	187
Duryea, Charles	583
Duryea, Frederick	583
Duryea, John	583
Duryea, Simon	389
Dusenberry, Henry	583
Dusenberry, Samuel	583
Dusenberry, William	583
Duston, Amos	583
Dustrider, John	583
Dutcher, Jacob	583
Dutton, George	187
Duvinney, William	583
Duychinck, James	583
Duychinck, John	(2) 337, (2) 344, 351
Dwire, Thomas	583
Dwyer, Charles	851
Dye, Amos	583
Dye, Daniel	583
Dye, James	583
Dye, John	583, 861
Dye, Joseph	583
Dye, Lawrence	583
Dye, Thomas	583
Dye, William	873
Eager, Archibald	187
Eagle, see Gage	
Eagles, Thomas	583
Eakin, Samuel	379
Eakman, Peter	583
Earl, Aaron	583

Name	Pages
Earl, David	583
Earl, Edward	583
Earl, Henry	187, 583
Earl, Israel	187
Earl, John	187, 476
Earl, Thomas	584
Earle, Morris	584
Early, Patrick	187
Early, Samuel	187, 584
Easey, John	584
Eastall, Joseph	584
Eastburn, Robert	584
Eastburn, Thomas	584
Eastlack, Francis	187, 584
Eastlick, Alexander	187
Easton, Moses	187
Easton, Peter	187
Easton, Samuel	187
Easton, Stephen	464
Eastwood, Amariah	187, 584
Eaton, Benjamin	61, 188
Eaton, Gideon	437
Eaton, John	584
Eaton, Thomas	584
Eben, Jabez	855
Eberhart, Adolph	188, 584
Eck, Samuel	584
Eckerson, Cornelius	584
Eckerson, Thomas	584
Eckles, John	136
Eckley, John	584
Eddy, Claeb	584, 838
Eddy, James	584
Eddy, John	584
Eddy, Samuel	584
Eddy, Thomas	855
Edgar, Archibald	584
Edgar, Clarkson	325, 343, 364
Edgar, David	38, 39, 40, 59, 80, 437
Edgar, James	584
Edgar, William	584
Edmeston, Samuel	847
Edmonds, Jacob	188
Edmonson, Hugh	443
Edmund, Samuel	584
Edsal, Benjamin	584
Edsal, James	(2) 584
Edsal, Joseph	584
Edsall, Jacobus	389
Edsall, James	188
Edsall, Richard	39, 96, 328, 390

Edwards, Aaron	(2) 584	Ellison, Samuel	586
Edwards, Daniel	845	Elmbly, Samuel	188
Edwards, David	390, 437	Elmer, Ebenezer	21, 22 (2) 31, 51, 73
Edwards, Jacob	188 (2) 584		
Edwards, Jasper	585	Elmer, Eli	320, 375
Edwards, Jesse	128, 188, 585	Elmer, Jonathan	586
Edwards, John	(2) 188, (3) 585, 873	Elmer, Moses G.	31, 51, 74
		Elmer, Nathan	586
		Elmer, Theophilus	26
Edwards, Joseph	128, (2) 585, 871	Elmer, Timothy	340, 364
		Elston, Andrew	586
Edwards, Michael	188	Elston, Jonathan	586
Edwards, Nathaniel	585	Elston, Josiah	586
Edwards, Richard	585	Elstone, Eli	586
Edwards, Thomas	443, 585	Elstone, Samuel	586
Effling, Frederick	443	Elvis, Jacob	586
Egbert, Abraham	188, 585	Elway, Jeremiah	586
Egbert, James	443, 585	Elwell, Amariah	188, 586
Egbert, John	585, 856	Elwell, David	188, 390, 586
Egbert, Lewis	188, 585		
Egbert, Thomas	344, 364	Elwell, John	586
Egberts, Abram	476	Elwell, Joseph	390
Egerton, Matthew	585	Elwell, Samuel	113, 586
Eghert, John	585	Elwell, Sawtel	390
Eglenton, Ebenezer	585	Ely, George	343, 352
Egmond, Lot	188	Ely, Joseph	586
Eiles, John	188	Ely, Moses	586, 861
Eldridge, Eli	340, 364	Eman, s, Benjamin	586
Eldridge, John	585	Embley, Ezekiel	586
Eldridge, Jonathan	585	Embley, John	189
Eldridge, William	585	Embley, Jonathan	586
Elholm, Cornelius	856	Emburgh, Jonathan	586
Elinore (alias Detmore), Robert	188	Emens, James	586
		Emens, John	464, 586
Ellason, Daniel	585	Emerson, James	189
Ellason, Joseph	585	Emerton, James	189
Ellason, Samuel	585	Emery, Jacob	586
Ellason, Seth	585	Emery, Thomas	189, 586
Ellender, Joshua	188	Emley, Ezekiel	425
Elliot, Daniel	188	Emley, Jonathan	586
Elliott, Daniel	585	Emley, Joseph	587
Elliott, Samuel	851	Emmel (or Hemmel), George	189, 587
Ellis, Christopher	586		
Ellis, Daniel	188	Emmons, ...	390
Ellis, Joseph	11, 19, 47, 341, 349, 375, (2) 586	Emmons, Abraham	189, 587
		Emmons, Amos	587
		Emmons, Benjamin	189, 587, 856
Ellis, Thomas	586	Emmons, Ezekiel	587
Ellis, William	324, 336, 337, 341, 364	Emmons, Isaac	587
		Emmons, Jacob	587
		Emmons, Jesse	587
Ellison, James	188	Emmons, Job	587

Emmons, John	(2) 189, (3) 587	Estall, John	588
		Estell, Joseph	390
Emmons, Lewis	128	Estill, John	588
Emmons, Nicholas	587	Estle, William	(2) 588
Emmons, Peter	587	Esty, Moses	390
Endicott, Jacob	443	Eules, John	190
Engart, Benjamin	189, 587	Eutell, Luther	588
Engle, Michael	465	Evans, Benjamin	(2) 588
Englehart, Henry	861	Evans, Crowell	588
English, David	587	Evans, David	190
English, James	377, 587	Evans, Emmanuel	190
English, John	(2) 189, 587	Evans, James	190, 588
		Evans, John	114, (2) 588
English, Joseph	587		
English, Mis.	587	Evans, Obadiah	190
English, Robert	587	Evans, Obediah	589
English, Thomas	587, 873	Evans, Samuel	844
Ennis, Daniel	451	Evans, Thomas	114, 465
Ennis, David	189	Evans, William	190, (3) 589
Ennis, John	587		
Ennis, (or Innis) Robert	189, 587	Eveland, Daniel	589
		Eveland, Peter	451
Ensley, Daniel	587	Evengen, William	589
Ensley, Henry	587	Everet, Godfrey	589
Ensley, John	587	Everet, Jacob	589
Ensly, Benjamin	856	Everet, John	589
Ensly, John	856	Everett, Abner	425
Ensminger, Henry	189	Everingham, John	(2) 589
Ent, Daniel, Jr.	588	Everingham, Nathaniel	589
Ent, Daniel, Sr.	587	Everingham, Stacy	190
Ent, Peter	390	Everingham, Thomas	589
Ent, Valentine	588	Everingham, William	190, 589
Eoff, Cornelius	588	Everitt, John	190
Errickson, Errick	588	Everitt, Samuel	451
Errickson, John	451	Everitt, Stacy	190
Errickson, Michael	588	Evers, ...	589
Errickson, Moses	189, 588	Everson, Barent	589
Errickson, Thomas	(2) 588	Everson, John	589
Erskine, Prince	588	Evett, William	589
Erskine, Robert	390	Evison, Bernard	589
Ervin, David	49, 73, 335, 378	Ewing, Abner	589
		Ewing, Abraham	589
Ervin, John	588	Ewing, George	104, 461, 589, 874
Ervin, Joseph	588		
Erwin, John	(2) 588	Ewing, James	375, 425
Erwin, Peter	189	Ewing, Joshua	390
Erwin, William	114, (3) 189	Ewing, Maskell, Jr.	452
		Ewing, Remington	190
Erwine, Robert	588	Ewing, Thomas	336, 340, 365, 377
Esdel, John	189		
Esler, Carrol	588	Ewler, Jacob	190, 589
Esler, Conrad	189	Ewman, Charles	190
Esler, John	465	Exsen, Abner	589
Esley, Moses, Jr.	588	Extell, Ebenezer	452
Essick, Stephen	190, 588		

Fagan, Henry	190		Farrow, John	590
Fagan, John	190		Farrow, Mark	191, 591
Fagan, Lawrence	190		Farrs, Joseph	191, 591
Fagan, Michael	136		Farver, Henry	191
Fagan, William	190		Fary, William	191, 591
Fairchild, Abiel	856		Faulkeson, Philip	591
Fairchild, Abijah	589		Faulkner, Peter	53, 104
Fairchild, Abner	390, 589		Faulkner, Robert	844
Fairchild, Abraham	371		Faulkner, William	16, 17, 80
Fairchild, Benjamin	589			
Fairchild, Hezekiah	589		Fauver, Joseph	476
Fairchild, Jonathan	589		Faver, Henry	191
Fairchild, Moses	590		Favin, Lawrence	191
Fairchild, Nathaniel	590		Fayer, Christian	591
Fairchild, Peter	590		Feaster, Henry	591
Fairchild, Stephen	590		Feather, John	591
Fairchild, William	425		Feathers, George	191, 591
Fairing, Charles	590		Feets, Peter	191
Falkner, Daniel	590		Fegan, John	591
Faney, David	190		Fegil (Trigel) John	861
Fannan, John	190		Fell, John	365
Fanning, James	190		Fell, Peter	339, 358, 591
Fanning, Lawrence	190			
Fantine, Rine	590		Fell, William	591
Fanver, Frederick	190, 590		Felter, Tunis	591
Fanver, George	590		Felty, George	591
Fanver, Henry	590		Fenemore, Samuel	832
Farey, Amariah	191, 590		Fenimore, Abraham	591
Farmer, George	61, 191 (2) 590		Fenimore, Benjamin	390, 842
			Fenimore, Daniel	591
Farmer, James	191		Fenimore, Henry	591
Farmer, Jasper	590		Fenimore, James	591
Farmer, Nathan	191, 590		Fenimore, Samuel	390
Farmer, Peter	590		Fenimore, Thomas	339, 365
Farney, George	191, 590		Fenton, George	(2) 591
Farnold, Peter	856		Fenton, John	61, 191
Farnsworth, Daniel	590		Fenton, Joshua	192
Farnum, Bezabul	465		Fenton, Peter	591
Farr, Abram	191		Fenton, Samuel	591
Farr, John	191, 590		Fenton, Thomas	(2) 591
Farr, William	191		Ferdon, Abram	591
Farral, Edward	191		Ferdon, Jacob	591
Farrand, Bethuel	590		Ferdon, Wilhelmus	591
Farrand, Daniel	590		Ferdone, Andrew	591
Farrand, James	590		Ferguson, Alexander	591
Farrand, Phineas	425		Ferguson, Hugh	591
Farrand, Samuel	590		Ferguson, Jeremiah	425
Farrell, James	191		Ferguson, John	592
Farrell, John	191, 590		Ferguson, Josiah	390
Farren, Enos	590		Ferguson, Jus	845
Farren, James	590		Ferguson, Samuel	592
Farren, Joseph	590		Ferguson, Thomas	192
Farren, Samuel	590		Ferlew, Nathan	592
Farrow, Abraham	590		Ferrat, Cornelius	592
Farrow, Abram	191		Ferrel, Absalom	592

Name	Page
Ferrel, Edward	592
Ferrill, James	192, 592
Ferrill, Morris	192
Ferris, Nathaniel	592
Ferris, William	592
Ferroll, Absalom	592
Ferroll, John	192
Ferver, Philip	592
Festor, Loadwick	592
Fetter, Jacob	592
Fich, Elnathan	592
Fid, Thomas	592
Fiddes, George	192
Fiddler, William	832
Fidler, John	592
Field, Benjamin	592
Field, Dennis	592
Field, Elnathan	592
Field, Hendrick	592
Field, Jeremiah	425
Field, Jeremiah B.	592
Field, John	592
Field, John B.	592
Field, Jonathan	592
Field, Richard	592
Field, Richard R.	592
Field, Seth	592
Field, Thomas	192, 592
Field, William	592
Fielder, William	592
Fielding, William	593
Fight, Leonard	593
Finch, John	192, 593
Finch, William	443
Findley, Robert	192
Findley, William	192
Fine, Abram	593
Fine, Frederick	845
Fink, Nicholas	593
Finley, James	593
Finley, John	128, 192, 593, 844
Finley, William	593
Finn, Thomas	192
Finnemore, John	873
Finnerty, Joseph	192
Firklin, Robert	192
Fish, John	593
Fish, Joseph	593
Fish, Thomas	593
Fisher, Bartholemew	848
Fisher, Charles	425, 465, 593
Fisher, Christopher	192, 593
Fisher, David	114, 593
Fisher, Felix	390
Fisher, Hendrick	14, 29, 96
Fisher, Henry	(2) 593
Fisher, Isaac	593
Fisher, Jacob	192, (3) 593
Fisher, John	(2) 192, 465, (3) 593, 856
Fisher, John H.	465
Fisher, Joseph	593
Fisher, Leonard	476
Fisher, Lewis	425
Fisher, Louis	593
Fisher, Moses	192, 593
Fisher, Peter	192, (2) 594, 861
Fisher, William	594
Fisker, Henry	594
Fisler, Jacob	594
Fisler, John	594
Fisler, Leonard	476
Fitch, Daniel	594
Fitch, John	437
Fitch, William	192, 594
Fite, John	594
Fithian, ...	390
Fithian, Aaron	594
Fithian, David	594, 856
Fithian, George	193, (2) 594
Fithian, Glover	29, 104, 193
Fithian, Isaac	193, 594
Fithian, Joel	390
Fithian, Jonathan	452
Fithian, Philip Vichers	(2) 336, 379
Fithian, William	594
Fitsimmons, James	594
Fitzgerald, ...	391
Fitzgerald, Henry	594
Fitzgerald, John	193, 594
Fitzgerald, Michael	193, 594
FitzRandolph, see Randolph, Fitz	
Flahaven, John	14, 29, 49, 50, 80
Flake, John	193
Flanagan, see also Flanningham	
Flanagan, Samuel	836
Flannagan, see Flanningham	

Flanningham, see also Flanagan or Flannagan		Ford, James	595, 856
		Ford, Jonathan	194
Flanningham, Samuel	21, 35, 36, 80, 341, 365	Ford, Mahlon	96
		Ford, Nathan	595
		Ford, Standish	844
Flat, John	594	Ford, Stephen	595, 873
Fleet, Jasper	594	Ford, Thomas	194, 595
Fleet, John	594	Ford, Timothy	595
Fleming, Jacob	425, 594	Ford, William	(3) 595
Fleming, Jeremiah	(2) 193, 594	Forden, James	194
		Fordham, Stephen	595
Fleming, John	(2) 193	Fordice, Samuel	595
Fleming, Lawrence	193	Fordier, Benjamin	595
Fleming, Samuel	391, 844	Fordyce, Henry	595
Fleming, Stephen	391	Fordyce, John	128, 595
Fleming, Thomas	594, 862	Foreman, Thomas M.	80
Fletcher, James	193, 594	Foreman, Walter	595
Fletcher, John	193, 594	Forgeson, Allar	194, 595
Fletcher, William	(2) 193, 594	Forgus, John	595
		Foriden, Henry	194
Flinn, Benjamin	465	Forker, Samuel	465
Flinn, John	193	Forman, Brigadier General	57
Flinner, Henry	193		
Flint, George	595	Forman, David	57, 64, (2) 335, 349, 375, 444
Flint, Joseph	595		
Flock, John	595		
Flood, Stephen	595		
Flowers, William	193, 595	Forman, Dennis	596
Floyd, Abraham	595	Forman, Isaac	596
Floyd, Joseph	194	Forman, Jonathan	38, 39, 49, 52, 54, 66, 329, 391, 460, 596
Foard, Nathan	839		
Fogg, Daniel	114		
Folk, Henry	595, 856		
Folk, Philip	444		
Foot, William	194	Forman, Joshua	596
Forbes, Uriah	595	Forman, Robert	596
Force, Henry	194	Forman, Samuel	337, 345, 352, (2) 596
Force, Isaac	595		
Force, Jacob	194		
Force, James	595	Forman, Samuel P.	425
Force, John	595	Forman, Teunis	465
Force, Jonathan	194	Forman, Tunis	114
Force, Joseph	194	Forman, William	465, 596
Force, Samuel	595	Forn, Jonathan	194
Force, Squire	595	Forsythe, Robert	834
Force, Thomas	476	Fort, Benjamin	596
Force, Thomas P.	595	Fort, Francis	596
Force, William	194, 595	Fort, Henry	596
Ford, Benjamin	194	Fort, John	596
Ford, Charles	595	Fort, Joseph	596
Ford, Chilleon	58, 71	Fort, Thomas	(2) 596
Ford, David	194	Fort, William	596
Ford, Jacob, Jr.	(2) 323, 345, 352	Forth, Francis	596
		Forth, Phineas	596

Fortner, Benjamin	596	Francisco, Peter	597
Fortune, William	194	Franklin, Elisha	597
Foster, Andrew	194	Franklin, John	597
Foster, Elias	596	Franks, David	196
Foster, Ephraim	(2) 425, 838.	Fraser, Christian	597
		Fraser, Cornelius	476
Foster, Ezekiel	340, 365	Frasey, Samuel	196, 597
Foster, Ichabod	(2) 194	Frazee, Abraham	196
Foster, Jeremiah	(2) 194, 596	Frazee, Benjamin	196, 597
Foster, Jacob	596	Frazee, Benoni	597
Foster, John	194, 596	Frazee, Henry	597
Foster, Jonathan	(2) 195, 596	Frazee, Hiram	597
		Frazee, Jonas	597
Foster, Judah	596	Frazee, Matthias	597
Foster, Nathan	195	Frazee, Morris	598
Foster, Nathaniel	596, 838, 856	Frazee, Moses	598
		Frazee, Reuben	598
Foster, Philetus	596	Frazer, Christian	598
Foster, Salathial	391	Frazer, Daniel	452
Foster, Salmon	391	Frazer, Henry	856
Foster, Samuel	(2) 195, 476, 596, 597	Frazer, James	856
		Frazer, Jeremiah	598
		Frazer, John	391
Foster, William	195	Frazer, Matthias	598
Fough (or Vought) Peter	195, 597	Frazer, William	425
		Frazier, Daniel	598
Foulks, John	597	Frazier, David	391
Fourat, Henry	597	Frazier, George	196
Fouratt, Daniel	114	Frazier, Zebedee	196
Fourt, Henry	597	Frazy, Benjamin	598
Fourt, Thomas	597	Freas, John	598
Fowler, see also, Wardell		Frease, Henry	476
		Fredenburgh, William	196, 598
Fowler, David	195	Frederick, John	598
Fowler, Davis	195	Fredon, Jacobus	136
Fowler, George	597	Freeland, see also Vreeland	
Fowler, Isaac	195, 597		
Fowler, Joseph	195	Freeland, Abraham	598, 873
Fowler, Robert	195	Freeland, Abram	(2) 598
Fox, Jacob	(2) 195, (2) 597	Freeland, Enoch	598
		Freeland, Garret	598
Fox, John	195	Freeland, Isaac	598
Fox, Joseph	195	Freeland, Jacob	598
Fox, Patrick	195, 597	Freeland, Jacob H.	598
Fox, Peter	195	Freeland, James	196, 598
Foy, Daniel	196, 597.	Freeland, John	482
Foy, John	(2) 196, 597	Freeland, Marinus	598
		Freeland, Peter	(2) 598
Frambris, Andrew	597	Freeland, Richard	196
Frambris, Nicholas	597	Freeland, Robert	598
Francis, Jacob	597	Freeling, John	598
Francis, William	196	Freeman, ...	391
Francisco, Anthony	597	Freeman, Alexander	598
Francisco, John	196, (2) 597	Freeman, Amos	(2) 598
		Freeman, Annanias	196

Freeman, Ashbel	598		Frisalear, James	600
Freeman, Benjamin	598, 856		Frister, Peter	600
Freeman, Calet	598		Frits, Peter	600
Freeman, Cyrus	598		Froon, George	600
Freeman, David	(2) 598, 599		Frost, John	(2) 197, 600
Freeman, Edgar	599, 872		Frost, Stephen	600
Freeman, Eleizer	599		Frothingham, Richard	840
Freeman, Elijah	391		Fry, John	600
Freeman, Henry	138, 482		Fry, William	600
Freeman, Israel	599		Fulker, Philip	391
Freeman, Jabez	196		Fulkerson, Caleb	197, 482, 600
Freeman, Jacob	196			
Freeman, Jedediah	196, 599		Fulkerson, Cornelius	600
Freeman, Jehiel	599		Fulkerson, Fulkert	600
Freeman, Jeremiah	599		Fulkerson, Henry	600
Freeman, John	196, 599		Fulkerson, Hons.	600
Freeman, Jonah	599		Fulkerson, John	197, 600
Freeman, Jonathan	599, 851		Fulkerson, Joseph	197
Freeman, Joseph	599		Fulkerson, Philip	391, 600
Freeman, Lott	196		Fulkerson, William	197, 600
Freeman, Matthew	327, 391, 599		Fullmore, John	600
			Fulmore, John	197
Freeman, Matthias	599		Fulper, William	197
Freeman, Melanthon	335, 377		Funerty, Joseph	197
Freeman, Michael	599		Furguson, John	844
Freeman, Moses	599		Furguson, Thomas	128
Freeman, Philip	196, (2) 599		Furguson, William	844
			Furling, Lawrence	874
Freeman, Samuel	465, (2) 599		Furman, Daniel	600
			Furman, Edward	600
Freeman, Silas	479, 599		Furman, Enos	600
Freeman, Thomas	862		Furman, Joshua	601
Freeman, William	(2) 599		Furman, Michael	601
Freeman, Zenus	599		Furman, Moore	834
Frees, Adam	599		Furman, Nathaniel	601
Frelinghuysen, Frederick	47, (2) 320, 334, 346, 352		Furman, Richard	851
			Furman, Robert	601
			Furman, Waters	601
French, Daniel	196, 599		Furman, William	601
French, David	599		Furter, David	197
French, Jeremiah	197, (2) 599		Fusler, Jacob, Jr.	601
			Fusler, Luke	601
French, John	848, 851		Fusler, Peter	601
French, Joseph	600			
French, Noah	832			
French, Samuel	600		Gaab, William	601
French, William	(2) 600		Gach, John	601
Freneau, Philip	465		Gad, Alexander	601
Frezby, Benjamin	600		Gad, William	601
Fricklin, Robert	197		Gaffin, John	197
Friend, Hendrick	600		Gage, Aaron	197
Fries, Henry	16, 96		Gage, Edward	197
Frisalear, Jacob	197, 600		Gage, (alias Eagle) John	601

Gaines, Elisha	601	Gardner, Samuel	602
Gait, Joseph	197	Gardner, Thomas	851
Gaithritt, John	197	Garey, William	602
Gale, Abel	601	Garkin, Abraham	198
Gale, Alexander	197	Garland, John	(2) 602
Gale, James	425	Garland, William	602
Gale, Joseph	(3) 197, 601	Garlaw, Jacob	603
		Garlinghouse, Benjamin	198, 603
Gallagher, Ebenezer	197	Garlinghouse, James	603
Gallagher, John	197, 601	Garlinghouse, John	198, 603
Gallidet, Peter	197	Garlinghouse, Joseph	198, 476
Galligher, Abraham	(2) 197	Garner, Benjamin	198
Gallihan, Abram	198	Garner, Jacob	603
Gallispy, James	479	Garner, James	198
Galloway, James	198, 601	Garnetson, see Garretson	
Galloway, John	601		
Galloway, Joseph	601	Garno, Henry	603
Gamberton, Charles	198, 601	Garno, Peter	603
Gamble, Calvin	198, (3) 601	Garon, Uriah	603
		Garrabrant, Garrabrant	198
Gamble, James	843	Garrabrants, Garrabrant	603
Gamble, Samuel	601	Garrabrants, John	603
Gana, Daniel	840	Garrabrants, Uriah	603
Gandy, David	602	Garratson, Jacob	603
Gandy, Edward	602	Garratson, Jeremiah	603
Gandy, Elias	602	Garratson, Joseph	603
Gandy, Enoch	602	Garratson, Lemuel	603
Gandy, John	602	Garrens, Thomas	198
Ganen, William	602	Garret, Robert	198, 603
Ganno, Daniel	602	Garret, William	603
Ganno, George	602	Garretse, Henry	391
Ganno, Isaac	602	Garretson (or Garnetson), Jacob	603
Gannon, William	198		
Gant, James	602	Garretson, Samuel	198
Gard, Alexander	602	Garrigues, David	603
Gard, Daniel	602, 856	Garrigues, Isaac	198, 603
Gard, Gershom	602	Garrigues, Jacob	603
Gard, Jacob	391	Garrigues, John	198, 603
Gard, John	602	Garrigus, David	851
Gardiner, Cornelius	198	Garrish, John	198, 452, 603
Gardner, Benjamin	481, 482, 862		
		Garrish, Joseph	603
Gardner, Christian	602	Garrison, Aaron	603
Gardner, Cornelius	128, (2) 602	Garrison, Abraham	198, 465
		Garrison, Abraham H.	603
Gardner, Elijah	602	Garrison, Amos	603
Gardner, George	602	Garrison, Benjamin	198, 603
Gardner, James	602, 856	Garrison, Bennet	198
Gardner, Jeremiah	602, 856	Garrison, Bernardus	603
Gardner, John	602, 848	Garrison, Burnet	198
Gardner, Jonathan	602	Garrison, Cornelius	603
Gardner, Joseph	(2) 602, 862	Garrison, Dirck	604
		Garrison, Elijah	604
Gardner, Jothan	602	Garrison, Garret	(2) 604
Gardner, Rufus	871	Garrison, George	(2) 604

Name	Page
Garrison, Jacob	604
Garrison, Joel	128, 604
Garrison, John	(3) 604
Garrison, Jonah	199, 604
Garrison, Joseph	(2) 199
Garrison, Josiah	604
Garrison, Matthias	199, (2) 604
Garrison, Morimus	604
Garrison, Peter	604
Garrison, Reuben	604
Garrison, Silas	199
Garrison, William	391, 604
Garrits, John	199, 604
Garritson, John	604
Garritson, Peter	604
Garritson, Rem	604
Garritson, Richard	604
Garritson, Samuel	604
Garroway, David	199
Garroway, William	199
Garthrite, John	604
Garthwaite, Henry	138
Garthwaite, Jeremiah	136
Garthwaite, John	199
Garton, David	604
Garwood, Samuel	199, 604
Gary, John	30
Gary, Martin	199
Gaskill, Abraham	199
Gaskill, Caleb	604
Gaskill, Samuel	425
Gaskill, William	(2) 199, 604
Gasling, Joseph	604
Gaspee, David	199
Gaston, Daniel	605
Gaston, Hugh	605
Gaston, Joseph	375
Gaston, Robert	37, 40, 80, 345, 358, 391, 605
Gaston, William	605
Gaulidet, Edgar	21, 36, 99
Gavan, Thomas	602
Gaven, John	605
Gavin, John	114, 199
Gearhart, Jacob	392
Gearhart, William	392
Gearson, Thomas	465
Geary, John	(2) 50, 104
Geddes, John	605
Gee, Rossel	605
Gelliland, John	605
Geloff, Benjamin	605
Gening, Benjamin	856
Gentry, William	605
Genung, Abraham	605
Genung, Ananias	605
Genung, Cornelius	605
Genung, Isaac	605
Genung, Jacob	199, 605
Genung, John	199
Genung, Stephen	605
George, John	114, 199, 605
Ghulick, Derrick	605
Ghulick, Ferdinand	605
Ghulick, John	605
Ghulick, Nicholas	605
Ghulick, Samuel	605
Gibbons, James	605
Gibbons, John	199
Gibbs, Caleb	60
Gibbs, John	199, (2) 605
Gibbs, Joseph	605
Gibbs, Martin	605
Gibbs, Samuel	605
Gibbs, Thomas	605
Gibbs, William	199
Giberson, John	605
Giberson, Joseph	606
Gibeson, James	606
Gibeson, Job	606
Gibeson, John	606
Gibson, David	606
Gibson, James	114, 200, 606
Gibson, Richard	606
Gibson, Thomas	114, 200, 851
Gibson, William	115, 136, 606
Giddeman, John	128
Giffen, Daniel	606
Giffens, Joshua	(2) 200
Giffers, Joshua	200
Gifford, Archibald	844
Gifford, Benjamin	606
Gifford, James	606
Gifford, John	(2) 606
Gifford, Timothy	606
Gifford, William	54, 55, 80

Name	Page
Gifford, William B.	21, 22, 36
Gilbert, ...	392
Gilbert, Thomas	606
Gildersleaves, Asa	200
Gildersleeve, Finch	57, 90
Gildersleve, Benjamin	606
Giles, James	90
Giles, Levi	606
Gili, Benajah	606
Gill, John	200, 606
Gillam, Isaac	392, 606
Gillam, James	606
Gillam, Jeptha	606
Gillard, Charles	606
Gillidet, Peter	200, 606
Gilliham, Abram	200
Gilliland, Daniel	465
Gilliland, David	426, 606
Gilliland, Matthew	606
Gillingham, James	606
Gillispie, William	200, 606
Gillman, Charles	606, (2) 607
Gillman, David	856
Gillman, Isaac	607
Gillman, John	200, 607
Gillman, John, Jr.	607
Gillman, Joseph	200
Gillman, Kent	839
Gillman, Moses	856
Gillmore, Daniel	200
Gillmore, John	200
Gillum, Ezekiel	607
Gilmore, Charles	(2), 607
Gilmore, David	607
Gilmore, John	607
Gilmore, Joseph	128
Gilmore, William	607, 851
Ginners, Edward	607
Ginners, Lawrence	607
Ginnons, William	200, 607
Given, Reese, Jr.	607
Given, Reese, Sr.	607
Given, William	607
Givons, William	607
Gladhill, Eli	200
Glann, James	200
Glashart, Jacob	392
Glass, James	862
Glassby, Job	392
Glenn, James	200
Glenn, Thomas	200, 607
Glinn, James	200
Glover, Charles	200
Glover, Thomas	607
Glue, Isaac	862
Goalder, Daniel	607
Goble, Aaron	856
Goble, Abraham	(2) 607
Goble, Enoch	607, 856
Goble, Ezekiel	465
Goble, George	201
Goble, Henry	607
Goble, Hugh	607
Goble, Jonas	856
Goble, Samuel	201, (2) 607
Goble, Silas	607
Goble, Simeon	452
Goble, Simon	426
Godden, Amos	607
Godden, David	608
Godden, John	201, 608
Godden, William	201, 608
Godfrey, James	608
Godown, John	608
Goeschius, John Mauritius	336, 339, 365
Goff, John	608
Goff, Joseph	608
Goff, Nathan	201
Goggin, Philip	201
Gold, Encrease	608
Gold, Joseph	608
Gold, Josiah	608
Gold, Robert	608
Gold, Squire	842
Gold, Timothy	608
Gold, William	608
Golden, David	608
Golden, John	608
Golden, Samuel	201
Golden, Tevis	608
Golder, Abraham	608, 832
Golder, Abram	608
Golder, Jacob	862
Goldersleaus, Asa	856
Goldin, John	873
Goldin, Samuel	608
Goldsmith, Josiah	608
Goldsworthy, John	201
Goldtrap, John	608
Goldy, John	115
Goldy, Nicholas	201
Gollahar, Ebenezer	608
Gollahar, Lewis	608
Gollet, John	608
Goltry, Thomas	608
Gonnel, Francis	608

Gonsalas, James	608	Gramo, Abram	610
Goodwin, ...	201	Grandin, William	465
Goodwin, Amos	608	Grandine, William	610
Gordon, ...	426	Granger, John	852
Gordon, Archibald	452	Grannon, Thomas	202
Gordon, Axchable	608	Grant, George	108, 202
Gordon, Bernardus	(2) 201, 608	Grant, John	(2) 202, (2) 610
Gordon, David	201, 392 609	Grant, Robert	610
		Grant, Thomas	610
Gordon, Ezekiel	608	Grant, Vincent	(2) 610
Gordon, George	201	Grant, William	610
Gordon, James	609	Gray, Abram	610
Gordon, John	609	Gray, Daniel	610
Gordon, Joshua	335, 373	Gray, Garret	202
Gordon, Kenneth	609	Gray, Henry	202, 610
Gordon, Peter	334, 365, 609, 836	Gray, Isaac	(2) 610
		Gray, Isaiah	610
Gordon, Samuel	609	Gray, Jacob	202
Gordon, Timothy	609	Gray, James	392
Gordon, William	22, (2) 36, 80, 201, (2) 609	Gray, John	610
		Gray, Joseph	202, 610
		Gray, Joseph, Sr.	610
		Gray, Josiah	610
Gore, James	609, 832	Gray, Samuel	202
Gorman, Joseph	452	Gray, William	(2) 610, 862
Gormley, James	609		
Gosling, Levi	609	Greatwood, Samuel	202
Gosling, Samuel	609	Greaves, Joshua	610
Gouger, Stephen	201	Green, see also Weeks	
Gould, Daniel	201, 609	Green -----	848
Gould, Jacob	609	Green, Ashel	610
Gould, John	609	Green, Benjamin	610
Gould, Joseph	609	Green, Ebenezer	862
Gould, Josiah	609	Green, Elihu	610
Gould, Robert	(2) 609	Green, George	392
Gould, Robert J.	609	Green, James	392, 610
Gould, Robert, Jr.	609	Green, John	(3) 202, 477, (2) 610
Gould, Timothy	465		
Gould, William	609		
Gould, William R.	609	Green, Joseph	202, 611
Goulder, Elias	609	Green, Nathaniel	202, 611
Goulder, Jacob	609	Green, Pierson	202
Goulder, William	609	Green, Robert	202, 611
Grace, John	201, 851	Green, Thomas	202, 611
Gracey, John	201	Green, William	(2) 611
Gracey, Matthew	201	Green, William R.	611
Graham, Daniel	202	Greene, Nathaniel	65
Graham, George	202, 609	Greenwood, Daniel	202, 611
Graham, Henry	136, 202	Greenwood, Joseph	852
Graham, James	609	Greeves, Robert	611
Graham, Richard	609	Gregory, Arthur	203
Graham, Thomas	202, 465	Gregory, Ebenezer	611
Graham, William	610	Gregory, John	611

Grey, Enoch	611	Growendyck, Samuel	342, 365
Grey, Henry	115	Grummond, David	612
Grey, John	203, 611	Grummond, Ichabod	832
Grey, William	852	Grummond, Joseph	612
Grice, Francis	871	Guard, Daniel	(2) 204, 612
Grier, Thomas	203		
Griffey, Edward	203	Guerin, Joshua	452
Griffey, Joseph	203	Guerine, Joseph	856
Griffey, Levi	203	Guering, Joshua	612
Griffin, Timothy	856	Guering, Moses	612
Griffin, William	203	Guering, Nathaniel	856
Griffings, Moses	611	Guering, Vincent	856
Griffins, Joshua	611	Guering, Vinson	612
Griffis, Abner	611	Guest, Henry	612
Griffith, Benjamin	(3) 611	Guest, John	612
Griffith, David	(2) 611	Guest, Moses	392
Griffith, John	611	Guest, William	392, 843
Griffith, Levi	203	Guild, Benjamin	612
Griffiths, William	203, 611	Guild, John	613
Griffy, Eddy	611	Guild, Ralph	21, 22, 100, 392
Griggs, Benjamin	611		
Griggs, Daniel	203	Guillam, Michael	613
Griggs, James	611	Guion, John	613
Griggs, Joakin	611	Guisebertson, Guisbert	392
Griggs, John	115, 465, 611	Gulaear, Lewis	613
		Gulick, Abraham	613
Griggs, Matthew	611	Gulick, Abraham J.	613
Griggs, Robert	203	Gulick, Abram	613
Griggs, Samuel	611	Gulick, Benjamin	613, 862
Griggs, Thomas	(2) 611	Gulick, Cornelius	613
Griggs, William	203, 611	Gulick, Henry	392
Grigson, Edward	203	Gulick, James	613
Grimes, ...	136	Gulick, Joakim	393
Grimes, Daniel	203, 611	Gulick, John	613
Grimes, George	203, 612	Gulick, Peter	613
Grimes, John	203, 612	Gulk, Joakim	613
Grimes, Jonathan	612	Gunion, Hugh	204, 613
Grimes, Richard	203, 612	Gunsauld, John	613
Grimes, Sheppard	203, 612	Guntterman, Conrad	393
Grindle, Jonathan	203, 612	Gurne, John	613
Griner, Peter	612	Gurril, John	204
Grixsion, John	203	Gurrill, John	204
Gromin, John	203, 612	Gustin, Benajah	613
Gromley, James	612	Gustin, John	613
Grommon, Ichabod, Jr.	612	Guy, John	204, 613
Groom, Moses	612	Guynep, Benjamin	204, 613
Grotecloss, Gilbert	204	Gwinop, George	613
Grove, John	612	Gwinop, John	613
Grove, Robert	612	Gwynnup, George	115
Grove, Samuel	452, 612		
Grover, Peter	612		
Grover, Stephen	612	Haas, John	613
Groves, Jacob	612	Hacket, Jeremiah	613
Growendike, John	612	Hacket, Samuel	36, 37
Growendike, Samuel	612	Hackett, Abraham	204

Name	Page
Hackett, Jeremiah	(2) 204
Hackett, John	843
Hackett, Joshua	204
Hackett, Luke	613
Hackett, Patrick	204, 613
Hackett, Samuel	100
Hackett, William	613
Hadden, Thomas	343, 358
Hadley, George	613
Hadley, Moses	204
Hagaman, ...	613
Hagaman, Adrain	613
Hagaman, Andrew	613
Hagaman, Dollwyn	614
Hagaman, John	614
Hagaman, Peter	614
Hagan, Charles	204
Hagan, James	204
Hagan, John	21, 22, 100
Hagan, Robert	22, 35, 36, 96
Hagarty, John	614
Hageman, Aaron	465
Hageman, Roliff	465
Hager, George	393
Hagerman, Barnt	614
Hagerman, Bennett	862
Hagerman, Garret	614
Hagerman, Henry	614
Hagerman, Joseph	480
Hagerman, Rulif	614
Hagerty, John	(2) 204
Hagerty, Michael	204
Hagin, David	614
Hagin, James	614
Haight, Joseph	339, 359
Haight, William	614, 872
Hailey, George	(2) 205, 614
Hailey, William	205, 614
Haines, Abram	614
Haines, Benjamin	614
Haines, Daniel	205
Haines, Jedediah	614
Haines, Job	614
Haines, John	205, 862
Haines, Joseph	205, 614
Haines, L. Aaron	614
Haines, Peter	205
Haines, Samuel	844
Haines, Thomas	205, 614
Haines, William	205
Hainey, William	614
Hair, George	426
Hairville, James	614
Halbert, John	393
Halbrook, William	115
Halburt, William	614
Haldron, Henry	205, 614
Hale, John	614
Hale, Thomas	393
Haley, Hugh	205
Haley, Jehu	205
Halfpenny, Isaac	614
Halfpenny, James	614
Halfpenny, John	614
Halfpenny, Thomas	205
Hall, ...	393
Hall, Charles	205, 614
Hall, Cornelius	205
Hall, David	205, 614
Hall, Edward	47, 346, 365
Hall, Gad	614
Hall, George	205, 426, (2) 615
Hall, Isaac	615
Hall, Jacob	205, (3) 615
Hall, James	128, 205, 615
Hall, John	128, (2) 615
Hall, Josiah	393, 615
Hall, Levi	862
Hall, Moses	205
Hall, Nathan	205
Hall, Nicholas	615
Hall, Peter S.	615
Hall, Richard	206
Hall, Seth	206, 615
Hall, Thomas	347, 365, 615
Hall, William	206, (2) 615
Hallet, James	38, 39, 40, 96, 444
Hallybirt, ...	848
Halsey, Abraham	615
Halsey, Benjamin	323, 465, 856
Halsey, David	615
Halsey, Ezra	426, 856
Halsey, Henry	615
Halsey, Hugh	(2) 206
Halsey, Isaac	375, 393, 615

Halsey, Jabez	615	Hance, John	207
Halsey, Joel	615, 856	Hancock, Andrew	207, 616
Halsey, John	615	Hancock, Cutlope	207
Halsey, Joseph	465	Hancock, John	10, 25
Halsey, Joseph, Sr.	615	Hand, ...	871
Halsey, Joshua	206	Hand, Aaron	616
Halsey, Josiah	206	Hand, Christopher	616
Halsey, Luther	31, 51, 52, 70, 206, 615	Hand, Constantine	207, 616
		Hand, Cornelius	207, 616
		Hand, David	452, 616
Halsey, Obadiah	615	Hand, Eleazer	207
Halsey, Stephen	(2) 615	Hand, Eleizer	616
Halsey, William	206, 616	Hand, Elijah	340, 352
Halsey, William, Jr.	616	Hand, Henry	340, 359
Halsey, Zephaniah	616	Hand, Hezekiah	617
Halstead, John	206	Hand, Japhet	617
Halstead, Josiah	206	Hand, Jeremiah	617
Halsted, Josiah	616	Hand, Jesse	375
Halsted, Matthias	(2) 13, 15, 71, 365	Hand, John	340, 365
		Hand, Jonathan	452
		Hand, Moses	617
Halt, William	616	Hand, Nathan	340, 373
Hambler, Jacob	616	Hand, Recompense	617
Hambler, John	206, 616	Hand, Silas	856
Hambleton, James	452	Handley, Ezekiel	617
Hambleton, John	206	Handley, Jeremiah	617
Hamer, James	206	Handley, Richard	207
Hamford, Andrew	206	Handlin, Matthias	617
Hamilton, ...	871	Handrix, John	617
Hamilton, Andrew	206	Hank, Tobias	617
Hamilton, Benjamin	206, 616	Hankins, Daniel	207, 617
Hamilton, George	206	Hankins, J.S.F.	617
Hamilton, James	(2) 206, 379, (2) 616	Hankins, John	862
		Hankins, Joseph	207, 617
		Hankins, Thomas	617
Hamilton, John	206, (2) 616	Hankins, William	617
		Hankinson, Aaron	347, 352
Hamilton, Robert	206	Hankinson, James	617
Hamilton, Thomas	206, (2) 207	Hankinson, John	617
		Hankinson, Joseph	617
Hamilton, William	207, 616	Hankinson, Kenneth	393
Hamlin, Isaac	862	Hankinson, Reuben	617
Hamlin, John	616	Hankinson, William	477, 617
Hammell, John	335, 378	Hannah, Preston	115
Hammill, John	426	Hannah, William	617
Hammond, Thomas	616	Hannas, Robert	617
Hampson, Daniel	616	Hanner, George	207, 617
Hampson, Daniel, Jr.	616	Hanness, William	207
Hampstead, Robert	207	Hanning, George	207
Hampton, James	(2) 616	Hansell, Anthony	617
Hampton, John	377, 393, 452, (2) 616, 852	Hansilpacker, William	617
		Hanton, Thomas	617
		Hanville, James	617
Hampton, Moses	616	Hanzey, Samuel	618

Hapler, Conrad	856	Harker, John	619
Harber, Edward	618	Harker, Jonathan	845
Harber, John	618	Harker, Joseph	393
Harber, Obadiah	618	Harker, Nathaniel	208, 619
Harberson, George	207	Harker, Earnest	844
Harbert, Daniel	618	Harley, Hugh	208
Harbert, James	465, 618	Harmer, James	208
Harbert, John	618	Harmon, Thomas	619
Harbert, Thomas	29, 104	Harparie, John	619
Harbough, Tuer	618	Harpending, Andrew	619
Harbourt, Edward	618	Harper, William	(2) 208, 619
HarCourt, Abram	207, 618		
Harcourt, William	618	Harr, James	619
Harculus, William	618	Harriman, Jacob	619
Hardcastle, John	115	Harriman, Samuel	393
Harden, John	207	Harring, Abraham	393
Harden, William	618	Harring, Abram A.P.	393
Hardenbrook, Isaac	618	Harring, Cornelius	393
Hardenbrook, John	618	Harring, George	208
Hardenbrook, Lewis	618	Harring, John D.	426
Hardenbrook, Lodowick	618	Harrington, William	619
Hardenbrook, Peter	207, (2) 618	Harriott, Asher	619
		Harriott, Ephraim	619
Harder, Christian	618	Harriott, George	393
Harder, Henry	618	Harriott, Samuel	619
Harder, Philip	618, 832	Harris, ...	393, 871
Harder, William	618	Harris, Amariah	444, 484
Hardey, William	618	Harris, Benjamin	619
Harding, John	207	Harris, Daniel	619
Hardly, Richard	618	Harris, David	619
Hardman, Michael	208, 618	Harris, Edmond	619
Hardwick, William	208, 618	Harris, Ephraim	619
Hardy, Isaac	208	Harris, Garret	465
Harford, John	208	Harris, George	208, 465
Haring, Abram	618	Harris, Isaac	377, 619
Haring, Abram J.	619	Harris, Jacob	28, 37, 49, 54, 73, 208, 619
Haring, David	619		
Haring, David P.	619		
Haring, Frederick	619		
Haring, Garret	619	Harris, James	(2) 452
Haring, Garret, F.	619	Harris, Jeremiah	619
Haring, Gertjee	619	Harris, John	208, 619, (2) 620, 832
Haring, John F.	465		
Haring, John J.	619		
Haring, Joseph A.	619	Harris, Matthias	426, 620
Haring, Peter A.	619	Harris, Moses	620
Haring, Peter G.	619	Harris, Reuben	620
Harker, ...	40, 96, 109	Harris, Samuel	208, 620
		Harris, Squire	620
Harker, Able	208, 619	Harris, Thomas	208, 620
Harker, Abraham	(2) 208	Harris, Walter	208, 620
Harker, Daniel	208, 347, 359	Harris, William	208, (3) 620
Harker, David	619	Harris, Winans	620

Name	Page
Harrison, Aaron	620
Harrison, Abiel	620
Harrison, Abijah	620
Harrison, Abraham	620
Harrison, Abram	620
Harrison, Adorrjah	620
Harrison, Amos	620
Harrison, Charles	393
Harrison, Daniel	477, 620
Harrison, David	620
Harrison, George	(2) 620
Harrison, Isaac	37, 96, 208, (2) 620
Harrison, Job	620
Harrison, John	115, 209, 620
Harrison, Jonathan	209
Harrison, Joseph	453
Harrison, Jotham	620
Harrison, Matthew	620
Harrison, Moses	621
Harrison, Reuben	426, 621
Harrison, Stephen	621
Harrison, Thomas	621
Harrison, William	209, 394, 621
Hart, Absalom	621
Hart, Asa	621
Hart, Asher	621
Hart, Cornelius D.	621
Hart, Daniel	621
Hart, Ebenezer	621
Hart, Frederick	209, 621
Hart, Jesse	375
Hart, John	621
Hart, John R.	621
Hart, Joseph	(2) 621
Hart, Levi	839
Hart, Nathaniel	621
Hart, Patrick	209
Hart, Philip	621
Hart, Ralph	477
Hart, Samuel	621
Hart, Stephen	621
Hart, Titus	621
Hart, William	477, 862
Harter, Peter	852
Harthaway, Thomas	209
Harthough, Lewis	484
Hartipee, William	394
Hartman, Christian	621
Hartman, Christopher	621
Hartman, Coonrad	621
Hartman, Cornelius	621
Hartman, Michael	209, 621
Hartseff, Zachariah	621
Hartshorn, David	622
Hartshorne, Lewis	622
Hartshorne, Richard	344, 373
Hartshough, Lewis	622
Hartshough, Lucas	622
Hartsough, Aug.	622
Harvey, Michael	842
Harwood, Thomas	129, 209
Hashorn, John	862
Haskell, Jonathan	622
Hatch, Herman	622
Hater, George	622
Hatfield, Aaron	622
Hatfield, Abner	622
Hatfield, Andrew	622
Hatfield, Daniel	622
Hatfield, Edward	622
Hatfield, Elias	622
Hatfield, John	622
Hatfield, John, Jr.	622
Hatfield, Joseph	622
Hatfield, Morris	622
Hatfield, Moses	622
Hatfield, Stephen	209
Hatfield, Thomas	862
Hatfield, Zopher	622
Hathaway, Benoni	47, 325, 345, 359
Hathaway, Isaac	856
Hathaway, Shadrack	115
Hathaway, Simon	209
Hathaway, Theodorus	209
Hathaway, Theophilus	209
Hathaway, Thomas	209
Hatheway, ...	622
Hatheway, Benjamin	622
Hatheway, Isaac	622
Hatheway, John	622
Hatheway, Jonathan	622
Hatheway, Joseph	622
Hattle, Peter	622
Hattonfield, Thomas	862
Haun, John	622
Haun, William	622
Hause, John	622
Hautenberg, Peter	622
Havens, Darling	623
Havens, Jesse	623
Havens, Moses	623
Havens, Thomas	465, 623
Haviland, John	426

Name	Page	Name	Page
Hawk, Jacob	(2) 623	Hazlet, Robert	394
Hawkenberry, Hermany	623	Hazlett, John	852
Hawkins, George	623	Hazlett, Samuel	21, 22, 100
Hawkins, John	209, 623		
Hawkins, Zachariah	623	Hazling, Richard	624
Hawlen, Nathaniel	623	Head, Francis	624
Hawn, John	852	Headdy, James	624
Hay, David	426	Headdy, Samuel	624
Hay, John	371	Headdy, Thomas	624
Hayback, Solomon	623	Headland, Cornelius	426
Haycock, Daniel	209	Headley, Carey	624, 856
Hayden, Jepaniah	623	Headley, Ephraim	624
Haydon, John	623	Headley, Francis	624, 856
Hayes, Abiel	623	Headley, Jacob	624
Hayes, David	209	Headley, James	466
Hayes, John	209	Headley, John	210
Hayes, Michael	(2) 209, 623	Headley, John F.	624
		Headley, Joseph	624
Hayes, Samuel	324, 326, 328, 336, 341, 366	Headley, Moses	210, 624
		Headley, Nathaniel	210
		Headley, Stephen	624
Hayley, John	623	Headly, Francis	347, 366
Hayman, ...	426	Heafland, Charles	426
Haynes, Frederick	210	Heard, General	25
Haynes, John	623	Heard, James	58, 81
Haynes, Joseph	466	Heard, John	59, 81, (2) 320, 444
Haynes, William	210		
Hays, Daniel	623		
Hays, David	(2) 623, 848	Heard, Nathaniel	15, 333, 334, (2) 335, 343, 349
Hays, John	481, (4) 623		
Hays, Joseph	623	Heart, Patrick	210
Hays, Robert	623	Heath, Andrew	624
Hays, Stephen	482	Heath, David	624
Hays, Thomas	90, 426	Heath, Richard	624
Hays, William	(2), 623	Heath, Richard, Jr.	624
Hayward, Bethuel	623	Heath, Thomas	624
Hayward, Daniel	623	Heaton, Jabish	624
Hayward, Ephraim	210, 623	Heaton, Thomas	444, 624
Hayward, Hiram	623	Heator, James	862
Hayward, Isaac	210	Heaviland, Job	210, 624
Hayward, Jonathan	623	Heaviland, Joseph	210, 624
Hayward, Silas	624	Hedd, Peter	624
Hayward, Simeon	624	Hedden, Abijah	624
Haywood, Eton	437	Hedden, Allen	624
Haywood, Jonathan	624	Hedden, Caleb	624
Haywood, Joseph	394	Hedden, David	624
Hazard, Charles	210	Hedden, Ebenezer	210, 625
Hazelton, Abraham	210	Hedden, Edward	625
Hazelton, Abram	210, 624	Hedden, Ephraim	625
Hazelton, Isaac	210	Hedden, James	371
Hazen, Abraham	624	Hedden, Jonas	625
Hazen, Moses	58	Hedden, Joseph	625
Hazen, Thomas	624	Hedden, Nehemiah	625

Hedden, Obadiah	625	Hendricks, ...	394
Hedden, Samuel	625	Hendricks, Abram	852
Hedden, Simon	453	Hendricks, Baker	626
Hedden, Thomas	625	Hendricks, Isaac	626
Hedden, Zadock	852	Hendricks, William M.	626
Hedden, Zephaniah	625	Hendrickson, Abraham	626
Hedgelin, ...	625	Hendrickson, Abram	626
Hedger (or Hedges) Joseph	210	Hendrickson, Auke	437
		Hendrickson, Benjamin	466
Hedges, see also, Hedger		Hendrickson, Cornelius	(2) 626
Hedges, Benjamin	625	Hendrickson, Daniel	345, 352, 394, 626
Hedges, Eli	625		
Hedges, Elias	466, 856	Hendrickson, David	(2) 426
Hedges, Gilbert	625	Hendrickson, Elias	(2) 626
Hedges, Jeremiah	625	Hendrickson, Garret	437
Hedges, Sylvenus	625	Hendrickson, Hendrick	626
Hegeman, Aaron	625	Hendrickson, James	129, 626
Hegeman, Benjamin	625	Hendrickson, John	129, 626
Hegeman, Peter	625	Hendrickson, Okey	626
Height, David	477	Hendrickson, Peter	626
Height, John	625	Hendrickson, Thomas	626
Heind, David	625	Hendrickson, William	626
Heingey, Samuel	625	Hendry, Samuel	16, 17, 32, 33, (2) 52, 81
Heisling, William	210, 625		
Heister, Jacob	210		
Heizer, Henry	625		
Helbert, David	625	Hendry, Thomas	342, 377
Helebrant, David	625	Heneman, Jacob	626
Helel, Leonard	625	Heneman, Richard	626
Heller, William	862	Henion, George	211
Helmes, Hance	625	Henly, William	627
Helmes, John	625	Henning, George	627
Helmes, Joseph	626	Hennion, Cornelius	20, 22, (3) 36, 81
Helms, William	17, 31, (2) 34, 52, 81, 394		
		Hennion, David	627
		Hennion, John	627
Helsifer, Christopher	210	Henns, Jacob	627
Heminover, Anthony	626	Henowil, John	627
Hemmel, see Emmel		Henry, Albert	862
Hemphill, Robert	626	Henry, Eleanor	76
Hendershot, Abram	626	Henry, George	627
Hendershot, Jacob	626	Henry, James	627
Hendershot, Michael	626	Henry, John	(2) 211, 627
Hendershot, William	626		
Henderson, David	626	Henry, Joseph	627
Henderson, Isaac	210	Henry, Peter	627
Henderson, John	394, 626, 848	Henry, Robert R.	75
		Hensminger, Henry	211, 627
Henderson, Patrick	(2) 210, 626	Hepburn, William	627
		Hepner, John	211
Henderson, Thomas	334, (2) 335, 359	Heppard, William	627
		Herbert, James	627
Henderson, William	211	Herbert, (or Hubbert) John	627, 862

Name	Page
Herbert, Obediah	627
Herbert, Robert	627
Herbert, Samuel	627
Herbert, Thomas	627
Herder, Christian	627
Herin, Gershom	627
Herony, Joseph	211
Herriman, Jacob	627
Herriman, Samuel	(2) 627
Herring, ...	394
Herrington, William	627
Herriss, John	627
Herrod, John	627
Herrod, Samuel	627
Herron, Charles	211
Herron, James	60, 81
Hervey, John	627
Hess, Michael	627
Hess, Peter, Sr.	628
Hessell, Frelick	628
Hessler, John	628
Hetfield, Daniel	466
Hetfield, Stephen	61, (2) 211, 628
Heward, Joseph	394
Hewes, William	628
Hewett, Benjamin	628
Hewett, Caleb	628
Hewett, Moses	628
Hewett, Samuel	628
Hewett, Thomas	628
Hewett, William	628
Hewit, Benajah	628
Hewitt, Benajah	211
Hewlings, Joseph	628
Hewlitt, Charles	628
Hewlitt, Charles	211
Hews, see also, Huse	
Hews, see also, Hush	
Hews, Alpheus	856
Hewyard, Benjamin	628
Hey, William	484
Heyers, Benjamin	628
Heyers, Reuben	628
Hibbets, James	628
Hibbey, Ephraim	211
Hibler, George	628
Hibler, Jacob	628
Hice, Jacob	628
Hice, Jasper	628
Hickley, Timothy	628
Hickman, Isaac	628
Hickman, James	628
Hickman, Thomas	628
Hicks, Joseph	211
Hick, Samuel	211, 629
Hickson, Amos	211, 629
Hickson, Andrew	211
Hickson, James	862
Hickson, Jonathan	211
Hickson, Matthew	211, 629
Hide, John	862
Hidglor, William	629
Hier, Hendrick	211, 629
Hier, Walter	211, 629
Hier, William	629
Higbee, Hendrick	211
Higbee, Obadiah	852
Higbee, Richard	394
Higbey, Absolom	629
Higbey, Edward	629
Higbey, Henry	629
Higbey, Isaac	629
Higbey, John	629
Higbey, Joseph	629
Higbey, Obadiah	629
Higbey, Philip	629
Higbey, Richard	629
Higday, George	629
Higgins, Azariah	466
Higgins, Benjamin	629
Higgins, Daniel	629
Higgins, Francis	852
Higgins, James	629
Higgins, Jediah	629
Higgins, John	(2) 17, 100, 212
Higgins, Jonathan	848
Higgins, Michael	212
High, Nathan	629
Hight, John	629
Hight, John N.	629
Hight, Nicholas	863
Hilcocks, James	212
Hill, Adam, Jr.	629
Hill, Daniel	629
Hill, Jacob	629
Hill, James	212, (2) 629
Hill, John	(2) 212, (2) 630
Hill, Martin	115
Hill, Peter	630
Hill, Samuel	212, (3) 630
Hill, Thomas	394
Hill, Uriah	630
Hill, William	630
Hilland, Henry	212
Hillebrant, Henry	(2) 212

Hilliard, Gershom	212	Hoagland, Abram	213, (2)
Hilliard, Thomas	212		631
Hillman, Daniel	630	Hoagland, Albert	631
Hillman, John	630	Hoagland, Amos	631
Hillman, Josiah	337, 359	Hoagland, Christian	466
Hillman, Samuel	(2) 630	Hoagland, Derrick	631
Hillman, Samuel A.	630	Hoagland, George	631
Hillman, Seth	630	Hoagland, Harm A.	631
Hillow, Jonathan	212, 630	Hoagland, Henry	631
Hillyard, William	630	Hoagland, Hermanus	631
Hilsey, Joseph	212, 630	Hoagland, Jacob	632
Hilsey, William	630	Hoagland, James	632
Hilyard, Simon	630	Hoagland, Johannes	632
Hilyer, James	630	Hoagland, John	213, (5)
Hilyer, John	630		632, 863
Hilyer, Simon	630	Hoagland, John C.	632
Hilyer, William	453	Hoagland, Joseph C.	632
Himeon, Adam	630	Hoagland, Lucas	632
Hinchman, John	630	Hoagland, Luke	632
Hinckley, Joshua	212	Hoagland, Martin	632
Hinds, Benjamin	852, 856	Hoagland, Oakey	339, 359,
Hinds, Dennis	212		836
Hinds, Esau	212	Hoagland, Peter	632
Hinds, Frederick	212, (2)	Hoagland, Richard	466
	630	Hoagland, Samuel	632
Hinds, John	(2) 212,	Hoagland, Teunis	632
	630	Hoagland, Tunis	632, 832
Hinds, Joseph	213, 630	Hoagland, William	632
Hinds, Robert	630	Hobbs, David	632
Hinds, Stephen	630	Hobbs, Elisha	213
Hinds, William	631	Hobbs, James	213, 632
Hines, Dennis	213, 631	Hockenberry, John	213, 632
Hink, John	631	Hodge, Francis	213
Hinkle, Jacob	213, 631	Hodge, Joseph	632
Hinley, William	631	Hoff, Abel	632
Hinman, Asabel	848	Hoff, Charles	633
Hinman, Samuel	394	Hoff, Dirck	633
Hire, Thomas	631	Hoff, John	466
Hires, John	631	Hoff, Nicholas	633
Hise, Jacob	631	Hoffman, Aaron	213
Hiss, Michael	631	Hoffman, Benjamin	213, 633
Hite, Christopher	213	Hoffman, Jacob	633
Hitman, John	631	Hoffman, John	633
Hixon, Abner	631	Hoffman, William	213, 633
Hixon, Amos	466	Hog, James	633
Hixon, James	213, 631,	Hogate, Philip	633
	863	Hogeland, Abraham	426
Hixon, Jediah	631	Hogeland, John	427
Hixon, John	213, 631	Hogencamp, Evert	633
Hixon, Joseph	213, 631,	Hogencamp, John	633
	863	Hogencamp, Martin	633
Hixon, Matthew	631	Hogg, Richard	213
Hixson, William	213	Holcomb, Elijah	213, 633
Hoagland, Abraham	327, 453,	Holcomb, George	343, 366,
	863		437

Holcomb, Jacob	427	Holmes, Joseph	634
Holcomb, Richard	633	Holmes, Samuel	634
Holden, Benjamin	(2) 214, (2) 633	Holmes, Stout	634
		Holmes, William (Indian)	(2) 214, (2) 634
Holden, Henry	214, 633		
Holden, Levi	394	Holshart, John	634
Holden, Richard	633	Holt, Daniel	214, 634
Holden, Thomas	214	Holt, Samuel	214
Holdren, Henry	633	Holton, Benjamin	634
Hole, Charles	633	Holton, Ephraim	634
Hole, Daniel	633	Holton, Joseph	634
Holeman, Thomas	633	Holton, Peter	634
Holl, Jacob	633	Holts, Daniel	832
Holl, Thomas	394	Homan, Andrew	634
Holland, James	214	Homan, Daniel	634
Holland, Thomas	214	Homan, David	634
Holliday, James	214	Homan, Evart,	634
Hollingshead, Francis	633	Homan, John	466
Hollingshead, James	394	Homan, Thomas	634
Hollingshead, William	633	Honny, William	634
Hollingsworth, Thomas	633	Hood, William	214
Hollinshead, Jacob	373	Hoof, John	214
Hollinshead, John	16, 31, 33, 52, 54, 68	Hook, Stephen	634
		Hook, Tobias	634
		Hooper, ...	116
Hollister, John	633	Hooper, Abram	863
Holloway, Benjamin	214, 633	Hooper, Daniel	453
Holloway, Elkanah	214, 634	Hooper, David	453
Holloway, Richard	634	Hooper, James	634
Holme, Benjamin	346, 352	Hooper, Joseph	634
Holme, Benjamin, Jr.	444	Hooper, Philip	634
Holme, John	346, 353	Hooper, Robert	214, 634
Holmes, Abijah	47, 336, 340, 359, 373	Hooper, Robert L.	842
		Hoops, Robert	334, 366
		Hope, ...	395
Holmes, Anthony	634	Hope, Adam	394
Holmes, Asher	47, 323, 325, (2) 326, 344, 353	Hope, William	863
		Hopewell, John	215
		Hopkins, Abijah	395, 427
		Hopkins, Benjamin	427
Holmes, Elisha	38, 39, 100	Hopkins, Caleb	329, 427
		Hopkins, Edward	634
Holmes, James	16, (2) 31, 38, 39, 73, 82, (3) 214, 377, 394, 634	Hopkins, Hugh	634
		Hopkins, John	215, 634
		Hopkins, Nathan	466
		Hopkins, William	859
		Hophire, Samuel	634
		Hoppen, Samuel	634
Holmes, John	14, 29, 50, 82, 214, 634, 863	Hopper, Abram A.	635
		Hopper, Andrew	635
		Hopper, Henry	215
		Hopper, John	53, 105, 395
Holmes, Jonathan	38, 39, 40, 52, 53, 82, 444	Hopper, John J.	635
		Hopper, Jonathan	395
		Hopper, Peter A.	635

Hopper, Richard	635	Horton, Joseph	395
Hopper, Rinard	215, 635	Horton, Joshua	(2) 635
Hopping, Ezekiel	635	Horton, Nathaniel	395
Hopping, John	635	Horton, Zephaniah	635
Hopping, Samuel	635	Hortwick, Barent	138, 482
Hopping, Silas	635	Hortwick, Barnabas	215
Hoppock, Cornelius	395	Hortwick, John	635
Hopsiker, Paul, see Hopsiker, Powles		Hortwick, Matthias	215
		Hortwick, Nathaniel	215
Hopsiker, Powles (or Paul)	215	Hosborn, Cooper	635
		Hosborn, John	636
Hopson, Jordan	116	Hosbrook, John	116
Hore, see Horn		Hottenbury, John	636
Horine, William	215	Hottman, George	215
Horn, Benjamin	39, 40, 54, 90, 215	Hough, William	375
		Houghland, John	636
		Houghton, Jacob	395
Horn, James	215	Houghton, Joab	325, 342, 359
Horn, (or Hore) John	635		
Horn, Moses	215	Houghton, Thomas	636
Horn, Ralph	215, 635	Houke, Tobias	636
Horn, Stephen	635	Houman, Asahel	466
Horn, William	635	Houseman, Jacob	444
Hornbaker, Philip	215, 635	Houseman, John	395
Hornbeck, Benjamin	427	Houseman, Mathew	216
Hornblower, James	635	Houseman, Thomas	216
Hornblower, Joseph	215	Housler, David	636
Hornblower, Josiah	215	Housman, John	636
Hornden, Jonathan	635	Houston, William C.	395
Horne, Joseph	635	Houten, Aaron	216
Horne, William	845	Houten, Cornelius	395
Horner, George	857	Hover, Henry	395
Horner, Samuel	(2) 635	Hover, Manuel	395
Horner, Timothy	635	Howard, Benjamin	216, (2) 636
Hornfoot, see also Horniford			
		Howard, Ebenezer	636
Hornfoot (or Horniford) Andrew	215	Howard, Elihu	216, 636
		Howard, Ephraim	136, 216, 481
Horniford, see also Hornfoot			
		Howard, Hiram	216, 636
Horniford (or Hornfoot) Andrew	635	Howard, John	216, (2) 636, 863
		Howard, Joseph	116, 395, 636
Hornler, John	857		
Horsebrook, John	635	Howard, Michael	216
Hort, Thomas	116	Howard, Samuel	216
Hortman, George	215	Howard, Simeon	216
Horton, ...	635	Howe, James	636
Horton, Benjamin	(2) 635	Howe, John	108, 460, 636
Horton, Caleb	395		
Horton, Daniel	635	Howell, Aaron	636
Horton, David	466	Howell, Absalom	636
Horton, Elijah	635	Howell, Arthur	636, 843
Horton, Jason	635	Howell, Asher	636
Horton, Jonathan	73, 335, 346, 377	Howell, Benjamin	636
		Howell, Caleb	832

Howell, Charles	453	Hudson, William	637, 857
Howell, David	(2) 636, 832	Huff, Andrew	637
		Huff, Benjamin	217, 637
Howell, Ebenezer	(2) 37, 68, (2) 336, 366	Huff, Bennum	637
		Huff, Derrick	637
		Huff, Isaac	637
Howell, Edward	116, 216	Huff, John	637
Howell, Elias	363	Huff, Moses	637
Howell, Ellet	444, 837	Huff, Nicholas	637
Howell, Ezekiel	(2) 636	Huff, Peter	217, 637
Howell, Henry	444	Huff, Richard	637
Howell, Israel	636	Huff, Thomas	638
Howell, Jacob	216, 637	Huff, Tunis	638
Howell, James	32, 105, 437	Huffman, John	638
		Huffman, William	481
Howell, Jeremiah	466	Hufty, Jacob	638
Howell, John	29, 50, 51, 82, 216, (2) 637	Hugg, John	638
		Hugg, Joseph	217
		Hugg, Richard	217
		Hugg, Samuel	320, 395
Howell, Jonathan	(2) 216, 637	Hugg, Thomas	396
		Huggins, John	638
Howell, Lewis	(2) 31, 74	Hughes, Alpheus	638
		Hughes, John	217, 638
Howell, Luther	637	Hughes, Memucan	375
Howell, Reading	342, 373	Hughes, Patrick	217
Howell, Richard	(2) 17, 31, (2) 51, 68	Hughes, Richard	217, 638
		Hughy, Will	638
		Hukey, John	638
Howell, Samuel	637, 857	Hulebart, Marties	638
Howell, Silas	13, 29, 82, 637	Hulfish, John	638
		Hulick, ...	396
Howell, Thomas	216, 637, 848	Hulick, Derrick	638
		Hulick, Henry	638
Howell, William	(2) 216, 637	Hulick, John	638
		Hulings, John	638
Howk, Philip	637	Hulit, George	638
Hoyle, Thomas	217	Hulit, John	638
Hubbard, Eliphalet	129	Hulit, Peter	466
Hubbard, Jacob	344, 377	Hulit, William	638
Hubbard, Jacobus	637	Hull, ...	396
Hubbell, John	217	Hull, Benjamin	217, 638
Hubbert, see Herbert		Hull, David	638
Hubbert, Ephraim	637	Hull, George	857
Hubble, John	116	Hull, Isaac	217, 348, 373, (2) 638
Hubbs, David	217, (2) 637		
Hubbs, James	637	Hull, Jacob	638
Huddy, Joshua	324, 395	Hull, Jahiel	217
Hudson, Abram	116	Hull, James	638
Hudson, John	217	Hull, Jeremiah	466
Hudson, Nathaniel	637	Hull, John	638
Hudson, Samuel	637	Hull, Josiah	217
Hudson, Thomas	637	Hull, Reuben	638

Hull, Samuel	116		Hunt, Oliver	640
Hull, Solomon	217		Hunt, Ralph	640, 840
Hullsiger, Christopher	217		Hunt, Richard	640
Huln, Matthew	638		Hunt, Samuel	640, 849
Huln, William	638		Hunt, Solomon	640
Huls, William	477		Hunt, Stephen	(2) 335, 346, 353
Hulsart, Benjamin	638			
Hulsart, Cornelius	638		Hunt, Thomas	640
Hulsart, Cornelius H.	639		Hunt, Varnell	640
Hulsart, Matthew	639		Hunt, Wilson	863
Hulsart, William	639		Hunter, Andrew	35, 53, 75, 217, 335, 379, 640
Hulse, Matthias	639			
Hulse, Timothy	639			
Hulshart, John	639			
Hulst, John	639		Hunter, Harman	217, 640
Hulst, William	639		Hunter, James	640
Humans, James	639		Hunter, John	640
Hume, John	639		Hunter, Joseph	217
Humes, James	639		Hunter, Richard	849
Hummell, Elijah	639		Hunter, William	852
Hummon, Isaac	639		Hunterdon, Gilbert	217, 640
Humphrevil, Timothy	466		Hunting, Matthew	640
Humphrie, Jacob	639		Hunting, Samuel	640
Humphries, David	217		Huntington, John	373, 836, 852
Humphries, John	639			
Humphries, Joseph	217, 639		Huntington, Samuel	396
Humphries, Thomas	639		Huntington, Simon	640
Hund, David	639		Huntly, John	218
Hund, Lewis	639		Hurd, Daniel	640
Hunds, Samuel	840		Hurd, David	640
Hunn, John S.	639		Hurd, Josiah	640
Hunn, Thomas	344, 366		Hurd, Stephen	640
Hunsted, Richard	116		Hurder, John	857, 863
Hunt, Abraham	342, 359		Hurley, James	90
Hunt, Benjamin	639, 863		Hurley, John	640
Hunt, Daniel	639		Hurley, Martin	(2) 30, 105
Hunt, David	477			
Hunt, Elias	444		Hurley, William	640
Hunt, Israel	639		Hurst, Andrew	640
Hunt, Jacob	217, 639		Huse (or Hews) Alpheus	640
Hunt, James	217, 482, 639, 848, 863		Hush (or Hews) Thomas	640
			Husk, Jonathan	218, 640
			Husted, Ephraim	641, 874
Hunt, Jesse	639		Husted, Hosea	218
Hunt, John	396, 639, 832		Husted, John	218, 641
			Husted, Reuben	218, 641
Hunt, John Jr.	640		Husten, Christory	641
Hunt, John S.	640		Huston, Hendrick	641
Hunt, John, Sr.	640		Huston, Robert	641
Hunt, Jonathan	466, 640		Hutch, John	(2) 218, 453
Hunt, Joseph	857			
Hunt, Josiah	116, 217		Hutchens, David	641
Hunt, Mansfield	640		Hutchens, William	641
Hunt, Nathaniel	342, 353, 375, 437		Hutchin, John	33, 34
			Hutchins, Gabriel	218

Hutchins, John	52, 53, 90	Ingersoll, Benjamin	642	
Hutchings, Isaac	641	Ingersoll, Ebenezer	642	
Hutchings, William	641	Ingersoll, John	642	
Hutchings, Abraham	641	Ingersoll, Joseph	437	
Hutchinson, Cornelius	641	Ingersoll, Joseph, Jr.	642	
Hutchinson, Ezekiel	641	Innes, James	642	
Hutchinson, John	(2) 641	Innis, see Ennis		
Hutchinson, Thomas	641	Inscho, Obadiah	863	
Hutchinson, William	218, 641	Insell, Samuel	642	
Hutsinger, Peter	641	Inskeep, Benjamin	453	
Hutson, Jacob	641	Inskip, John	396, 842	
Hutton, John	641	Inslee, Henry	832	
Hutton, Timothy	427	Inslee, John	642	
Huyler, Adam	396	Inslee, Joseph	642	
Huyler, John	396	Insley, Henry	857	
Huysman, Jacobus	641	Irelan, Amos	642	
Hyer, Jacob	344, 353, 836	Irelan, David	642	
		Irelan, Edmond	642	
Hyer, Jacob, Jr.	53, 105	Irelan, George	642	
Hyland, Henry	218	Irelan, Japhet	642	
Hyler, see Huyler		Irelan, Jonathan	642	
Hyler, Adam	871	Irelan, Joseph	642	
Hyler, John	641	Irelan, Reuben	642	
Hyler, Nicholas	641	Irelan, Thomas	642	
Hyler, William	641	Ireland, Daniel	218	
Hyre, William	641	Ireland, Dayton	218	
		Ireland, Edward	437	
		Ireland, James	642	
		Ireland, John	642	
Idle, Jacob	641	Ireland, Thomas	116, 218, 642	
Ihnetler, George	641			
Iller, John	218	Irons, Garrett	642	
Imell, John	129	Irons, James	642	
Imlay, David	328, 396	Irvin, James	218, 642	
Imlay, Ezekiel	453	Irvine, Andrew	427	
Imlay, Gilbert	427	Irvine, William	68, 218	
Imlay, Isaac	437	Irving, James	843	
Imlay, James H.	366	Irwin, William	218	
Imlay, Jonathan	641	Isleton, Jonathan	218, 477, 642	
Imlay, Robert	642			
Imlay, William	453	Isleton, Matthew	642	
Imlay, William E.	396	Isleton, Samuel	642	
Imlay, William Eugene	21, 82	Ivens, Abel	218	
Incell, John	218	Ivins, Abel	643	
Indian, see Cromwell, Oliver, Cuffey, William, Dillap, James, Holmes, William		Ivins, Solomon	218, 643	
		Jack (Negro)	863	
		Jacks, John	643	
Ineel, John	218	Jackson, ...	396	
Ingalson, Daniel	642	Jackson, Benjamin	466	
Ingalson, Isaac	642	Jackson, Charles	373	
Ingard, Benjamin	642	Jackson, Daniel	219, 643	
Ingersol, Benjamin	477	Jackson, Hugh	643	

Name	Page
Jackson, John	(2) 219, 643, 842
Jackson, Lewis	643
Jackson, Nathan	871
Jackson, Richard	117
Jackson, Samuel	219
Jackson, Stephen	396, 643
Jacobs, John	219, 643
Jacobs, Joseph	219
Jacobus, ...	396
Jacobus, Cornelius	643
Jacobus, Henry	219, 643
Jacobus, James	(3) 643
Jacobus, John	219, (2) 643
Jacobus, Richard	643
Jaggers, Jermiah	643
Jaggers, Nathan	643
James, Daniel	219
James, David	117
James, Elias	643
James, Jehiel	643
James, John	643, 844
James, Levi	643
James, Lewis	138
James, Robert	466, 643
James, Thomas	219, 643
James, Uriah	643
James, William	643
Jameson, Robert	219
Jamison, Alexander	219, 643
Jamison, David	219
Jamison, Thomas	219
Jamison, William	219
Janes, Phineas	644
Jaques, Moses	47, 341, 353
Jaquet, Peter	466
Jaquett, Peter	852
Jaquish, ...	396
Jaquish, Jonathan	644
Jaquish, Samuel	644
Jaraloman, Henry	396
Jaraloman, Jacobus	396
Jaraloman, John	453
Jarman, Azariah	644
Jaroleman, Halmack	644
Jaroloman, James	396
Jarvis, Philip	427
Jasper, Richard	219, 644
Jay, John	219
Jay, Joseph	219, 427
Jeans, Elias	644
Jefferies, James	644
Jefferies, John	(2) 644
Jeffers, Aaron	644
Jeffers, Caleb	644
Jeffers, David	219
Jeffers, Francis	644
Jeffrey, Francis	644
Jeffrey, Garret	480
Jeffrey, Henry	644
Jeffrey, Humphrey	219, 644
Jeffrey, John	644
Jemison, Isaac	644
Jemison, John	219, (2) 644
Jenkens, James	219
Jenkins, Benjamin	219
Jenkins, Ephraim	326, 396
Jenkins, James	220
Jenkins, John	852
Jenkins, Jonathan	396
Jenkins, Joseph	644, 832
Jenkins, Josiah	477
Jenkins, Nathaniel	33, 34, (2) 52, 105, 220
Jenkins, Tully	220
Jenkins, Zachariah	644
Jennings, Edward	644
Jennings, Jacob	336, 377,
Jennings, John	220, (2) 6
Jennings, Joshua	644
Jennings, Lawrence	644
Jennings, William	220, 466
Jennins, Luke	220
Jenny, John	645
Jenung, Jacob	220
Jermon, Reuben	366
Jerry, Jonathan	645
Jervis, Robert	645
Jess, Samuel	220, 645
Jewell, George	220, 645
Jewell, Hopewell	220
Jewell, Hubbard	220
Jewell, Ichabod	645
Jewell, John	(2) 645
Jewell, Mitchell	645
Jewell, Nathaniel	645
Jewell, Samuel	220, 645
Jewell, Seth	220
Jewell, William	220, 645
Jewett, Phoenix	220
Jewitt, Theunis	220
Jimerson, Daniel	852
Jimerson, Hugh	852
Jimerson, John	852

Jingley, Lemuel	645	Johnson, Jacob	427
Jinners, William	645	Johnson, James	33, 34, 105, (2) 221, 397, 427, (3) 646, 842, 852
Jinnings, John	645		
Jinnings, Joseph	645		
Jinson, James	645		
Job, John	220		
Job, Joseph	645		
Job, Peter	645	Johnson, John	(2) 117, 129, 138, (3) 221, (7) 646, 647, (2) 863
Job, Richard	220, 645		
Job, William	129		
Jobbs, William	117		
Jobes, Ezekiel	129		
Jobes, John	220		
Jobes, Robert	645	Johnson, John Jacob	647
Jobs, John	138, 220	Johnson, John R.	647
Jobs, Richard	110, 220	Johnson, Jonathan	(2) 647
Jobs, Samuel	220, 645	Johnson, Joseph	221, (5) 647, 852
Jobs, William	645		
Johnes, Isaac	645	Johnson, Lambert	453
Johnes, John	221	Johnson, Lawrence	647
Johnes, William	852	Johnson, Levi	61, 222
Johns, John	645	Johnson, Levy	222
Johnson, see also, Johnston		Johnson, Lewis	(2) 222, (2) 647
Johnson, Abner	221, 645, 646	Johnson, Martin	117, 647
		Johnson, Matthew	117, 647
Johnson, Adrian	221	Johnson, Matthias	328, 453
Johnson, Ananias	427	Johnson, Michael	647
Johnson, Ander	646	Johnson, Moses	863
Johnson, Andrew	221, 437	Johnson, Nathaniel	(2) 647
Johnson, Barney	221	Johnson, Othniel	222
Johnson, Barrent	646	Johnson, Peter	(2) 222, 466, (2) 647
Johnson, Benjamin	221, 646		
Johnson, Caleb	646		
Johnson, Cato	221	Johnson, Philip	(2) 335, 353
Johnson, Christopher	397		
Johnson, Cornelius	397	Johnson, Richard	14, 100, 345, 366, 647, 863
Johnson, Daniel	(2) 646		
Johnson, David	397, 646		
Johnson, Enoch, see Johnson, Erick		Johnson, Robert	222
		Johnson, Samuel	(2) 222, (2) 647, 852
Johnson, Enoch	646		
Johnson, Ephraim	646		
Johnson, Erick (or Enoch	221	Johnson, Samuel C.	129
		Johnson, Seth	38, 39, 54, (2) 55, 82, 453
Johnson, Gershom	847		
Johnson, George	(2) 221		
Johnson, Hendrick	221, 646		
Johnson, Henry	129, 221, 348, 373, 397, (2) 646	Johnson, Sylvanus	648
		Johnson, Thomas	(2) 222, 427, (3) 648
Johnson, Isaac	129, (2) 221, (3) 646	Johnson, Uzal	648

Johnson, William	(2) 222, 397, 466, 477, (8) 648, 832	Jones, Daniel	223, 467, (4) 649
		Jones, David	223, 342, 366, 649
Johnston, see also Johnson		Jones, Ebenezer	223
		Jones, Elijah	649
Johnston (or Johnson), Abraham	397, 648	Jones, Enoch	650
		Jones, Henry	223, 224, (4) 650
Johnston, Andrew	648		
Johnston, Benjamin	648	Jones, Hugh	650
Johnston, Caleb	648	Jones, Isaac	117, 224, (2) 650
Johnston, Cornelius	467		
Johnston, Daniel	648	Jones, Israel	650
Johnston, David	648, 844	Jones, James	(3) 224, (5) 650
Johnston, Heathcote	397		
Johnston, Hendrick	648	Jones, John	129, 224, (2) 650
Johnston, Henry	222, 648		
Johnston, Isaac	222, 648	Jones, Jonas	650
Johnston, Jabez	648	Jones, Jonathan	224, 650
Johnston, Jacob	(2) 648	Jones, Joseph	117, 467, (2) 650
Johnston, John	222, (2) 648		
		Jones, Joshua	224, 650
Johnston, John Jr.	649	Jones, Josiah	650
Johnston, Jonathan	649	Jones, Lawrence	650
Johnston, Joseph	222, (2) 649	Jones, Michael	224
		Jones, Moses	650
Johnston, Lawrence	832	Jones, Peter	852
Johnston, Levi	222	Jones, Ralph	438
Johnston, Lewis	467	Jones, Reuben	650
Johnston, Matthew	222	Jones, Richard	224, 650
Johnston, Matthias	649	Jones, Samuel	117, (2) 224, 467, (3) 651, 863
Johnston, Moses	649		
Johnston, Peter	467		
Johnston, Samuel	222, (2) 649		
		Jones, Stephen	(2) 651
Johnston, Uzal	341, 377	Jones, Thomas	371, 651, 841
Johnston, William	223, (4) 649		
		Jones, Timothy	224, 345, 377
Johnston, Windsor	223, 649		
Johnstone, George	649	Jones, Timothy, Jr.	651
Joiner, Michael	223	Jones, William	224, 397, (2) 651, 849, 852
Jolley, Lewis	649		
Jonas, John	223, 649		
Jones, Abiel	649	Jones, Zebulon	397
Jones, Abraham	223, 649	Jonet, Phoenix	224
Jones, Abram	649	Jonner, Samuel	224, 651
Jones, Alexander	(2) 223	Jordan, Felix	224
Jones, Ambrose	(2) 223, 649	Jordan, John	651
		Jordon, Felix	651
Jones, Anthony	223	Jordon, Frederick	224
Jones, Armstrong	223	Jordon, James	224, 651
Jones, Asa	223	Jordon, Jesse	852
Jones, Azariah	117	Jordon, John	651
Jones, Benjamin	649	Jordon, Michael	224, 651
Jones, Cornelius	649	Jordon, Richard	224

Jorney, John	651	Kelly, George	652
Joslin, Jeremiah	651	Kelly, Jacob	225
Joslin, Jeremy	224	Kelly, Jared	225
Joy, James	224	Kelly, Jeremiah	652
Juel, Licha	651	Kelly, Jesse	652
Justice, Jesse	225	Kelly, John	48, 225, 367, (2) 652
Justice, Joseph	467	Kelly, Matthew	225
Kaighn, John	225, 651	Kelly, Oliver	652
Kaighn, Samuel	375, 397	Kelly, Patrick	(2) 225, 652
Kain, Edward	225	Kelly, Samuel	652
Kaits, Philip	225	Kelly, Uriah	652
Kallender, Philip	651	Kelly, William	652
Kapenbaugh, Philip	849	Kelsey, Benjamin	117, 652
Kaper, Thomas	651	Kelsey, Daniel	652
Kark, James	477	Kelsey, Enos	324, 336, 347, 366, 379, 834, 841
Karney, Gilbert	225		
Karr, see also Carr			
Karr, Peter	225, 651	Kelsey, John	652
Karr, (or Kerr) Walter	225	Kelsey, William	375, 397
Kauzcriss, Jacob	857	Kelso, Robert	837
Kayn, John	427	Kelson, Thomas	652
Kean, John	842	Kelty, Michael	226, 652
Kearney, see also Carney		Kelty, William	226, 652
Kearney, Lawrence	225	Kemble, Nathan	226
Keatheart, Robert	651	Kemble, Nathaniel	226
Keeler, Lewis	651	Kemble, Peter	653
Keelor, Thomas	225	Kemp, John	653
Keen, Benjamin	427	Kempburn, Peter	226
Keen, Edward	225, 651	Kemper, Daniel	835
Keen, Jacob	225	Kemper, Jacob	14, 15, 96
Keen, James	397, 652		
Keen, Nicholas	329, 397, 871	Kempton, Peter	226, 653
		Kenan, Thomas	653
Keen, Reuben	652	Kendall, Clayton	653
Keenon, Peter B.	225, 652	Kendle, James	653
Keeper, Thomas	652	Kennan, Joseph	467
Keesler, William	652	Kennan, Peter	835
Keet, David	225	Kennard, John	226
Kehela, Thomas	652	Kennedy, Charles	130
Keilson, David	652	Kennedy, Henry	653
Keisler, John	225, 652	Kennedy, James	653
Kelley, John	346	Kennedy, John	839
Kellison, William	652	Kennedy, Thomas	(2) 653
Kellory, John	652	Kenney, Abraham	428
Kelly, Abraham	652	Kenney, Peter	467
Kelly, Abram	652	Kenny, Jacob	226
Kelly, Bartholemew	225	Kenny, William	653
Kelly, Carpenter	467	Kent, David	226
Kelly, Daniel	225	Kent, Elias	226
Kelly, David	225, (2) 652	Kent, Jacob	226, 653
		Kent, James	653

Kent, Jonas	226	Kilsey, John	227, 654
Kent, Joshua	226	Kilsey, Joseph	227
Knet, Phineas	653	Kimble, Caleb	227, 654
Kerlin, John	454	Kimble, Jacob	654
Kernine, Eder	226	Kimble, Stephen	654
Kerr, see also, Carr		Kincard, George	227, 654
Kerr, see also, Karr		Kindle, Joseph	654
Kerr, Ebenezer	653	King, Aaron	654
Kerr, John	397, 863	King, Abel	844
Kerr, Joseph	840, 863	King, Abraham	481
Kerr, Nicholas	653	King, Abraham H.	480
Kerr, Walter	653	King, Abram	654
Kerr, Watson	653	King, Alexander	654
Kerr, William	38, 40, 105, 454, 653	King, Andrew	(2) 654
		King, Anthony	130, (2) 227, (2) 654
Kerrey, John	226, 653		
Kerrill, William	653	King, Aurey	655
Kersey, William	37, 54, 55, 90	King, C. Victor	327
		King, Constant Victor	371
Kershaw, Abraham	653	King, David	(2) 655
Kershaw, George	653	King, Francis	655
Kesler, John	653	King, Frederick	345, 374
Kested, Henry	653	King, George	(2) 655, 833, 840
Kester, John	653		
Ketcham, David	226	King, Henry	397
Ketcham, James	653	King, Hugh	871
Ketcham, John	226, 653	King, James	655
Ketcham, Levi	653	King, John	(2) 655
Ketcham, Solomon	653	King, Joseph	37, 59, 70, 72, 136, 227, 335, 372, 655
Ketcher, John	226		
Kettle, Joseph	(2) 226		
Keyt, John	653		
Kibby, Ephraim	117, 226, 654		
		King, William	227, 655
Kibler, George	226, 654	Kingfield, Conrad	227
Kibler, Matthias	654	Kingman, Thomas	655
Kidd, Daniel	654	Kingsland, Abraham	655
Kidd, Peter	654	Kingsland, Abram	655
Kidney, John	397, 438	Kingsland, Isaac	227, 655
Kiers, Edward Wm.	836	Kingsland, John	655
Kies, Joseph	654	Kingsland, William	655
Kilander, Philip	226	Kinnan, John	655
Kilborn, Moses	118	Kinnan, William	849
Kiler, Adam	226	Kinnebaugh, James	227, 655
Killenar, Philip	654	Kinned, Peter	655
Killey, John	227, 654	Kinney, Daniel	(2) 227, (2) 655
Killey, Patrick	227		
Killis, William	227	Kinney, Jacob	655
Kilpatrick, Andrew	654	Kinney, John	22, 35, 37, 100
Kilpatrick, Hugh	654		
Kilpatrick, James	136, 227, 481	Kinney, Peter	438
		Kinney, Thomas	22, 105, 397, 857
Kilpatrick, Samuel	(2) 227, (2) 654		
		Kinney, William	857

Kinny, ...	655	Kittle, Joseph	656
Kinny, John	655	Klicknor, George	656
Kinny, Simon	655	Kline, Jacob	656
Kinsey, James	227, (2) 655	Kline, John	656
		Knap, David	228
Kinsey, James, Jr.	228	Knapp, David	228, 656
Kinsey, James, Sr.	228	Knapp, Thomas	118, 482
Kinsey, John	228	Kneeler, Thomas	228
Kinsey, Jonathan	38, 39, 82, 398,	Knight, John	849
		Knight, Samuel	863
Kinsey, Shadrach	228	Knight, William	228
Kinsley, James	(2) 655	Knolton, Robert	428
Kint, Henry	655	Knowles, Jesse	656, 657
Kip, Richard	836	Knox, Joseph	(2) 657
Kipp, Amos	656	Kohler, Peter	852
Kipp, Cornelius	656	Kollock, Shepherd	90
Kipp, Robert	656	Kreager, Jacob	467
Kirby, Isaac	656	Krim, John	657
Kirby, Jacob	656	Kruser, Francis	398
Kirkendall, Andrew	656	Kuleman, Johannes	657
Kirkendall, Benjamin	398	Kurer, John	228, 657
Kirkendall, Samuel	398, 656	Kurtin, Joshua	657
Kirkendall, Simon	398	Kuyper, Hendricus	398
Kirkendall, Stephen	656	Kyson, Frederick	228
Kirkhoff, Bernice	438		
Kirkpatrick, Alexander	(2), 656	Labagh, Isaac	657
Kirkpatrick, Andrew	398	Labaw, Charles	657
Kirkpatrick, David	57, 83, 656	Lacey, Isaac	228, 657
		Lacey, Isaiah	228
Kirkpatrick, Hugh	656	Lacey, Jacob	228
Kirkpatrick, James	136, 228	Lacey, Joseph	228
Kirkpatrick, John	398, 656	Lacey, Josiah	229
Kirkpatrick, Samuel	228, 656	Lacey, Samuel	229
Kirkpatrick, William	656	Lacke, William	873
Kise, Peter	656	Lacount, John	857
Kitchel, Matthias	139	Lacy, Abraham	657
Kitchel, Obadiah	398	Lacy, Cornelius	657
Kitchell, Aaron	656, 857	Lacy, David	657
Kitchell, Asa	656	Lacy, Emanuel	657
Kitchell, Benjamin	656	Lacy, Jacob	657
Kitchell, Daniel	656	Lacy, Thomas	657
Kitchell, David	656	Lacy, William	657
Kitchell, Isaac	656	Ladner, Robert	657
Kitchell, James	228, 656	Lafayette, General	42
Kitchell, John	656	Lafever, Alinert	657
Kitchell, Moses	656, 844	Lafever, Minard	229, 657
Kitchell, Phineas	656	Lafever, Myndert	657
Kitchell, Uzal	656	Lafever, Naphtali	229, 657
Kitchen, Henry	228	Lafferty, Denice	657
Kite, John	228	Lafferty, Dennis	657
Kithim, John	228	Lafferty, John	(2) 657
Kittle, Abraham	228	Lafler, Coonrad	657
Kittle, Jacob	656	Lafler, John	657

Laforge, Levi	657	Lambertson, Thomas	659
Lahey, John	229	Lambord, Samuel	659
Lahy, John	657	Lame, George	659
Lain (or Lane), John	130	Lamor, Mack	659
Lain, Abram	658	Lampson, Thomas	659
Lain, Daniel	658	Lan, William	229
Lain; John	229, 658	Lancaster, Joseph	659
Laine, Job	229	Lance, ...	467
Laine, John	658	Lance, George	659
Laing, Abram	658	Lance, Peter	659
Laing, Benjamin	398	Land, George	659
Laing, Daniel	229	Land, James	659
Lair, John	130	Land, John	659
Laird, Richard	118, 467, 658	Lander, Peter	229
		Lander, Philip	660
Laird, Robert	658	Landon, Benjamin	229
Laird, William	229, (2) 658	Landon, David	467
		Landon, Edward	660
Lake, Andrew	658	Landon, James	229, 660
Lake, Benjamin	658	Landon, Laban	230
Lake, Daniel	658	Landon, Labau	61
Lake, Garret	658	Landon, Nathaniel	660
Lake, George	658	Landon, Samuel	118
Lake, Isaac	658	Landon, Thomas	660
Lake, John	229, 477, 658	Lane, see also, Lain	
		Lane, ...	428
Lake, Joseph	229, 658	Lane, Aaron	17, 32, 33, (2) 52, 90, 660
Lake, Nathan	658		
Lake, Spencer	229, 658		
Lake, Thomas	658		
Lake, William	(2) 658	Lane, Abraham	14, 30, 100, 428
Lamar, Mark	229		
Lamb, Jacob	658	Lane, Cornelius	398, 660
Lamb, John	58	Lane, Derick	38
Lamb, Patrick	658	Lane, Derrick	33, 40, 51, 52, 53, 83, 445
Lamberson, Chris	658		
Lamberson, David	658		
Lamberson, Thomas	659		
Lambert, ...	467	Lane, Ezekiel	660
Lambert, David	229, 659	Lane, Gilbert	481, (2) 660
Lambert, Isaac	659		
Lambert, James	229, 659	Lane, Guisbert	660
Lambert, Jeremiah	659	Lane, Hendrick	660
Lambert, Joseph	229, 659	Lane, Henry	660
Lambert, Lancelot	229	Lane, Isaac	660
Lambert, Lott	229, 659	Lane, Jacob	(3) 660
Lambert, Samuel	229, 659	Lane, John	230 (4) 660
Lambert, William	229, 659		
Lambertson, Cornelius	659	Lane, Mathew	398
Lambertson, David	659	Lane, Matthias	660
Lambertson, Elijah	659	Lane, Michael	230
Lambertson, Garret	659	Lane, Reuben	660
Lambertson, John	659	Lane, Tunis	660
Lambertson, Joshua	659	Lane, William	230, (2) 660
Lambertson, Simon	659		

Laney, George	230		Laughhead, James	662
Langden, Benjamin	230		Laughhead, William	662
Lange, William	660		Lawkerman, Thomas	662
Langley, David	230		Lawrence, Abram	662, 852
Langley, Elnathan	230		Lawrence, Benjamin	38, 39, 101
Langley, Jasper	230			
Langley, John	230		Lawrence, Daniel	230, (2) 662
Langley, Thomas	661			
Langstaff, Henry	661		Lawrence, Elisha	353, 836
Langstaff, James	661		Lawrence, Elisha, Jr.	345, 360
Langstaff, John	661		Lawrence, George	662
Lanning, Daniel	661		Lawrence, Isaac	662
Lanning, David	661		Lawrence, Israel	662
Lanning, Elijah	661		Lawrence, Jacob	460
Lanning, Henry	661		Lawrence, Jock	230
Lanning, James	661		Lawrence, John	230, 662
Lanning, John	661		Lawrence, Nathaniel	230
Lanning, Levi	836		Lawrence, Thomas	230, 662
Lanning, Ralph	445		Lawrence, William	662, 857
Lanning, Robert	661		Lawrie, James	16, 31, 32, 34, 83
Lany, William	661			
Lapee, William	230			
Lapley, John	230		Lawson, Andrew	857
Lard, John	661		Lawson, John	230, 662
Lard, Samuel	118, 661		Lawyer, (or Sawyer) James	231, 662
Lard, William	661			
Larew, James	661		Layton, John	231
Larey, Jacob	230		Layton, Peter	398
Large, John	661, 863		Layton, Samuel	662
Large, Jonathan	661		Layton, Thomas	662
Larison, Roger	467		Lazalear, Nicholas	863
Larison, William	467		Lazear, Henry	231
Larrison, John	661		Lazerlier, Benjamin	663
Larrison, Peter	857		Leach, Abner	663
Larrison, Thomas	661, 857		Leach, Richard	663
Lasader, Benjamin	661		Leadbetter, George	231
Lasender, Jacob	661		Leader, Patrick	231, 663
Lasey, Abraham	661		Leah, Nathan	663
Lashells, George	661		Leahy, see Leigh	
Lashells, John	661		Leak, John	398
Lassier, John	661		Leake, Amos	663
Last, Isaac	661		Leake, Nathaniel	663
Last, Peter	661		Leake, Recompense	118
Latham, James	662		Leake, William	663
Latimer, John	662		Leaman, Ephraim	663
Laton, Thomas	662		Leaman, George	231
Latourett, Cornelius	662		Leaman, Godfrey	663
Latourett, Peter	662		Leaming, Thomas	340, 372
Latourett, Peter, Jr.	662		Leapy, John	231
Latourett, Peter, Sr.	662		Leard, Richard	663
Latourrette, Peter	230		Leard, William	663
Latter, Lewis	662		Learnard, David	857
Lattleally, Samuel	662		Leary, Cornelius	663
LaTurrette, Daniel	118		Leary, Daniel	231

Leary, Dennis	231	Leigh, Samuel	664
Leary, William	428	Leighton, John	231
Lecroy, Job	231	Leister, John	664
Leddle, William	663	Lemmon, Isaiah	664
Lee, Abel	663	Lemmon, Thomas	664
Lee, Charles	663	Lenen, Thomas	232, 664
Lee, Daniel	663	Leniton, Henry	232, 664
Lee, David	118, 663	Lenner, Levi	664
Lee, Ebenezer	663	Lennington, Thomas	836
Lee, Ephraim	663	Lenox, Toby	864
Lee, Giles	438	Leonard, Azariah	232, 665
Lee, Henry	57	Leonard, David	665
Lee, Israel	663	Leonard, Elias	665
Lee, John	(2) 231, (3) 663	Leonard, Elijah	232, 665
		Leonard, Henry	665
Lee, Joseph	231, (2) 663	Leonard, James	232, (2) 665
Lee, Moses	663	Leonard, John	232, (2) 665
Lee, Paul	428, 663, 839, 852	Leonard, Joshua	232, 665
Lee, Philip	663	Leonard, Nathan	232
Lee, Richard	664	Leonard, Nathaniel	21, 36, 51, 54, 55, 83, 398, 665, 844, 852
Lee, Samuel	664		
Lee, Thomas	231, 664, 864, 873		
Lee, Timothy	231		
Lee, Walter	664	Leonard, Samuel	232, 467, (2) 665
Lee, William	(2) 664, 874		
		Leonard, Silas	665
Leedes, James	231	Leonard, Stephen	232, 665
Leeds, Daniel	664	Leonard, Thomas	467
Leeds, Enoch	428	Leonard, William	232, (2) 665, 864
Leeds, Felix	664		
Leeds, James	664	Leonard, Zephaniah	232
Leeds, Jeremiah	438	Leppo, Paul	665
Leeds, Nehemiah	664	Lequear, William	665
Leeds, Robert	664	Lerghouser, Jacob	232
Leeds, Thomas	664	Leshier, John	665
Leeds, William	231, 664	Lesse, Moses	665
Leffer, John	664	Lester, Samuel	665
Lefferty, Henry C.	664	Leterah, Cornelius	665
Leffler, Philip	231, 664	Letson, John	665
Leford, Vincent	231, 664	Letson, Thomas	665
Leforge (or Liforg), Benjamin	664	Letts, Elijah	665
		Letts, Elisha	666
Leforge, Levi	664	Letts, Francis	477
Lefoy, Abraham	664	Letts, John	232, (2) 666
Legaree, William	664		
Legear, William	232	Letts, Nehemiah	666
Legrange, John	231	Letts, William	666
Legur, William	231	Leverick, Robert	666
Leigh, Elijah	467, 664	Levick, Robert	232
Leigh (or Leahy) John	664, 836	Levings, Richard	666
		Levins, John	232
Leigh, Joseph	844	Levy, Asher	(2) 50, 105

Levy, Thomas	666		Lindley, Caleb	667	
Lewis, see Luis			Lindley, Daniel	667	
Lewis, Barnett	666		Lindley, Joseph	667	
Lewis, Barney	666		Lindley, Moses	233	
Lewis, Benjamin	232, 666		Lindsay, Alexander	667	
Lewis, Daniel	232		Lindsey, Benjamin	840	
Lewis, David	232		Lindsey, Thomas	843	
Lewis, Edward	233, 428, (2) 666, 839, 843		Lindsley, Benjamin	445, 836	
			Lindsley, Daniel	667	
			Lindsley, David	667	
Lewis, Ezekiel	666		Lindsley, Ebenezer	667	
Lewis, Francis	666		Lindsley, Eleazer	(2) 56, 66, 345, 360	
Lewis, Irenius	666				
Lewis, Jacob	233, 666, 852		Lindsley, Ephraim	667	
Lewis, James	233, 666		Lindsley, James	233	
Lewis, John	233, 666		Lindsley, John	398, 857	
Lewis, Joseph	376, 836		Lindsley, John, Jr.	667	
Lewis, Levi	666		Lindsley, Jonathan	667	
Lewis, Richard	233, 666		Lindsley, Joseph	345, 367	
Lewis, Robert	233		Lindsley, Joseph, Jr.	667	
Lewis, Samuel	666		Lindsley, Moses	857	
Lewis, Thomas	666		Lindsley, Philip	667, 857	
Lewis, William	233, 339, 360, 666		Lindsley, Samuel	667	
			Lindsley, Ziba	667	
Leye, ...	467		Lineday, Walter	667	
Leyoc, Benjamin	844		Linen, John	233	
Lezear, Hillebrant	233		Liner, Isaac	667	
Lezear, Peter	233		Lines, Anthony	667	
Liber, John	233		Lines, Benjamin	667	
Lickram, Jacob	666		Lines, Coonrad	667	
Liddle, Robert	118, 428		Lines, John	667	
Liforg, see Leforge			Lines, Peter	667	
Light, James	833		Lines, William	667	
Light, Peter	666		Ling, Isaac	233	
Light, Thomas	666		Lining, Job	667	
Lightning, John	233		Linn, Dominick	667	
Likens, Andrew	118, 667		Linn, James	346, 367, 668	
Likens, Jacob	233				
Likens, John	864		Linn, John	467	
Likings, William	667		Linn, Joseph	347, 37?, 668	
Lile, John, Jr.	667				
Lile, John, Sr.	667		Linn, Robert	668	
Lile, Moses	667		Linnington, Henry	233	
Lilley, John	233		Linsey, Thomas	233, 668	
Lillie, Nathan	233		Lintner, Andrew	864	
Limar, Mark	233		Linwood, John	233, 668	
Limbarger, Gabriel	667		Lipehite, John	234	
Limbergh, John	667		Lipes, John	234, 668	
Liming, Job	667		Lippencott, Daniel	668	
Linch, Lawrence	233		Lippencott, Jacob	234, 668	
Linch, William	233		Lippencott, John	234, 668	
Lincoln, John	667		Lippencott, Jonathan	398	
Lincorn, Jacob	667		Lippencott, Samuel	668	
Lincorn, John	667		Lippencott, William	(2) 668	

Lipps, Paul	668	Lloyd, James	234, 669
Lisk, Abram	668	Lloyd, John	118, 234, 235, 669, 843
Lisk, John	234, (2) 668		
List, John	864	Lloyd, Joseph	136, 235
Litson, John	668	Lloyd, Richard	21, 58, 83
Littell, Eliakim	398		
Littell, Henry	668	Lloyd, Thomas	669
Little, ...	668	Lloyd, William	467
Little, Andrew	852	Load, Thomas	235
Little, Benjamin	234, 668	Lobdell, Thomas	669, 864
Little, Christopher	398	Loboc, Charles	669
Little, Christy	668, 857	Locey, Jesse	235, 669
Little, Cornelius	668	Locey, Moses	235, 669
Little, David	668	Lock, Andrew	852
Little, Ebenezer	668	Lock, David	235
Little, Eleazer	59, 91	Lock, Francis	399
Little, Enos	234	Lock, John	669
Little, Ephraim	234	Lock, Jonathan	669
Little, Henry	668	Lock, Philip	235
Little, Jacob	234	Lockade, James	235, 669
Little, James	864	Locker, John	235, 669
Little, John	342, 376, 668	Lockhard, James	235
		Lockwood, James	669
Little, John, Jr.	668	Lockwood, Jehiel	669
Little, John, Sr.	668	Lockwood, John	669
Little, John R.	668	Lockwood, Justice	669
Little, Jonathan	668	Lockwood, Silas	670
Little, Joseph	234, 668	Locy, Cornelius	670
Little, Nathaniel	234, (2) 669	Locy, John	670
		Loder, Daniel	235
Little, Noah	669	Loder, Zenas	235
Little, Robert	(2) 234, 669	Loder, Zenus	670
		Lodge, John	670
Little, Samuel	234, 669	Lodwick, Conrad	235, 670
Little, Simeon	234	Lofbrey, Abraham	235
Little, Theodore	96	Lofler, Jacob	670
Little, Theophilus	399	Lofler, Philip	670
Little, Thomas	399	Logan, David	840
Little, William	669, 844	Logan, Hugh	670
Livers, Gershom	669	Logan, James	235, 670, 849
Living, Richard	669		
Livingston, Henry B.	66	Logan, Robert	118
Livingston, James	60	Logan, Stoffel	670
Livingston, John L.	872	Logan, Thomas	670
Livingston, Robert	428	Logan, William	235, (2) 399
Livingston, Robert James	669		
		Loiskerom, Jacob	670
Livingston, William	338, 349, 669	Lomarson, Lawrence	445
		Lombard, Justin	235
Lloyd, Bateman	39, 40, 53, 54, 55, 83, 399, 844	Lomberson, John	670
		London, Samuel	235
		Lonely, ...	842
		Long, Ansey	670
Lloyd, David	234, 669	Long, Cornelius	670

Long, George	235, 670	Lorton, James	671	
Long, Henry	670	Lorton, John	671	
Long, John	670	Losbrey, Abraham	236	
Long, Joseph	118, 235	Losey, Abraham	236	
Long, Moses	670	Losey, Abram	671	
Long, Richard	235	Losey, Amos	671	
Long, Silas	670	Losey, Cornelius	671	
Longhouse, Jacob	118, 670	Losey, Jesse	236, 671	
Longley, Jasper	61, 235	Losey, John	672	
Longstreet, Aaron	399, 438, (2) 670	Losey, Philip	672, 857	
		Losey, Timothy	236	
Longstreet, Christian	399	Losey, William	672	
Longstreet, Elias	14, 29, 83	Lott, Abraham	(3) 672	
		Lott, Abram	482	
Longstreet, Gilbert	47, 428	Lott, Andrew	672	
Longstreet, James	670	Lott, Bartholemew	672	
Longstreet, John	(2) 670	Lott, Cornelius	399	
Longstreet, Samuel	671	Lott, Daniel	460	
Longstreet, William	849	Lott, Eli	236	
Longwell, John	671	Lott, George	445	
Longworth, Thomas	671	Lott, Gershom	672	
Lonitun, Jacob	852	Lott, Henry	672	
Loofborrow, David	236	Lott, John	672	
Looker, Eleazer	236	Lott, Peter	30, (2) 49, 50, 51, 71, 672	
Looker, John	236			
Looker, Nathaniel	671			
Looker, Othneil	671			
Loose, Eleazer	671	Lott, Richard	344, 360	
Loose, Jesse	236	Loughberry (or Luffberry) Abram	119	
Loose, Shubal	671			
Loper, Abraham	118, 428	Loughborough, John	672	
Loper, Abram	671	Lounsberry, Abraham	236	
Loper, Isaac	236	Lounsberry, Walker	236	
Loratt, Cornelius	671	Lountinhirger, Jacob	852	
Loratt, Peter	671	Love, Alexander	130	
Lord, Asa	671	Love, Cornelius	236	
Lord, David	671	Love, Job	672	
Lord, Ichabod	671	Love, John	236	
Lord, John	671	Love, William	236	
Lord, Jonathan	671	Loveberry, Elias	672	
Lore, Daniel	454	Lovel, Esail	672	
Loree (or Loring) Ephraim	35, 53, 54, 75	Lovelace, Gershom	236	
		Lovelace, Lott	236, 672	
Lorey, Cornelius	671	Loveland, Charles	672	
Lorey, Jesse	236	Loveland, Samuel	672	
Lorey, John	671	Lovett, Aaron	864	
Lorey, John, Jr.	671	Lovett, Francis	236	
Lorie, Ephraim	671	Low, Abraham	(2) 672	
Lorie, James	671	Low, Alexander	467	
Lorie, Job	671	Low, Benjamin	672, 864	
Lorie, Samuel, Jr.	671	Low, Cornelius	672, 844, 857	
Lorie, Solomon	671			
Lorie, Sylvanus	671	Low, Henry	454	
Loring, see Loree		Low, Job	857	
Lorkyer, John	236	Low, John	(2) 672	
		Low, Joseph	857	

Low, Peter	38, 40, 97, 438	Lugston, John P.	673
Low, William	672	Luif, John	673
Lowden, Anthony	445	Luis (or Lewis), William	673
Lowden, John	857	Luke, John	673
Lowden, William	672	Luker, Benjamin	673
Lowder, John	857	Luker, David	673
Lowder, William	857	Luker, Eleizer	673
Lowe, ...	399	Luker, Isaac	673
Lowe, Cornelius D.	672	Luker, John	237, 673
Lowe, William	399	Luker, Johnson	673
Lown, Richard	672	Luker, Othnel	673
Lownsberry, Samuel	673	Luker, Thomas	673
Lowrance, Daniel	857	Lum, Israel	673
Lowrey, Stephen	842	Lum, John C.	673
Lowrey, Thomas	345, 353	Lum, Matthew	673
Lowrey, William	836	Lum, Matthias	673
Lowry, Thomas	673	Lum, Samuel	673
Lowsadder, Benjamin	673	Lum, Stephen	674
Loxley, Abram	837	Lumley, Samuel	237
Loyd, David	454	Lummes, Ephraim	340, 367
Lozier, John	454, 673	Lummis, Jonathan	130
Lozier, Peter	673	Lummis, Joseph	674, 874
Lucas, John	445, (2) 864	Lumnes, Joseph	136
Lucas, Simon	329, 399	Lun, Eleizer	674
Luce, Henry	17, 32, (2) 34, 84, 399	Lunn, James	454
		Lunny, Philip	237, 674
		Lupardus, Christian	399
Luce, Joseph	864	Lupardus, William	674
Lucre, Benjamin	857	Lupp, ...	400
Lucus, ..	399	Lupton, John	237, 674
Ludlam, Abraham	236, 673	Lurton, Jonathan	674
Ludlam, Christopher	445	Lusbay, Abram	674
Ludlam, Henry	438	Luse, Benjamin	674
Ludlam, Jacob	29, 105, 673	Luse, Eleazer	428
		Luse, Francis	53, 105
		Luse, Israel	428
Ludlam, Jonas	673	Luse, Nathan	345, 360
Ludlam, Norton	428	Luse, Samuel	674
Ludlam, Samuel	673	Luse, Shubal	674
Ludlam, Watson	236, 673	Luse, Walter	468
Ludlam, Ziba	673	Luse, William	468
Ludlow, ...	399	Lusk, Israel	237, 674
Ludlow, Abram	236, 673	Luther, Lewis	674
Ludlow, Cornelius	335, 345, 360	Luyster, John	674
		Luyster, John P.	674
Ludlow, Joseph	237, 673	Luyster, Peter	674
Ludlow, Richard	673, 842	Luzear, Henry	237
Ludlow, Watson	237	Lyall, Thomas	130
Ludlow, Winser	237, 673	Lyde, John	237
Ludlum, Cornelius	852	Lydecker, Garret	400
Ludlum, Matthias	852	Lye, William	237
Lue, Thomas	673	Lyle, Jacob	674
Luffberry, see Loughberry		Lyle, John	367
		Lyle, Moses	468

Lyman, Benjamin	674	McBride, John	242, 681
Lynch, Dennis	237	McBride, William	468
Lynch, Henry	674	McBurney, James	242
Lynch, William	237	McCabe, Henry	242
Lyns, Daniel	674	McCafferly, Joseph	242
Lyon, Aaron	674	McCafferty, Joseph	681
Lyon, Abraham	38, 39, 40, 84, 400	McCaghan, John	242, 681
		McCain, John	(2) 242, (2) 681
Lyon, Abram	674	McCalla, William	834
Lyon, Asher	674	McCalley, Alexander	242
Lyon, Benjamin	674	McCalsner, John	681
Lyon, Charles	842	McCam, John	681
Lyon, Daniel	674	McCanley, Edward	681
Lyon, David	237, 674, 840	McCann, Henry	242
		McCann, John	242, 681
Lyon, Ebenezer	674	MacCarey, Andrew	675
Lyon, Eros	674	McCarle, see McCarrol	
Lyon, Gideon	237, 675	McCarrol (or McCarle) David	242
Lyon, Henry	(2) 237, (2) 675	McCarron, Hugh	681
Lyon, Isaac	675	McCarter, Charles	74
Lyon, James	237	McCarter, Francis	853
Lyon, Jedediah	130	McCarter, John	840, 843
Lyon, Jediah	237	McCarty, Clark	844
Lyon, John	675	McCarty, Dennis	242, 681
Lyon, Joseph	675	McCarty, Hugh	242, (2) 681
Lyon, Matthias	400, 675		
Lyon, Moses	675	McCaskey, Cornelius	844
Lyon, Nathan	237	McCauley, David	400
Lyon, Nathaniel	237, 675	McChesney, James	681
Lyon, Samuel	675	McChesney, Robert	681
Lyon, Solomon	237, 675	McChesney, Samuel	681
Lyon, Stephen	675	McClain, Archibald	682
Lyon, William	675	McClain, John	242, 682
Lyon, William C.	238	McClanin, William	439
Lyons, Elias	238, 675	McClean, John	682
Lyons, Elisha	238	McClean, Robert	242, 682
Lyons, Enos	238	McCleary, Daniel	242, 682
Lyons, John	238	McCleary, Michael	682
Lyons, Jonas	238	McClellan, James	682
Lyons, Serring	238	McClow, Cornelius	682
Lyons, William	238	McClure, Alexander	242, 682
Lyram, Jacob	675	McClure, Andrew	119, 840
		McClure, John	242
		McColem, Duncan	682
McAdams, William	681	McColem, Hugh	682
McAfee, Benjamin	681	McCollam, John	682
McAfee, Richard	681	McCollester, William	242, 682
McAnally, Patrick	241	McCollom, David	243
McArthur, Thomas	681	McCollom, John	243, 682
McBath, see McRoath		McCollough, Joseph	682
McBath, Andrew	241	McCollough, Robert	682
McBetts, William	834	McCollum, ...	468

Name	Page
McCollum, Cornelius	454
McCollum, John	91, 243, 682
McCollum, Patrick	468
McCollum, Samuel	243
McComb, James	379
McComb, John	844
McCombs, John	130
McConally, Patrick	243
McConigal, William	243
McConnally, Patrick	682
McConnel, Francis	243
McConnel, Hugh	243
McConnel, James	243
McConnell, Adam	682
McConnell, Hugh	682
McConnell, Robert	682
McCormick, Dennis	243, 682
McCormick, Stephen	682
McCourby, Daniel	401
McCourney, Matthew	346, 374
McCowen, Constant	243
McCowen, Daniel	853
McCowry, Malcolm	836
McCoy, Adam	243
McCoy, Charles	429
McCoy, Daniel	243, 682
McCoy, Ganen	401
McCoy, Gavin	682
McCoy, James	243, 468
McCoy, Joseph	(2) 243, 682
McCoy, Reuben	243, 683
McCrackin, Philip	(2) 243
McCrah, William	243
McCray, James	683
McCrea, Philip	119
McCroy, Thomas	244, 683
McCrum, Michael	119
McCue, ...	468
McCugo, Edward	119, 468
McCullock, Abraham	244, 683
McCullock, Robert	119
McCullom, Jonas	683
McCullough, Benjamin	401
McCullough, Joseph	429
McCullough, Robert	244
McCullough, William	849
McCully, James	244
McCully, John	244
McCully, William	244
McCurdy, Daniel	244
McCurry, Mahlon	346, 374
McDade, Charles	244
McDade, William	(2) 244, 683
McDaniel, Benjamin	244, 683
McDaniel, Cornelius	244, (3) 683
McDaniel, Edward	683
McDaniel, John	(2) 244
McDaniel, R.	842
McDaniel, William	244
McDermot, Cornelius	244, 683
McDermott, Cornelius	683
McDermott, William	683
McDonald, Alexander	244, 683
McDonald, Benjamin	244, 245, 683
McDonald, Daniel	243, 367
McDonald, Elizur	683
McDonald, George	109
McDonald, James	245, 683
McDonald, John	(2) 245, 683
McDonald, Richard	347, 367
McDonald, William	20, 22, 101, 245
McDonel, John	683
McDowell, Andrew	429
McDowell, Ephraim	683
McDowell, Thomas	683
McDuffee, Daniel	683
McDuffee, James	683
McDuffee, Robert	683
McDuffey, Archibald	245
McDuffy, Archibald	683
McDuffy, Randall	245
McDugal, William	683
McElhaney, John	683
McElrath, Thomas	684
McEowen, William	684
McEwen, Daniel	684
McEwen, George	846
McEwen, John	56, 71, 842
McEwen, William	846
McFadden, Connolly	684
McFadden, Conolly,	245
McFadden, James	245, 684
McFadden, John	245, 684
McFarland, George	38, 40, 106, 454
McFarland, John	684
McFarland, John M.	684
McFarland, Samuel	445, 684
McFarland, Thomas	245
McFarlin, John	245

McGalliard, William	468	McKin, Andrew	685
McGee, Abram	684	McKindrick, Robert	247
McGee, Daniel	245, 684	McKiney, John	864
McGee, James	245, 401, 684	McKinley, George	853
		McKinneg (alias McKinney) David	685
McGee, John	684		
McGee, Robert	245, 684	McKinney, see also McKinneg	
McGee, Thomas	684		
McGee, William	245, 684	McKinney, ...	685
McGill, James	245, 684	McKinney, Abraham	401
McGill, John	245, 684	McKinney, John	247, 839
McGill, Patrick	684	McKinney, Joseph	(2) 247, 685
McGill, Robert	684		
McGill, William	246, 684	McKinney, Matthew	685
McGillon, ...	684	McKinney, Mordecai	(2) 685, 853
McGinness, Gabriel	684		
McGinness, James	684	McKinney, Patrick	247
McGinness, John	684	McKinney, Timothy	247
McGinnis, Arthur	246	McKinsey, John	247
McGinta, John	246	McKinstry, John	685
McGintrey, John	684	McKinstry, Matthias	685
McGintry, John	246	McKnight, Joseph	685
McGlaughlin, George	401	McKnight, Richard	401
McGlocklin, Charles	246	McLain, John	685
McGlocklin, John	246	McLane, Angus	247
McGongue, George	246	McLane, John	247
McGonigal, George	246, 684	McLane, Patrick	247
McGool, John	864	McLane, Robert	247, 685
McGronigal, John	684	McLaughlin, Charles	247
McGuire, Daniel	246	McLaughlin, Collin	120
McGuire, James	246	McLaughlin, Daniel	247, 685
McGuire, Michael	246	McLaughlin, Hugh	247
McGuire, Patrick	246	McLaughlin, John	247
McGurn, see McQuin		McLean, Francis	864
McHenry, Charles	246, 685	McLean, Hugh	(2) 247
McHolland, Patrick	246	McLean, John	833
McHughs, Edward	246	McLure, Andrew	120, 685
McIlrath, Samuel	685	McLure, James	(2) 248, 685
McIlroy, William	468		
McInnelly, Patrick	246	McMackin, Andrew	685
McIntire, Joseph	246	McMahan, Abner	248
McIntyre, John	246	McMahan, David	248, 685
McKasson, John	685	McMahon, Jeremiah	248, 686
McKay, William	685	McManis, Christian	248
McKee, Gibbs	246	McManis, Christopher	120
McKenney, Cornelius	685	McManis, Kinney	120, 686
McKenney, Timothy	685	McManners, Moses	686
McKenney, William	246, 685	McManners, William	686
McKenny, Malcolm	247	McManus, William	686
McKenny, Timothy	247	McMaslen, Hugh	248
McKenway, Michael	685	McMichael, William	(2) 21, 97
McKey, Joseph	685		
McKim, Nathaniel	120	McMillan, John	248
McKimmy, William	685	McMillen Charles	120

M'Mires, Andrew	14, 29, 30, 85	Magee, Joseph	675
McMortry, Robert	686	Magee, Michael	675
McMullan, John	248	Magee, Thomas	238, 675, 676
McMullen, John	(2) 686	Maggraw, Barney	676
McMullen, William	248	Magie, William	238
McMullin, John	248	Magill, Robert	676
McMurry, Daniel	686	Magill, William	836
McMurton, Thomas	248	Magway, John	676
McMurtrey, see also Murtry		Mahan, Jeremiah	676
		Mahan, Richard	676
McMurtrey, Thomas	248, 686	Mahl, Frederick	238
McMurtry, Thomas	686	Mahone, Daniel	238
McNeal, Henry	248, 686	Mailer, Gershom	676
McNeal, John	248	Mainer, Andrew	676
McNealy, James	248	Maines, Andrew	238
McNealy, John	248	Mains, Andrew	676
McNeil, ...	367	Mains, Jonathan	676
McNeil, Hector	109, 686	Mains, William	676
McNelly, Simeon	248	Maitland, ...	400
McNichols, Archibald	248	Major, John	238
McNight, James	248	Malaby, Cornelius	676
McNight, Lewis	686	Malaby, Thomas	238, 676
McOrwin, Samuel	248	Malat, Peter	676
McPeatz, Jonathan	249	Malcolm, John	238, 676
McPherson, Joseph	249	Malick, Andrew	400
McQuay, John	249	Malick, John	239, 676
McQuillom, James	249, 686	Mallatt, Abraham	239
McQuin (or McGurn), James	840	Manary, Abram	676
		Mancy, David	676
McRoath (or McBath), Andrew	686	Mandeval, Giles	676
		Mandeville, Henry W.	676
McSperry, Matthew	249, 686	Mandeville, Yellis	676
McTeer, William	686	Manfort, Henry	676
McVey, Christopher	249, 839	Manheart, John	239
McVickers, Duncan	401	Manley, Benjamin	676
McWhorter, Alexander	76	Mann, Abraham	239
McWilliams, John	686	Mann, Amos	679
Mackay, Joseph	400	Mann, Elisha	119, 239
Mackendow, John	238	Mann, Henry	239
Mackey, John	238, 340, 353	Mann, Isaac	676
		Mann, Richard	239
Mackey, Joseph	675	Manners, John, Sr.	676
Mackin, Nicholas	238	Manning, Andrew	676
Maclick, Leonard	675	Manning, Benjamin	(3) 676
Maclick, Peter	675	Manning, Clarkson	677
Madden, John	238	Manning, David	677
Maffatt, Archibald	400	Manning, Enoch	677
Maffatt, William	400	Manning, Ephraim	677
Maffit, Bartholemew	238	Manning, Isaac	445, 677
Magdelen, Abraham	675	Manning, James	438
Magee, Ezekiel	675	Manning, Jeremiah	400
Magee, James	675	Manning, John	239, 454, 677
Magee, John	(3) 675		

Manning, John, Sr.	677	Marsh, Jesse	454
Manning, Phineas	677	Marsh, John	119, (2) 678
Manning, Reuben	400		
Manning, Samuel	677	Marsh, Joseph	839
Manning, Thomas	119, 239, 677	Marsh, Joshua	468
		Marsh, Noah	428
Manning, William	400	Marsh, Ralph	438, 844
Mans, Andry	677	Marsh, Samuel	240, 678
Mapes, Edmond	677	Marsh, Stephen	678
Mapes, Frederick	119	Marsh, William	678, 853
Mapes, John	239, 677	Marshall, John	678
Mapes, Joseph	239, (2) 677	Marshall, Joseph	678
		Marshall, William	678
Mapes, Phineas	239	Mart, Andrew	678
Mapes, William	239, 677	Marters, James	240
Mapey, (or Massey), Benjamin	239	Martin, Absalom	37, 50, 51, 84
Maple, John	864	Martin, Alexander	240, 678, 873
Maple, Stephen	677		
Maple, Thomas	864	Martin, Benjamin	(2) 678
Maple, William	677, 864	Martin, Caleb	678
Marcelles, Eden	677	Martin, Daniel	130, 240, 678
Marical, George	677		
Marill, Uriah	239	Martin, David	(2) 240, (3) 678
Marinus, David	400		
Marius, Sylvester	677	Martin, Edmund	678
Mark, John	239	Martin, Eliacum	678
Marks, David	239	Martin, Enos	678
Marks, William	239	Martin, Ephraim	37, 64, 335, 347, 353, 468
Marlalt, Richard	460		
Marlatt, John	239, 677		
Marlatt, Peter	239, 677	Martin, George	240
Marlin, Nathaniel	677	Martin, Gershom	(2) 678
Marlin, Robert	239	Martin, Irenias	678
Marmaduke, William	677	Martin, Isaac	678
Marriner, ...	871	Martin, Jacob	40, 84
Marriner, William	677	Martin, James	(2) 240, (2) 678, 679
Marrot, Levi	239		
Marryott, Samuel	857		
Marselles, Edo	677	Martin, Jeremiah	679
Marsh, ...	428	Martin, John	(2) 38, 97, 240, 438, 468, (2) 679, 864
Marsh, Abraham	428		
Marsh, Benjamin	677		
Marsh, Charles	678		
Marsh, Christopher	400	Martin, Joseph	(2) 679
Marsh, Daniel	835	Martin, Joshua	679
Marsh, Ephraim	678, 853	Martin, Leonard	679, 839, 864
Marsh, Ephraim, Jr.	47		
Marsh, George	239, 678	Martin, Lewis	679
Marsh, Henry	844	Martin, Merrick	679
Marsh, Jabish	678	Martin, Michael	679
Marsh, James	678	Martin, Moses	679
Marsh, Jehiel	678	Martin, Mulford	679

Martin, Nathan	679		Matterson, Aaron	680
Martin, Nathaniel	679		Mattewman, Luke	874
Martin, Oliver	240		Matthews, Daniel	680
Martin, Reuben	679		Matthews, Ely	680
Martin, Robert	240, 679		Matthews, Garret	680
Martin, Samuel	481		Matthews, Henry	680
Martin, Thomas	(2) 240, 679		Matthews, James	241
			Matthews, John	428
Martin, William	61, (3) 240, (3) 679, 842		Matthews, Pearse	680
			Matthews, Richard	454
			Matthews, Robert	(2) 680
Martinus, Cornelius	679		Matthews, William	680
Marts, William	678, 679		Mattison, Aaron	241, (2) 680
Mary, Edward	679			
Mase, Samuel	679		Mattison, Jacob	241, 680
Mash, Samuel	240		Mattison, Joseph	428
Mash, Simeon	29, 30, 106		Mattox, John	241
			Mattox, Luke	857
Mashat, Peter	679		Mattox, William	241, 680
Mashatt, James	454		Maule, Uriah	241
Maskell, Daniel	340, 367		Mawe, Rynear	680
Maskell, Street	119		Maxfield, David	680
Mason, Andrew	119, 679		Maxon, John	681
Mason, David	679		Maxwell, Anthony	57, 84
Mason, Isaac	240, 679		Maxwell, Brigadier General	63
Mason, John	76, 379			
Mason, Joseph	679		Maxwell, General	41, 55
Masore, William	679		Maxwell, Isaac	681
Massacker, John	680		Maxwell, James	17, 32, (2) 34, 84
Massey, see also Mapey				
Massey, Benjamin	680		Maxwell, John	400, 681
Massey, Samuel	240, 680		Maxwell, Robert	429
Masters, Benjamin	680		Maxwell, William	16, 41, 64, 67, 68, (2) 69, 347, 353
Masters, Clement	241			
Masters, Edward	680			
Masters, Jesse	680			
Masters, John	241			
Masters, Joseph	680		May, Andrew	241
Masters, Stephen	241		May, Edward (Rev.)	241, 681
Masters, William	119, 680		May, Moses	681
Masterson, Uriah	680		Maybeck, John	681
Matchett, William	241		Mayberry, Thomas	853
Mathers, James	241		Maybury, Joseph	241
Mathews, Henry	853		Mayer, Jacob	241
Mathis, Jeremiah	864		Mayhew, David	681
Mathis, Pierce	864		Mayhew, John	681
Matintock, John	680		Mayhew, Richard	241
Matlack, Joseph	400		Maylord, Abram	849
Matlack, Samuel	438		Mayps, John	241
Matlock, Jacob	680		Maze, Edward	130
Matson, John	680		Mead, Daniel	249, 686
Mattacks, David	680		Mead, Giles see also Mead, Yellis	
Mattacks, Jesse	680			

Mead, Giles	29, 30, 50	Meloby, Thomas	250, 687
Mead, James	120	Melsom, James	250
Mead, John	(2) 249, 401	Melvin, Daniel	687
		Melvin, George	687
		Melvin, John	687
Mead, Stephen	249, 686	Melvin, Thomas	687
Mead, William	249	Mencow, see Midsco	
Mead, Yellis (or Giles)	14, 84	Menely, Jesse	250
		Menfort, Henry	687
Mealigh, John	686	Menfort, Peter	688
Means, Robert	686	Mengas, Moses	250
Meare, George	686	Mengen, Joseph	120
Mears, Robert	249	Menley, James	401
Meculick, Robert	686	Menny, Thomas	250
Mecum, John	849	Mercer, John	13, 15, 28, 30, 85
Mecum, Thomas	346, 367		
Mecum, William	346, 367		
Medagh, Emanuel	249, 686	Mericus, Stephen	250
Medagh, Manuel	686	Merlett, John	688
Medagh, Morris	249	Merrell, Benjamin	688
Medagh, Moses	249, 687	Merrell, David	688
Medio, Conrad	249	Merriam, Joseph	250
Medler, ...	401	Merrick, John	(2) 250, 688
Meeker, Amos	687	Merril, Andrew	688
Meeker, Benjamin	687	Merril, Richard	688
Meeker, Caleb	480	Merrill, Andrew	250
Meeker, Cory	249, 687	Merritt, Abram	688
Meeker, Daniel	687	Merritt, Caleb	688
Meeker, David	687	Merritt, Levi	250, 688
Meeker, Isaac	687	Merritt, Samuel	688
Meeker, Isaiah	687	Merry, Samuel	688
Meeker, James	687	Marryman, Joseph	250
Meeker, John	687	Mershon, Aaron	688
Meeker, Jonathan	687	Mershon, Andrew	688, 849
Meeker, Joseph	14, 84, 687	Mershon, Asher	688
		Mershon, Benjamin	688
Meeker, Josiah	687	Mershon, Henry	439, 480, 688
Meeker, Michael	(3) 249, (2) 687		
		Mershon, Robert	688
Meeker, Obadiah	401	Mershon, Timothy	688
Meeker, Robert	250, 687	Mershon, William	688
Meeker, Samuel	325, 347, 367, 429	Mersural, Jacob	439
		Meseroll, Peter	836
Meeker, Thomas	250	Messerol, Abram	688
Meeker, Timothy	468	Messerol, Charles	(2) 688
Meeker, Uzal	57, 91	Messerol, Jacob	688
Meeker, William	687	Messerol, John	688
Meelish, John	687	Messerol, Nicholas	688
Meeservie, Conrad	687	Messerol, Peter	688
Meginnis, Timothy	864	Messerol, William	688
Mehelm, John	11, 19, 339, 343, 354, 834	Messeroll, Abraham	468
		Messler, Abram	689
		Messler, Cornelius	689
Melatt, Abram	250	Messler, Peter	689
Melligan, William	687	Messler, Simon	468

Meyer, John	843	Miller, Jonathan	690
Meyers, Charles	689	Miller, Joseph	(2) 251, 468, 690
Mickel, John	689		
Mickle, Reuben	130, 250	Miller, Lewis	690
Middagh, Cornelius	689	Miller, Luke	690
Middagh, Daniel	689	Miller, Malahar	690
Middagh, Sepherin	689	Miller, Malaher	251
Middah, Derrick	346, 360	Miller, Marion	690
Middaugh, Solomon	429	Miller, Marsh	690
Middlesworth, James	849	Miller, Melsher	251
Middlesworth, Tunis	849	Miller, Mercer	690
Middlesworth, John N.	689	Miller, Moreen	690
Middleton, Joel	689	Miller, Morris	468
Middleton, John	689	Miller, Moses	690
Middleton, Joseph	250	Miller, Noah	251, (2) 690
Middleton, Thomas	(3) 689		
Middleworth, John	853	Miller, Prime	690
Midsco, (or Mencow) Conrad	250, 689	Miller, Robert	251, 690
		Miller, Samuel	690, 691
Miers, John	(2) 689	Miller, Silas	853
Miers, Michael	689	Miller, Stephen	691
Milburn, John	689	Miller, Theophilus	691
Milburn, Timothy	689	Miller, Timothy	691
Miles, George	250, 689	Miller, William	401, 455, (2) 691, 865
Miles, Sage	689		
Miles, Samuel	837		
Miles, William	689	Millet, Joset	833
Milford, ...	689	Milligan, James	691
Millard, Stephen	468	Mills, Cornelius	251, 691
Miller, ...	864	Mills, Edward	251, 468
Miller, Abner	689	Mills, Isaac	251
Miller, Benjamin	250, (4) 689	Mills, ...J.	844
		Mills, Jedediah	251, 429
Miller, Clark	250, 690	Mills, Jeremiah	401
Miller, Eleazer	(2) 690, 853	Mills, John	(2) 251, (3) 691, 853
Miller, Enoch	690		
Miller, Francis	690	Mills, Morgan	251
Miller, Frederick	250, 690	Mills, Nehemiah	468
Miller, George	690	Mills, Reuben	251
Miller, George D.	690	Mills, Richard	251
Miller, Henry	250	Mills, Samuel	691, 839
Miller, Holse	690	Mills, Timothy	691
Miller, Ichabod	690	Millson, James	251
Miller, Isaac	690	Milspaugh, Christian	251
Miller, Isaac, Jr.	690	Minard, (or Minor), Benjamin	401
Miller, Israel	454		
Miller, J.	844	Minard, Outerkirk	251
Miller, Jacob	864	Minor, see also Minard	
Miller, Jedediah	690	Minor, William	(2) 691
Miller, Jediah	477	Minsher, Moses	251
Miller, John	(2) 120, 327, 454, (3) 690, 853, 865	Minster, Moses	691
		Minteor, Samuel	691
		Minthorn, George	691
		Minthorn, John	108, 120

Minthorn, Lemuel	327, 329	Montgomery, Hugh	853
	455, 691	Montgomery, James	429
Minthorn, Philip	120	Montgomery, John	252, 692
Minthorne, Lemuel	251	Montgomery, William	345, 367,
Minthorne, William	251		692
Mires, Albertus	691	Montjoy, James	252
Mires, Cornelius	691	Mooers, Samuel	693
Mires, George	691	Moon, Jacob	693
Mirkle, Reuben	251	Moon, John	252
Misket, Peter	691	Mooney, Barnet	108
Misner, Luke	429	Mooney, John	(2) 252,
Misner, Peter	853		693
Mitchell, Alexander	38, 39,	Mooney, Nicholas	693
	40, 50,	Mooney, Samuel	693
	85, 439	Mooney, William	252, 693
Mitchell, Benjamin	691	Moore, Abijah	693
Mitchell, Edward	251, 691	Moore, Abram	693
Mitchell, George	691	Moore, Andrew	693
Mitchell, Jacob	251	Moore, Arthur	693
Mitchell, James	691	Moore, Azariah	401
Mitchell, John	(2) 252,	Moore, Benjamin	693
	(4) 691,	Moore, Caleb	252, 693
	692	Moore, Daniel	252, 693
Mitchell, Joseph	692	Moore, David	693
Mitchell, Martin	252, 692	Moore, Edward	693
Mitchell, Reuben	252	Moore, Eli	455
Mitchell, Richard	252	Moore, Elijah	252, 693
Mitchell, Thomas	252, 692	Moore, Eliphalet	252
Mitchell, William	252, 692	Moore, Elisha	865
Mitop, James	252	Moore, Gershom	865
Mix, John	692	Moore, Henry	252, 477,
Mixon, John	692		693
Moffatt, Batholemew	692	Moore, Isaac	693
Moffatt, Samuel	692	Moore, Israel	693
Moffatt, William	401, 692	Moore, Jacob	253
Molatt, Gideon	252, 692	Moore, James	253, (2)
Monfort, Hendrick	692		402, (3)
Monfort, Henry	692		693, 865
Monfort, Isaac	252, 692	Moore, Jedediah	693
Monfort, Peter	692	Moore, Jesse	693
Monfort, William	865	Moore, John	(2) 253,
Mongen, John	120		468, (3)
Monks, James	692		693, (4)
Monson, Ezekiel	692		694, 844
Monson, Josiah	692	Moore, Jonathan	61, (2)
Monson, Solomon	692		253, (2)
Monson, Stephen	692	Moore, Joseph	(2) 253,
Montanye, Abram	(2) 692		(3) 694
Montanye, Edward	692	Moore, Josiah	253, 694
Montanye, Edward, Jr.	692	Moore, Loammix	694
Montanye, Isaac	692	Moore, Martin	865
Montanye, Joseph	692	Moore, Matthias	253, (2)
Montawney, Isaac	137		694
Montgomery, Alexander	429	Moore, Moses	439, 694
Montgomery, Burnett	468	Moore, Nathan	468

Moore, Nathaniel	469, 865	Morril, Elijah	696
Moore, Patrick	694	Morris, ...	402, 696
Moore, Philip	694	Morris, Abram	696
Moore, Phineas	694	Morris, Daniel	254, 696
Moore, Prine	694	Morris, David	254, 696, 833
Moore, Resarrick	694		
Moore, Rynear	694	Morris, Dennis	696
Moore, Sackett	694	Morris, Elisha	696
Moore, Samuel	445, (2) 694	Morris, Ephraim	696
		Morris, Frazee	696
Moore, Stephen	694, 853	Morris, Isaac	696, 853
Moore, Thomas	253, 694	Morris, Israel	379
Moore, William	(2) 253, (2) 695	Morris, Jacob	696
		Morris, James	(2) 254, 696
Moorehead, George	695		
Moorehouse, Benjamin	695	Morris, John	254, 328, 455, (4) 696, 853
Moorehouse, James	695		
Moorehouse, Jonathan	253		
Moorehouse, Samuel	695	Morris, Jonathan F.	13, 15, 75, 106, 378
Moorehouse, Simeon	(2) 695		
Moran, Thomas	253, 695		
Morehead, Andrew	695	Morris, Joseph	13, (3) 28, 68, 696
Morehouse, Jacob	(2) 253		
Morehouse, Joshua	254		
Morehouse, Simeon	254	Morris, Laney	833
Morford, ...	455	Morris, Lewis	696
Morford, Daniel	695	Morris, Nathaniel	696
Morford, John	(2) 695	Morris, Randolph	696
Morford, Joseph	695	Morris, Reuben	696
Morford, Lewis	865	Morris, Robert	254, 696
Morford, Noah	695	Morris, Samuel	696
Morford, Stephen	695	Morris, States	696
Morgan, Abraham	469	Morris, Stephen	254
Morgan, Abram	695	Morris, Sylvester	696
Morgan, Adam	695	Morris, Thomas	(2) 254, 696, 697
Morgan, Anthony	695		
Morgan, Charles	(2) 254	Morris, Timothy	254, 697
Morgan, Cornelius	695	Morris, William	480, 697
Morgan, Daniel	42, (2) 695	Morrison, Daniel	697
		Morrison, Isaac	14, 29, 30, 85
Morgan, Enoch	695		
Morgan, James	402, (2) 695	Morrison, James	254, 697
		Morrison, John	697
Morgan, James, Jr.	327, 455	Morrison, Samuel	697, 835, 853
Morgan, John	254, 695		
Morgan, Jonathan	696	Morrison, Samuel, Jr.	853
Morgan, Nicholas	329, 429	Morrison, William	697
Morgan, Philip	696	Morrow, ...	469
Morgan, Samuel	254, 696	Morrow, John	697
Morley, George	254	Morrow, Samuel	469
Morrel, Benjamin	696	Morse, Amos	402
Morrel, Joseph	455	Morse, James	254
Morrel, Thomas	402	Morse, Jonas	697
Morrell, Thomas	(2) 37, 68	Morse, Joshua	697

Name	Page
Morse, Nehemiah	439
Morse, Nicholas	697
Morse, Philip	255
Morse, Randolph	697
Morton, George	842
Morton, James	697
Morton, Joseph	697
Moser, Reuben	697
Moses, George	697
Moses, Randolph	697
Mosher, Reuben	255
Moslander, Sharon	697
Moss, ...	402
Moss, David	865
Moss, Isaac	836
Moss, James	(2) 697
Moss, John	697
Moss, Philip	255
Motomore, Thomas	255
Mott, Christian	697
Mott, Christopher	697
Mott, James	345, 368
Mott, John	20, 36, 48, 85, 402, 697
Moulton, Daniel	697
Mount, Elijah	697
Mount, Evert	697
Mount, Ezekiel	698
Mount, George	255, 477
Mount, Hezekiah	698
Mount, Humphrey	698
Mount, James	698
Mount, Jesse	698
Mount, John	429
Mount, Joseph	698
Mount, Matthew	698
Mount, Moses	698
Mount, Nathaniel	698
Mount, Richard	698
Mount, Samuel	469
Mount, Thomas	657
Mount, William	698
Mountre., John	255
Mow, William	698
Mower, Constant	255
Moylan, John	841
Moylan, Stephen	59
Muchmore, David	698
Muchmore, John	698
Muchmore, William	698
Muire, John	255, 698
Muirherd, Andrew	865
Muirheed, John	255
Muirheid, George	698
Muirheid, John	698
Muirheid, Jonathan	469
Muirheid, William	698
Muler, Frederick	698
Mulford, Abram	698
Mulford, Benjamin	698
Mulford, David	429
Mulford, Enoch	698
Mulford, Ezekiel	698
Mulford, Forman	255, 698
Mulford, Furman	698
Mulford, Isaac	429
Mulford, James	698
Mulford, John	699
Mulford, Jonathan	699
Mulford, Joseph	699
Mulford, Lewis	699
Mulford, Samuel	699
Mulford, Thomas	402
Mullaky, John	699
Mullen, James	699
Mullen, John	699
Mullen, Patrick	699
Mullen, William	699
Mullet, George	255
Mullford, Timothy	699
Mulliner, Moses	255
Mulloner, Joseph	699
Mumford, David	255, 699
Mummey, John	853
Munday, Benjamin	699
Munday, Clawson	699
Munday, Clerkson	699
Munday, Gabriel	699
Munday, Henry	699
Munday, Levi	699
Munday, Martin	699
Munday, Nicholas	699
Munday, Peter	699
Munday, Reuben	699
Munday, Samuel	699
Muney (or Murrey) Dave	699
Muning, Charles	255
Munjoy, James	699
Munn, Amos	699
Munn, David	699
Munn, John	91, 699
Munn, Samuel	699
Munnion, John	699
Munson, Daniel	699
Munson, John	335, 345, 354
Munson, Joseph	865

Munson, Josiah	(2) 700	Nagle, Barent, Jr.	701
Munson, Moses	402, 844	Nail, John	701
Munson, Solomon	255	Nance, John	256, 701
Munson, Stephen	402	Nance, Thomas	256
Munson, Uzal	255	Naphis, Peter	701
Murdock, James	255, 700	Nash, ..	91
Murdock, John	(2) 255, 700	Nash, Francis	41
		Naugle, Barent, H.	701
Murdock, Thompson	121	Naugle, Barent, J.	701
Murdock, William S.	255	Naugle, David	701
Murdock, William T.	255	Naugle, Isaac	701
Murdry, James	700	Navey, Samuel	256
Murphy, Daniel	255, 700	Navius, Christian	701
Murphy, George	700	Navius, Christopher	701
Murphy, James	256	Navius, David	701
Murphy, John	256, 700	Naylor, Amos	701
Murphy, Robert	700	Neal, Thomas	256, 701
Murphy, Thomas	700	Neally, John	701
Murphy, William	(2) 256, (3) 700	Neally, William	701
		Nealy, Abraham	56
Murray, James	256, (2) 700	Nean, William D.	256
		Neaves, Thomas	256, 701
Murray, Joseph	700	Nebbard, Eliphalet	256, 701
Murray, Patrick	700	Neely, Abraham	85
Murray, Robert	700	Neff, Jacob	701
Murray, Thomas	700	Nefies, Albert	853
Murray, William	256, 700	Nefies, Peter	469
Murrel, William	700	Neglee, Samuel	17, 32, 33, (2) 52, 91
Murrey, see Muney			
Murroll, Nathaniel	865		
Murtis, Stephen	256	Negro, see Andrew Ceaser, Dick, Jack, Pomp, Will	
Murtry, see also McMurtrey			
Murtry, Thomas	256	Neifes, Garret	701
Musbrook, John	256, 700	Neifes, Garret W.	701
Myatt, Jean Baptist	256	Neifes, John	701
Myer, Henry	121	Neifes, William	701
Myers, Albertus	700	Neigent, Jonathan	701
Myers, Benjamin	700	Neigh, James	256
Myers, Cornelius	700	Neil, Daniel	(2) 320, 402
Myers, Henry	481		
Myers, John	402, 469, (2) 700	Neil, Robert	327, 402
		Neilson, John	343, 350, 834
Myers, Michael	700		
Myers, Peter	839	Nelson, Alexander	702
Myers, Stephen	256	Nelson, Davis	(2) 701
Myler, Cornelius	700	Nelson, Gabriel	(2) 702
Myrick, Joseph	701	Nelson, James	702
Myselor, Simon	701	Nelson, Joseph	(2) 702
		Nelson, Nehemiah	702
		Nephies, Jacob	702
Naberling, Christian	256, 701	Nephies, John	702
Naby, Peter	701	Nephies, Martin	702
Nagle, ...	402	Nervelin, Daniel	702

Nesbit, Nathaniel	702	Newton, Gilbert	703
Nesbit, Robert	702	Newton, John	445
Nesbit, Samuel	702	Newton, Silas	121, 257, (2) 703
Neslor, John	256		
Nestler, John	257, 702	Newton, Thomas	257
Neston, John	257	Newton, William	703
Nestor, John	257, (2) 702	Niblack, John	853
		Niblick, John	257
Nestor, Michael	257	Nice, Richard	703
Nevelling, John	379	Nicebank, John	703
Neviers, John	702	Nicholas, Benjamin	703, 853
Nevies, Cornelius	702	Nicholds, Jonathan	121
Nevies, Martinus	702	Nichols, Benjamin	703, 849
Nevil, John	702	Nichols, Cornelius	703
Neville, John	702	Nichols, Humphrey	703
Nevins, Garret	257	Nichols, Jacob	703
Nevins, John	702	Nichols, John	703
Nevins, Joseph	702	Nichols, Jonathan	121
Nevious, David	833	Nichols, Robert	403
Nevius, Abraham	347, 368	Nichols, Thomas	257, 703
Nevius, David	469	Nichols, William	121
Nevius, Peter	402, 469	Nicholson, Peter	840
Nevius, Peter, Jr.	702	Nickles, Wilson	703
Nevius, Peter, Sr.	702	Nickleson, John	704
Newark, Thomas	(2) 320, 420	Nickolds, Lewis	704
		Nickson, Alexander	704
Newberry, William	483	Nicola, Lewis	62
Newbod, Barzillai	368	Nielson, David	704
Newcastle, ...	121	Nielson, Davis	704
Newcomb, Andrew	402	Nielson, Gabriel	704
Newcomb, Brigadier General	368, 369	Nifins, Garret	257, 704
		Nile, Benjamin	704
Newcomb, Dayton	403	Nimnough, Neal	257
Newcomb, Ethan	703	Ninemaster, Michael	704
Newcomb, Reuben	257, 703	Niverson, John	704
Newcomb, Silas	(2) 28, 64, 335, 340, 350	Nivins, Ruloff	704
		Nivison, Nathan	704
		Nixon, George	257, 704
Newcomb, Webster	703	Nixon, Isaac	257, 704
Newell, Hugh	703	Nixon, James	257
Newell, James	469	Nixon, John	704
Newell, Theodore	703	Nixon, Richard	(2) 257, (2) 704
Newenham, James	257		
Newent, Daniel V.	703	Nixon, Robert	257, 344, 368, 704
Newgen, Richard	703		
Newkirk, Cornelius	403	Nixon, Thomas	372
Newkirk, John	703	Nixon, William	257, 704
Newkirk, Mathew	853	Noble, George	257, 704
Newman, John	703	Noble, Thomas	704
Newman, Reuben	703	Noe, Amos	704
Newman, Samuel	703	Noe, Andrew	704
Newman, Thomas	703	Noe, James	258, 705
Newman, William	257, 703	Noe, John	705
Newton, Charles	257	Noe, Lewis	258, (2) 705

Noe, Marsh	705	Nutter, John	258
Noe, Peter	705	Nyce, John	706
Noe, Samuel	258	Nyce, William	403
Nolt, Philip	258		
Nonan, John	705		
Norcross, Benjamin	258, 705	Oader, Morris	258
Norcross, James	705	Cake, Jacob	706
Norcross, John	705	Cakey, Abram	706
Norcross, Joseph	705	Oakley, George	857
Norcross, William	20, 22, (2) 36, 97, 836	Oakley, John	258, 706
		Oatman, Andrew	865
		Oave, Peter	258
Norkett, Dennis	258	Obart, George	258, 706
Norman, Benjamin	258	Obart, John	259, 706
Norman, James	258	Obart, Peter	706
Norman, Obediah	705	Obert, George	706
Normonton, William	258	Obert, Henry	403, 469
Norris, Bethuel	705	O'Briant, John	259
Norris, Burns	478	O'Bryan, John	259
Norris, Burrows	705	O'Bryan, Patrick	259
Norris, David	705	Ockerman, Garline	706
Norris, George	429	Ockerman, John	706
Norris, Gershom	865	Ocletree, John	706
Norris, Henry	705	Odel, Garret	706
Norris, James	705	O'Flaherty, John	259, 706
Norris, John	258, 469	Ogbron, William	706
Norris, Libbius	705	Ogden, Aaron	13, (2) 28, (2) 50, 69, 842
Norris, Peter	258, 705		
Norris, Thadeus	705		
Norris, Thomas	705		
Norris, Walter	705	Ogden, Abraham	360
Norris, William	(2) 705	Ogden, Barne	57, 91
Norris, Ziba	121	Ogden, Benjamin	259, 706
North, John	705	Ogden, David	(2) 706
Northall, William	705	Ogden, Eleizer	707
Northrup, Joseph	705	Ogden, Eliakim	706
Northup, David	705	Ogden, Eliakum	(2) 259
Norton, Caleb	705	Ogden, James	403
Norton, Jacob, Jr.	705	Ogden, Jedediah	259, 455
Norton, James	258, 705	Ogden, John	(4) 707, 865
Norton, Jonathan	705		
Norton, Oliver	706	Ogden, Jonathan	(2) 707, 865
Nortwick, John	483, 706		
Nortwick, Simon	706	Ogden, Joseph	707
Nott, Philip	258	Ogden, Ludlow	259
Nottman, George	258	Ogden, Matthew	259
Nowey, Samuel	258	Ogden, Matthias	13, (2) 28, 49, 64, 707
Nowlen, John	469		
Nugent, James	833		
Nugent, Richard	258, 706	Ogden, Moses	57, 106
Nukler, Thomas	706	Ogden, Nathan	259
Nukless, Wilson	706	Ogden, Nathaniel	71
Nun, John	706	Ogden, Noah	137
Nunn, Thomas	706	Ogden, Oliver	707

Ogden, Samuel	(2) 259, 340, 360		Orman, Benjamin	708
			Orman, James	260
Ogden, Samuel, Jr.	259		Orman, Stephen	708
Ogden, Simeon	707		Orr, Alexander	429
Ogden, Stephen	259, 707, 857		Orr (or Ord) John	57, 91 (2) 260, (2) 708
Oglesbie, Robert	707			
O'Hara, ...	403		Orril, Arnold	708
O'Harra, George	707, 839		Orsman, Benjamin	260
Ohe, John	707		Orsman, John	260
O'Kelly, Ephraim	259, 707		Osband, Squire	708
Okeson, Nicholas	853		Osband, Stephen	708
Olban, George	865		Osborn, Adonijah	260
Olden, John	707		Osborn, Abraham	430
Olden, Thomas	259, 478		Osborn, Amos	261
O'Lefferty, Henry	259, 707		Osborn, Daniel	708
Olewine, Lawrence	259, 707		Osborn, David	261, (2) 708
Oliphant, James	403			
Olischant, John	853		Osborn, Ethan	708
Oliver, Allen	707		Osborn, Howell	430
Oliver, David	259, 707		Osborn, J ...	430
Oliver, James	(2) 707		Osborn, Jedediah	261
Oliver, Jeremiah	259		Osborn, Joel	261
Oliver, Jerome	707		Osborn, John	261, 708
Oliver, John	260, 403, 707, 837		Osborn, John B.	469
			Osborn, Jonathan H.	481
Oliver, Joseph	260, 707		Osborn, Joseph	261
Oliver, Nicholas	260, 707		Osborn, Luke	261, 708
Oliver, Samuel	260, 403, 857		Osborn, Nehemiah	(2) 708
			Osborn, Samuel	261
Oliver, William	91, 707		Osborn, Stephen	261, 708
Olp, John	707		Osborn, Thomas	430, 708
Oman, Charles	260		Osborne, Abner	708
O'Mara, Charles	260		Osborne, Elisha	261
O'Mock, see Aumoch			Osborne, Henry	708, 865
O'Neal, Conrad	260		Osborne, Ichabod	261, 708
O'Neal, Daniel	260		Osborne, Jesse	261, 708
O'Neal, Henry	260, 707		Osborne, Samuel	478
O'Neal, John	260, 708		Osborne, Stephen	709
O'Neal, Neal	260, 708		Osburn, Abner	709
O'Neil, A	260, 708		Osburn, Abram	709
O'Neil, Henry	260		Osburn, Cornelius	709
O'Neil, John	260		Osburn, Elias	709
Opaike, William	260		Osburn, Hand	709
Opdycke, Albert	403		Osburn, Henry	709
Opdyke Luther	455		Osburn, Jacob	709
Oppey, Christopher	708		Osburn, Joel	261, 709
Orun, Cooper	708		Osburn, John	709
Oram, Darby	260, 874		Osburn, Joseph	261, 709
Orchard, John	708		Osburne, Nathaniel	131
Ord, see also, Orr			Osman, John	(2) 261
Ord, John	121		Osman, Joseph	261
Ore, John	708		Osmon, John	709
Organ, John	260		Osmun, Benajah	(2) 31, 52, 53, 91

Name	Pages	Name	Pages
Osmun, Benjamin	131	Palmer, Richard	262, 839, 865
Otto, Bodo	341, 354		
Otto, Bodo, Jr.	337, 378	Palmer, William	710
Otto, Frederick	74	Pamerly, Isaac	262
Otson, John	261, 709	Pamly, see Pannely	
Outgelt, Frederick	709	Pancoast, Joseph	403
Outwater, Francis	261, 709	Pangborn, Jonathan	262, 710
Outwater, John	327, 403	Pangborn, Joseph	262, 710
Overfelt, Conrad	709	Pangborn, Limis	710
Overt, George	709	Pangborn, Nathaniel	710
Overteur, Henry	709	Pangborn, Peter	(2) 710
Owen, David	709	Pangborn, William	(2) 710
Owens, James	261, (2) 709	Pannely (or Pamly) Isaac	262
Owens, Stephen	261, 709	Panner, William	711
Oyers, Benjamin	709	Panoman, Peter	711
		Panton, John	262
		Parcel, John	833
Pace, Michael, Jr.	262, 709	Parcel, Peter	833
Pack, David	709	Parcell, Anthony	137
Pack, Isaac	709	Parcell, Jacob	711
Pack, Philip	709	Parcell, Peter	711
Pack, William	262, 709	Parcell, Thomas	262, 711
Packer, George	709	Pardun, Thomas	262
Packer, Jacob	262, 709	Pardunn, Thomas	711
Packer, John	709	Parent, Daniel	262
Packston, William	710	Parent, William	469, 865
Paddleford, Edward	710	Parke, William	439
Padgett, David	710	Parker, ...	121, 712
Padgett, Thomas	121, 710	Parker, Abraham	455
Page, Ambrose	710	Parker, Abram	711
Page, Daniel	262	Parker, Amariah	853
Page, David	403	Parker, Azariah	478, 711
Page, Thomas	710	Parker, Benjamin	711
Page, Timothy	710	Parker, Daniel	430
Pagg, Daniel	840	Parker, David	711
Pain, Isaac	710	Parker, Elisha	711
Pain, John	403, 710	Parker, George	711
Pain, Stephen	710	Parker, Gershom	(2) 262
Painter, George	121	Parker, Isaac	455
Painter, John	446	Parker, Jacob	262, 711
Pairs, Samuel	710	Parker, James	711
Paiser, John	710	Parker, John	403, (4) 711
Pall, John	262		
Palmer, Anthony	262, 710	Parker, Joseph	(4) 711
Palmer, David	710	Parker, Joseph, Jr.	711
Palmer, Edmund	710	Parker, Joseph, Sr.	711
Palmer, James	710	Parker, Mark	711
Palmer, John	469	Parker, Nathaniel	262, 711
Palmer, Jonathan	833	Parker, Robert	711
Palmer, Joseph	865	Parker, Samuel	(2) 711
Palmer, Philip	262, 710, 853	Parker, Samuel F.	335, 368
		Parker, Stephen	711
Palmer, Philip, Jr.	710	Parker, Thomas	131, 711

Parker, William	262		Parsons, Robert, Jr.	439	
Parkes, Daniel	712		Parsons, Samuel	263, 469	
Parkes, Joseph	712		Parsons, Stephen	713	
Parkes, Noah	712		Partrick, John	713	
Parkes, Paul	712		Parvin, Benajah	857	
Parkhurst, Abraham	712		Parvin, Benjamin	263, 713	
Parkhurst, Caleb	712		Parvin, David	874	
Parkhurst, John	85, 131, 712		Parvin, Jeffrey	874	
			Parvin, Jeffry	713	
Parkhurst, Solomon	712		Parvin, Matthew	109	
Parkinson, Aaron	712		Passant, see Parsons		
Parkinson, Henry	91		Passell, Nicholas	713	
Parkinson, Jonathan	712		Patchen, Daniel	713	
Parkinson, Sylvanus	712		Paten, James	263	
Parks, Joseph	262		Paterson, Andrew	263	
Parks, Zebulon	121		Paterson, James	131	
Parmer, Daniel	712		Paterson, John	263	
Parmer, George	262		Paterson, Robert	853	
Parr, Benjamin	263, 712		Patrick, Samuel	713	
Parr, Jesse	712		Patten, James	713	
Parr, John	263, 712		Patten, John	404, 713	
Parr, Mathias	712		Patten, Joseph	843	
Parr, Thomas	712		Patten, Thomas	263, 713	
Parrent, John	712		Patterson, ...	57, 92	
Parrent, Robert	712		Patterson, Edward	20, 22, 35, 37, 97	
Parrit, Silas	30, 50, 51, 91				
Parrot, Adoniram	131		Patterson, John	(2) 713	
Parrot, William	16, 32, 33, 97		Patterson, Jonathan	713	
			Patterson, Lemuel	713	
Parrott, David	712		Patterson, Reuben	713	
Parrott, John	712		Patterson, Robert	336, 368 378, 469	
Parrott, Joseph	712				
Parrott, William	712		Patterson, Thomas	20, 35, 85	
Parry, John	712				
Parsail, see also, Pursell			Patterson, Watson	713	
			Patterson, William	20	
Parsail (or Pursel), Swain	263		Patterson, Zachariah	263	
			Patton, James	430, 849	
Parse, John	712		Paul, After	263	
Parse, Jonathan	712		Paul, Benjamin	461, (2) 713	
Parsel, Jacob	712				
Parsel, Mathias	712		Paul, David	404	
Parsel, William	712		Paul, James	34, 52, 5 92.	
Parshall, Israel	712				
Parsonet, John	712		Paul, John	263, (2) 713	
Parsons (or Passant) Abraham	446				
			Paul, Joseph	713	
Parsons, David	263		Paul, Richard	713	
Parsons, Harmon	263		Paulshamus, Abraham	469	
Parsons, John	(2) 263, 430, (2) 713		Pawpe, Robert	713	
			Paxon, William	(2) 713	
			Paxton, James	76, 84፻	
Parsons, Matthew	263		Payne, George	342, 36፻	

Paynton, William	713	Peirce, Ward	430
Peach, William	714	Peirie, James	264
Peachy, Benjamin	263, 714	Peirson, Azel	404
Peairs, John	404	Peirson, David	404, 715
Pearce, Adam	263, 714	Peirson, John	264
Pearce, Benjamin	714	Peirson, Mathew	715
Pearce, Michael	714	Peirson, Stephen	455, 715
Pearce, Samuel	714	Peirson, Thomas	264
Pearce, William	263, 714	Peirson, William	715
Pearsall, Anthony	263	Pell, Gilbert	469
Pearson, Benjamin P.	714	Pelters, Philip	264
Pearson, Daniel	714	Pelton, Joseph	715
Pearson, David	378, 714	Pemberton, Robert	57, 86
Pearson, Elihu	714	Pence, William	264, 715
Pearson, James	840	Penington, Nathan	264
Pearson, John	38, 39, 40, 86, 714	Pennington, John	715
		Pennington, Nathan	(2) 715
		Pennington, William	58
Pearson, Joseph	714	Pennington, William S.	101
Pearson, Mathew	714	Penton, Abner	404
Pearson, Matthias	263, 714	Penton, Clark	715
Pearson, Theophilus	714	Penton, James	131, 715
Pearson, Thomas	714	Penton, Joseph	715
Pearson, Timothy	714	Penwell, David	715
Pearson, William	263	Penyard, Joseph	715
Pease, Jonathan	264	Penyard, Samuel	715
Pease, Samuel	714	Peor, James	715
Peck, Constant	22, 97	Pepper, William	264
Peck, Daniel	714	Peran, Henry	264
Peck, David	264	Percil, John	469
Peck, James	714	Periam, Joseph	28, 73
Peck, John	31, (2) 51, 52, 92, 404	Perill, John	715
		Perill, Peter	715
		Perkins, ...	871
Peck, Joseph	714	Perkins, Eleazer	264, 715
Peck, Moses	264, 714	Perkins, Jacob	325, 339, 368
Peck, Nathan	714		
Peck, Stephen	714	Perkins, Samuel	716
Peckin, Samuel	714	Perkins, Thomas	716
Peep, Samuel	714	Perkins, William	716
Peer, David	714	Perlee, Peter	716
Peer, Isaac	715	Pern, Silas	865
Peer, John	455	Perrine, Andrew	716
Peer, Jonathan	264, 715	Perrine, Daniel	(2) 716
Peet, Herm	715	Perrine, Henry	(2) 716
Peffer, David	715	Perrine, James	(4) 716, 865
Pegg, Daniel	715		
Peidrick, Benjamin	715	Perrine, James D.	716
Peigant, Robert	715	Perrine, Job	716
Peigent, Robert	264	Perrine, John	469, (3) 716
Peir, Cornelius	715		
Peir, James	715	Perrine, Joseph	716
Peirce, John	264	Perrine, Lewis	716
Peirce, Jonathan	715	Perrine, Mathew	716
Peirce, Samuel	715	Perrine, Nicholas	716

Perrine, Peter	404, 716	Pettit, Edward	718
Perrine, Silas	716	Pettit, Jesse	718
Perrine, William	264, 716	Pettit, Nathaniel	342, 368
Perriton, Jonathan	853	Pettitt, Jabez	265
Perry, Daniel	716	Petty, Andrew	718
Perry, Henry	(2) 264	Petty, Daniel	718
Perry, John	264, (2) 716	Petty, David	718
		Petty, John	404
Perry, Joseph	716	Petty, Peter	470
Perry, Jotham	264, 717	Pew, Benjamin	265
Perry, Moses	717	Pew (or Pue,) Benoni	265
Perry, Noah	717	Pew, Joseph	718
Perry, Samuel	717	Pew, Reuben	265
Perry, Thomas	264, 717	Pew, William	265
Perry, William	717	Phagons, James	718
Persal, Jacob	717	Phares, Amariah	718
Persall, John	430	Phares, Andrew	718
Perse, Samuel	717	Phares, John	455, 718
Persee, John	717	Phares, Robert	718
Persifelt, Christian	717	Phelps, ...	718
Person, Abram	866	Phelps, Joel	834
Persons, Nicholas	264	Philhower, Christian	718
Perstider, John	265	Philhower, Christopher	718
Petemus, Joseph	265	Phillips, Amos	265
Peters, Amos	469	Phillips, Benjamin	839
Peters, John	717	Phillips, Berin	839
Peters, Levi	(2) 265	Phillips, David	718
Peters, Philip	265, (2) 717	Phillips, Elias	342, 372
		Phillips, Francis	265
Peters, Richard	717	Phillips, Frederick	131
Peterson, Abraham	265, 717	Phillips, Henry	342, 368
Peterson, Abram	717	Phillips, Hugh	718
Peterson, David	717	Phillips, Jacob	(2) 265, 844
Peterson, Derick	368		
Peterson, Derrick	340	Phillips, Joel	718
Peterson, George	717	Phillips, John	33, 106, 266, (2) 404, (3) 718
Peterson, Henry	265, 717		
Peterson, Hessel	717		
Peterson, Jacob	265, 717		
Peterson, John	(2) 404	Phillips, Jonathan	16, 32, 33, 34, 52, 86, 404
Peterson, Peter	(2) 265		
Peterson, Reuben	717		
Peterson, Samuel	265, (2) 717		
		Phillips, Joseph	(2) 335, 342, 354, 478, 718
Peterson, Thomas	(2) 717		
Peterson, William	430		
Peterson, Zachariah	265	Phillips, Lott, Jr.	718
Pett, Joseph	718	Phillips, Lott, Sr.	718
Pette, Robert	718	Phillips, Palmer	470
Pettemore, Jonathan	718	Phillips, Philip	404
Pettenger, Richard	718	Phillips, Ralph	719
Pettit, Benjamin	718	Phillips, Simon	842
Pettit, Daniel	718	Phillips, Theo	719
Pettit, David	718	Phillips, Thomas	719, 833

Philmelie, David	719	Pierson, Shadrack	720
Philpot, Abraham	719, 874	Pierson, Stephen	720
Philwell, David	719	Pierson, Sylvanus	720
Piatt, Abram	719	Pierson, Timothy	720
Piatt, Daniel	14, 29, (2) 49, 69	Pierson, Uriah	720
		Pierson, William	(2) 720
		Piggett, Samuel	720
Piatt, Jacob	14, 28, 29, 49, (3) 50, 86, 404	Pigney, William	266
		Pike, Asher	720
		Pike, James	720
		Pike, Jeremiah	720
Piatt, John	719	Pike, John	720
Piatt, John D.	483	Pike, Nathaniel	844
Piatt, William	(2) 50, 86	Pike, Thomas	720
		Pike, Thomas M.	720
Pick, William	266	Pike, Zebulon	59, 86
Pickell, Mathias	719	Pinkney, William	266, 720
Pickens, Alexander	266, 719	Pinton, James	266
Picket, Francis	719	Pipes, John	38, 39, 101, 439
Picket, George	266, 719		
Picket, Robert	266	Pirney, Peter	266
Pidcock, Charles	719	Pitman, Jonathan	720
Pidcock, Jonathan	719	Pitney, Mahlon	(2) 720
Pidgeon, Isaac	719	Pittenger, Abram	720
Pier, Isaac	719	Pittenger, John	405, 720
Pier, Jacob	719	Pittenger, Richard	470
Pierce, Francis	266	Pittenger, Samuel	720
Pierce, George	405, 719	Pittman, Jonathan	405
Pierce, John	266	Pitts, William	720
Pierce, Jonathan	719	Pittson, Andrew	720
Pierce, Thomas	266	Pitney, Peter	266
Pierce, Ward	719	Plahames, Cornelius	430
Pierson, Aaron	719	Platt, David	405
Pierson, Abram	719, 844	Platt, Francis	720
Pierson, Benjamin	405, 719	Platt, John	430
Pierson, Caleb	121, 266, 719	Platt, Joseph	721
		Platt, Samuel	721
Pierson, Daniel	21, 101	Plough (or Plow), Jacob	266, 721
Pierson, David	266, 470, 719		
		Ploughman, Moses	721
Pierson, Elihu	720	Plow, see Plough	
Pierson, Enos	720	Plowman, John	874
Pierson, Ephraim	720	Plum, Abram	721
Pierson, Erastus	720	Plum, Isaac	721
Pierson, Harman	266	Plum, John	721
Pierson, Jabez	720	Plum, Samuel	721
Pierson, John	266, 720	Plumb, David	266
Pierson, Joseph	(2) 720	Plumb, Stephen	131
Pierson, Josiah	405	Plumbley, Jacob	267
Pierson, Matthew	266	Plume, Isaac	456
Pierson, Nicholas	266, 720	Plumley, Jacob	(2) 721
Pierson, Robert	266, 720	Plummer, James	267, 721
Pierson, Samuel	266, 405, 720	Plummer, John	267, (2) 721

Poarch, Thomas	721	Post, Francis	405
Poke, John	721	Post, Garret	139, 405
Poland, John	121	Post, George	722
Polhemus, James	721	Post, Hendrick	470
Polhemus, John	14, 28, 29, 69	Post, Henry	267, (2) 722
Polhemus, Lefford	721	Post, Jacob	722
Polhemus, Nathan	721	Post, Jacobus	368
Polhemus, Nathaniel	405	Post, James	722
Polhemus, Tobias	405	Post, Jediah	722
Poling, Richard	721	Post, John	(2) 722
Poling, Samuel	721	Post, John C.	722
Polk, Jacob	267	Post, John H.	722
Polk, Joab	267	Post, John J.	722
Polk, Job	131, 267, 721	Post, John P.	722
		Post, Joseph	723
Pollard, John	721, 866	Post, Josiah	723
Pollard, Thomas	267	Post, Merselus	723
Polmer, Daniel	460	Post, Peter	478
Pomeroy, John	844	Post, Philip	723
Pomp (Negro)	866	Post, Ralph	723
Pool, Benjamin	721	Post, Thomas	723
Pool, David	721	Post, Tunis	723
Pool, Jacob B.	480	Post, William	267, 723
Pool, James	721	Posteda, Daniel	866
Pool, John	267, (2) 721	Postens, Charles	723
		Postens, Jacob	723, 853
Pool, John, Jr.	721	Poster, Charles	723
Pool, Robert	267	Postley, Richard	723
Pool, Thomas	722	Potter, Amos	267, 723
Pool, William	470	Potter, Caleb	723
Poord, Joseph	722	Potter, David	324, 340 350
Pope, Birney	722		
Pope, Christian	722	Potter, Enoch	723
Pope, Christopher	722	Potter, Gilbert	723, 866
Pope, Jeremiah	722	Potter, Isaac	723
Pope, John	267	Potter, Jacob	460
Pope, Samuel	722	Potter, John	405
Porter, Abner	267	Potter, Joseph	267, (2) 723, 843
Porter, James	838		
Porter, John	722	Potter, Matthew	405
Porter, Joseph	722	Potter, Moses	723
Porter, Nathaniel	47, 405, 722	Potter, Paul	723
		Potter, Reuben	343, 368 723
Poryn, Peter	722		
Post, Aaron	722	Potter, Robert	723
Post, Abraham	430, (2) 722	Potter, Russel	723
		Potter, Samuel	20, 86, 267, 341, 354, 849
Post, Abram	430		
Post, Adrian	722		
Post, Ausey	722	Potter, Silas	723
Post, Caleb	267, 722	Potter, Stephen	723
Post, Cornelius H.	722	Potter, Thomas	122, 267, 723
Post, David	722		

Potter, Zanas	723	Preston, Joseph	268, 725
Potts, Isaac	267, 723	Preston, Levi	405
Potts, Jasper	132, 267	Prevost, Daniel	725
Potts, Jonathan	723	Price, Abner	725
Potts, Samuel	723	Price, Abram	725
Potts, William	267, 723	Price, Anthony	430
Poules, Jacob	723	Price, Benjamin	268, 725
Pouleson, Jacobus	723	Price, Charles	725
Pouleson, Lawrence	724	Price, David	725
Pouleson, Martin	724	Price, Edward	268, 725
Poulesse, Jacobus	456	Price, Elijah	139
Poulson, Lawrence	267	Price, Ephraim	725
Pound, Benjamin	724	Price, Ezekiel	268
Pound, Cornelius	724	Price, Farrington	725
Pound, John	724	Price, George	(2) 725
Pound, John, Sr.	849	Price, Isaac	268, 725
Pound, Jonathan	724	Price, Jacob	725
Pounder, William	267, 724	Price, James	866
Pounds, Hezekiah	724	Price, Jeremiah	725
Poweel, Thomas	483	Price, John	(4) 268, (3) 725
Powell, Elkanah	446		
Powell, Isaac	840	Price, Jonathan	725
Powell, John	724	Price, Joseph	268, (2) 725
Powell, Reuben	456		
Powell, Richard	724	Price, Levi	725
Powell, Thomas	110, 724	Price, Nathaniel	268
Powels, Jacob	267	Price, Philip	268, 725
Powelson, Abram	724	Price, Price	725
Powelson, Cornelius	724	Price, Ralph	725
Powelson, Hendrich	724	Price, Rice	268, (2) 725
Powelson, Henry	724		
Powelson, John	724	Price, Richard	725, 837
Powelson, Martin	724	Price, Samuel	268, 725
Powelson, Monah	724	Price, Stephen	122, 268
Powelson, Powell	724	Price, Thomas	268, 725, 839, 845, 866
Powelson, Richard	724		
Powers, George	(2) 268, 724	Price, Thompson	726, 866
Powers, John	268, 724	Price, William	269, 405, 726
Powers, Thomas	268		
Powles, Powles	724	Price, Zachariah	726
Powleson, James	724	Pricket, Francis	726
Powlson, John	470	Pricket, Isaac	726
Prall, Garrison	853, 866	Pricket, John	726
Prall, John	430, 724, 866	Pricket, Stephen	726
		Pricket, William	726
Prall, William	724	Prickett, Azariah	269
Pratt, ...	405	Prickett, John	269
Pratt, Cornelius	268, 724	Prickett, Robert	269
Prendergrass, Thomas	132	Pridmore, Daniel	726
Preston, Abijah	724, 874	Pridmore, John	269, 726
Preston, Ebenezer	724	Pridmore, William	726
Preston, Isaac	340, 354, 724, 874	Prigmore, John	866
		Prigmore, William	(2) 726
Preston, John	725	Primmer, Adam	726

Prince, William	269		Quick, Benjamin	727
Printy, William	269		Quick, David	727
Prior, John	726		Quick, Eleazer	269, 727
Prior, Lemon	269		Quick, Garret	727
Prior, Moses	726		Quick, Henry	269, 727
Pritten, Adoniram	269		Quick, Jacob	727, 857
Probasco, Garret	(2) 726		Quick, Jacobus	406
Probasco, Hendrick	405		Quick, James	406, 727
Probasco, Peter	726		Quick, Joakim	456
Proctor, Robert	269		Quick, John	269
Prouse, Adam	726		Quick, Manuel	727
Prout, James	269		Quick, Moses	270
Provost, David	470, (2) 726		Quick, Peter	727
			Quick, Peter, Sr.	727
Provost, Jasper	726		Quick, Samuel	270, (2) 727
Provost, John	726			
Provost, Jonathan	726		Quick, Tunis	727
Provost, Peter	(2) 726		Quick, William	270, 727
Prudden, Adoniram	269		Quicksel, William	727
Prudden, Amos	726		Quigg, Henry	270
Prudden, Boyse	726		Quigley, David	270, 727
Prudden, John	726		Quigley, Isaac	853
Prudden, Joseph, Jr.	727		Quigley, John	728
Prudden, Samuel	269		Quigley, Joseph	406
Prymon, Samuel	727		Quigley, Moses	728
Pryor, Thomas	269		Quigley, Robert	406
Psandler, Joshua	269, 727		Quigley, Thomas	406, 871
Pubit, William	269		Quigley, William	728
Pue, see Pew			Quill, John	270
Pulaski, Cassamer	62		Quimby, John	270
Pulis, John	470		Quimby, Josiah	20, 101, 483
Pull, John	727			
Pullenger, Richard S.	727		Quimby, Samuel	728
Pumyea, Peter	406		Quin, David	728
Purcell, Thomas	727		Quodoir, Peter	728
Purdy, Richard	727			
Pursel, see Parsail				
Pursel, Swain	269		Raberger, John	270, 728
Pursum, John	727		Race, Andrew	270, 728
Purvis, George	406		Racy, Philip	728
Putnam, Israel	65		Radley, William	270
Putnam, Peter	269, 406		Radnan, John	270
Pyatt, ...	406		Raferty, John	728
Pyke, Robert	727		Rafferty, John	270
			Raffsnyder, Joseph	270
			Raims, William	270
Quack, Peter	727		Rain, John	270, 728
Quackenboss, Isaac	269, 727		Rall, Matthias	270
Quackenbush, Cornelius	727		Ralph, Leroy	728
			Ramsden, William	728
Quackenbush, Peter	727		Ramsen, William	728
Quay, John	430		Randle, David	270, 728
Queen, David	727		Randle, John	270, 728
Quick, Abraham	347, 354		Randle, Rufus	270

Randle, William	270, 728	Raverty, John	271, 729
Randolph, Abijah	728	Ray, David	729
Randolph, Asa	728	Ray, James	271
Randolph, Asher Fitz	327, 329, 406	Ray, John	729
		Ray, Josiah	729
Randolph, Barzilla F.	728	Rayman, James	271, 729
Randolph, Brazilla	728	Raymond, James	122, 271
Randolph, Daniel	728 (2)	Raynor, Jonathan	729
Randolph, Daniel F.	728	Raynor, Matthew	430
Randolph, Dennis	728	Read, see also, Reed	
Randolph, Ephraim	728	Read, ...	406
Randolph, Esieh F.	728	Read, Charles	324, 337, 339, 354
Randolph, Ezekiel F.	728		
Randolph, F.	728	Read, Daniel	446
Randolph, James	728, 729	Read, David	729
Randolph, James F.	729	Read, Ephraim	271
Randolph, John	729	Read, George	271, 729
Randolph, Joseph	406	Read, Giles	271
Randolph, Joseph F.	729	Read, John	271
Randolph, Lewis Fitz-	329, 456	Read, Thomas C.	20, 75
Randolph, Malachi	729	Read, William	730
Randolph, Malachi F.	729	Reader, William	730
Randolph, Michael	729	Reading, Charles	406
Randolph, Nathaniel Fitz	406	Reading, Jacob	730
		Reading, Jeremiah	730
Randolph, Nehemiah	729	Reading, John	22, 36, 37, 97
Randolph, Phiaeas	(2) 729		
Randolph, Phineas Fitz	729	Reading, Samuel	17, 34, 49, 52, 69, 271
Randolph, Reuben	406		
Randolph, Robert	729	Reading, Thomas	21, 86
Randolph, Rufus	271, 729	Reading, Wright	730
Randolph, Samuel	343, 368, 729	Ready, John	271
		Reamer, George	730
Randolph, Samuel F.	729	Reamer, John	730
Randolph, Simeon	853	Reamer (or Reams), Paul	271, 730
Randolph, Simon	729		
Randolph, Stella F.	729	Reams, see Reamer	
Randolph, Thomas F.	729	Reanalds, James	730
Randolph, Zedekiah	833	Reardon, John	271, 730
Randolph, Zedkiah Fitz	729	Reather, John	730
		Recey, Philip	730
Rankin, Thomas	132	Reckless, Anthony	60, 92
Rankins, James	271	Reckless, Robert	730
Rap, Conrad	729	Reclaw, John	730
Rapalye, Jeromus	729	Redding, Chris	730
Rape, Christopher	406	Redford, Joseph	730
Rapp, Solomon	271	Redman, John	271
Rappleyea, Jacobus	729	Redner, Nicholas	866
Rardon, John	271	Reeas, ...	866
Rarity, John	271	Reed, ...	406
Rase, John	729	Reed, Aaron	(2) 730
Rattan, Samuel	(2) 729	Reed, Abner	730
Raul, Matthias	271	Reed, Amos	271

Reed, Benjamin	730	Reeves, Moses	731
Reed, Bowes	336, 339, 354	Reeves, Paul	272
		Reeves, Thomas	(2) 732
Reed, Daniel	439	Reid, see also Reed	
Reed, Enoch	730	Reid, Ephraim	732
Reed (or Read), Ephraim	730	Reid, John	470, 732
		Reid, Jonathan	732
Reed, General	366	Reid, Richard	732
Reed, George	866	Reiler, Thomas	272
Reed, Henry	132, (2) 271	Remington, Clement	272
		Remington, John	732
Reed, Isaac	271, 730	Remsen, William	407
Reed, Isaiah	271	Rennard, Thomas	732
Reed, James	272, 730	Reock, Abraham	732
Reed, Jesse	853	Reock, Jacob	272, 732
Reed (or Reid), Job	731	Reock, John	732
Reed, John	30, 39, 40, 54, 57, 92, 101, 106, 272, (2) 456, 470, 731	Rew, John	732
		Reynearson, Garret	(2) 732
		Reynolds, Abijah	272
		Reynolds, George	17, 31, 34, 48, 101, 407
		Reynolds, James	272, 732
Reed, Jonathan	731	Reynolds, John	(2) 273, (3) 732
Reed, Joseph	334, 350, 731		
		Reynolds, Michael	273
Reed, Joshua	731, 866	Reynolds, Robert	732
Reed, Lewis	272, 731	Reynolds, Samuel	(2) 732
Reed, Obediah	731	Reynolds, Thomas	47, 339, 354
Reed, Peter	731		
Reed, Richard	(2) 731	Reynolds, William	(2) 732
Reed, Robert	272	Reynord, Henry	273, 732
Reed, Thomas	60, 74, (2) 272, 731	Rhea, Aaron	30, (2) 50, 106
		Rhea, David	16, 31, 66, 329, 374, 431, 837
Reed, William	(2) 731, (3) 272		
		Rhea, David, Jr.	344, 372
Reeder, Andrew	407	Rhea, James	273
Reeder, Isaac	731, 853	Rhea, John	470
Reeder, John	(2) 731	Rhea, Jonathan	33, 34, 52, 53, 92
Reeder, William	731, 866		
Reemer, Lewis	731		
Reepley, Baltis	731		
Reerdon, John	272	Rhea, Robert	407, 732
Reese, David	272	Rhodan, Thomas	732
Reeves, David	272, 731	Rhodes, Charles	376
Reeves, Hosea	731	Riall, Isaac	733
Reeves, Isaac	407	Ribbets, William	132, 733
Reeves, James	731	Ribble, George	407
Reeves, John	32, 106, (2) 272, (4) 731	Ribble, William	733
		Ribeck, William	273
Reeves, Joseph	470	Ribeth, William	273, 733
Reeves, Joshua	139, 731	Rice, Daniel	273

Rice, Isaac	273	Riggs, Zenus	734
Rice, James	122	Right, John	274
Rice, Michael	273, 733	Riker, Gerardus	456
Rice, Richard	733	Riker, Jacob	734
Rice, Thadeus	273	Riker, James	470
Rice, William	273, 407, 871	Riker, John	734
		Riker, John B.	37, 74
Rich, Jacob	273	Riker, John Jacob	274, 734
Rich, Joseph	273, (2) 733	Riley, Daniel	734
		Riley, Jacob	734
Richards, ...	470	Riley, James	122, 274
Richards, James	273	Riley, John	274
Richards, Martin	733	Riley, Joseph	137, 274, 734
Richards, Samuel	122		
Richards, Thomas	733	Riley, Patrick	734
Richardson, Jacob	733	Riley, Roger	407
Richardson, James	273, 733	Rinehart, Godfrey	343, 369
Richardson, John	273, (3) 733, 872	Rinehart, Philip	274
		Ringo, William	734
Richardson, Joseph	273, 733	Rino, Ephraim	734
Richardson, William	733	Rino, William	734
Richerson, Richard	733	Risley, Aun	734
Richman, Richard	733	Risley, David	734
Richman, William	733	Risley, Jeremiah	446
Richmond, Abraham	833	Risley, Joseph	734
Richmond, Daniel	733	Risley, Morris	734
Richmond, John	874	Risley, Nathaniel	734
Richmond, Jonathan	840	Risley, Samuel	734
Richmond, William	273, 733	Risley, Thomas	734
Richow, Abram	733	Riston, Paulus	734
Rickar, Philip	273	Ritner, Nicholas	853
Ricker, John N.	733	Rivers (or Bevens), Davis	274
Rickey, Benjamin	733		
Rickey, Cornelius	273, 733	Rivets, George	734
Rickey, Israel	407	Roach, Nicholas	341, 378
Riddin, Christopher	273	Roads, William	734
Riddle, John	733	Robards, Ichabod	734
Rider, John	733	Robarts, John	431
Ridler, William	733	Robbins, Isaac	734
Riffe, Matthias	273	Robbins, Jesse	735
Riffner, Adam	274, 733	Robbins, Job	866
Riggins, James	734	Robbins, John	735
Riggins, Richard	734	Robbins, Joseph	735
Riggs, Alexander	274	Robbins, Moses	735
Riggs, Arund	734	Robbins, Thomas	735, 866
Riggs, Benjamin	734	Robbins, William	735
Riggs, Bethual	407	Roberts, ...	108
Riggs, Cyrenus	734	Roberts, Aaron	735
Riggs, Gideon	734	Roberts, Adam	735
Riggs, Jonathan	734	Roberts, Amos	470
Riggs, Joseph	734	Roberts, Cornelius	845
Riggs, Perminus	734	Roberts, Edmund	735
Riggs, Smith	734	Roberts, Ichabod	(2) 735
Riggs, Thomas	734	Roberts, Jacob	274

Roberts, James	735	Rockafellow, Chris	853
Roberts, Jesse	274	Rockefellow, Christ	737
Roberts, John	137, 274, (2) 735	Rockefellow, Peter	456, 737
Roberts, Joseph	(2) 735	Rockefellow, William	737
Roberts, Matthew	(2) 735	Rockhill, William	122, 132, 737
Roberts, Moses	735	Rockley, George	275
Roberts, Palmer	431	Rockwell, William	122
Roberts, Peter	845	Rodes, Allen	737
Roberts, Samuel	735	Rodgers, David	275
Roberts, Sayre, see Roberts, Sears		Rodgers, James	(2) 55, 106, 275, 737
Roberts, Sears (or Sayre)	735	Rodgers, Samuel	737
Roberts, Stephen	274, (2) 735	Rodon, John	275
		Roe, Asabel	737
Roberts, Thomas	122, 736	Roe, Joel	275
Roberts, William	274, 736	Roe, Michael	275
Robertson, Amos	866	Roelf, Levi	275
Robertson, George	736	Roff, Ebenezer	737
Robertson, Isaac	274, (2) 736	Roff, John	737
		Rogers, David	138, 275, 483, 737
Robertson, James	(2) 274, (2) 736	Rogers, Henry	275, (2) 737
Robertson, John	274, (2) 736	Rogers, James	(2) 275, 483, 737, 845
Robertson, Joseph	736		
Robertson, Richard	736		
Robertson, Robert	15, 29, (2) 30, 98	Rogers, Jedediah	737
		Rogers, John	737
		Rogers, Nathan	737
Robertson, Thornton	736	Rogers, Nathaniel	737
Robeson, Benjamin	736	Rogers, Patrick	737
Robeson, Caleb	736	Rogers, Richard	737
Robeson, James	736	Rogers, William	275, 833
Robeson, Jeremiah	736	Rolan, George	737
Robeson, Joseph	736	Roland, Peter	737
Robeson, Thomas	736	Rolde, John	737
Robeson, William	736	Rolen, James	737
Robine, Thomas	274	Roler, George	737
Robins, Moses	274	Roler, Philip	275, 737
Robins, Thomas	274	Roler, William	737
Robins, William	275	Roles, James	737
Robinson, Andrew	736	Rolf, Elisha	737
Robinson, Caleb	736	Rolf, Henry	738
Robinson, Cornelius	275	Rolf, John	738
Robinson, Daniel	275	Rolf, Tera	738
Robinson, Edmund	736	Rolffe, Zerah	738
Robinson, Edward	275	Roliston, Aaron	738
Robinson, Hamilton	736	Roll, John	470, 738
Robinson, Isaac	275, 736	Roll, John, Jr.	738
Robinson, Jeremiah	736	Roll, Matthias	275
Robinson, John	(2) 275, 736	Rolle, Moses	738
Robinson, Solomon	275	Rollins, Amariah	738

Rollins, Stephen	738	Rosier, Abraham	276
Rolls, William	738	Ross, ...	276, 407
Rolph, Henry	275	Ross, Andrew	276, 460, 739
Rolph, Jonathan	276, 738		
Rolph, Richard	276, 738	Ross, Casper	739
Rolph, Sterney	276	Ross, Daniel	739
Rolton, Joseph	132	Ross, David	854
Romer, Benjamin	276, 738	Ross, Eliakim	132, 276
Romeo, Christopher	276	Ross, Ephraim	739
Romine, Benjamin	470	Ross, Ezekiel	739
Romine, Elias	407	Ross, Finley	739
Romine, Nicholas	738	Ross, George	14, 32, 34, 101
Romine, Samuel	738		
Roney, Robert	738	Ross, Isaac	276, (2) 739, (2) 740
Roobe, Matthew	276		
Roof, Adam	738		
Roof, Ephraim	738	Ross, Jackson	740
Rooker, Jacob	276	Ross, James	740
Rooler, George	738	Ross, John	21, 35, 52, 54, 55, 69, 123, 339, 360, 478, (3) 740, 854
Rooler, William	738		
Roome, Henry	738		
Roome, Samuel	738		
Roomer, John	738		
Roosa, Cornelius	738		
Roper, James	276		
Rorah, Casper	738	Ross, Joseph	276, (2) 740
Rorick, see Rowick			
Rorick, William	866	Ross, Levi	276
Rorits, William	738	Ross, Matthew	456
Rosbrook, John	738	Ross, Nathaniel	480
Rosco, William	840	Ross, Peter	132, 276
Rose, Charles	739	Ross, Robert	47, 407
Rose, Ezekiel	739	Ross, Stephen	740
Rose, John	(2) 276, 739	Ross, William	125, 277, 740
Rose, Jonathan	(2) 739	Ross, Zachariah	740
Rose, Joseph	276, (2) 739	Rossburg, John	740
		Rossburgh, John	277
Rose, Joseph R.	854	Rossell, Andrew	740
Rose, Richard	276, (2) 739	Rossell, Elias	277, 740
		Rossell, John	740
Rose, Thomas	137, 461, 739	Rossell, Zachariah	277
		Rostoinder, Thomas	740
Rose, Timothy	739	Rounsevale, John	277
Rose, William	122, (2) 739	Rounsifer, John	277
		Row, Christopher	740
Rosebroom, Garret	739	Row, Philip	431
Rosebroom, Hendrick	739	Rowan, Hugh	740
Rosebroom, Henry	739	Rowan, James	842
Rosecrans, Alexander	739	Rowan, John	407
Rosecrantz, Jacob	(2) 36, 87, 328, 431	Rowe, Henry	446
		Rowe, John	277
Rosekranz, John	348, 354	Rowick (or Rorick), Gasper	740

Rowland, George	845		Runyard, Job	742
Rowland, Jacob	740		Rush, George	132
Rowland, Samuel	740		Rush, Henry	278
Rowlen, George	740		Rush, John	278
Rowlin, William	277		Rush, Peter	742
Rowlison, Aaron	740		Rush, William	470
Rowlinson, William	740		Russel, Casper	278
Roy, John	277, 740		Russel, Edward	278
Roy, Patrick	277, 740		Russel, John	278, 470
Royal, ...	740		Russel, Richard	278
Royal, David	277, 740		Russell, Caleb	742
Royal, John	277, 740		Russell, Casper	742
Rozell, Benjamin	866		Russell, Daniel	742
Robart, John	277, 740		Russell, John	742
Ruckman, David	741		Russell, Newton	742
Ruckman, John	741		Russell, Richard	742
Ruckman, Samuel	277, 741		Russell, Thaddeus	278, 742
Ruckman, William	277, 741		Russell, William	278, 742
Rude, Noah	741		Russell, Zachariah	278
Rudnown, Enoch	741		Rutan, Abraham	456
Rudrow, Enoch	741		Rutan, Daniel	742
Rue, Henry	741		Rutan, John	742
Rue, Job	741		Rutan, Paul	742
Rue, John	741		Rutan, Peter	92
Rue, Lewis	34, 106		Rutan, Samuel	278
Rue, Matthew	(3) 741		Ryall, David	278
Rue, Matthias	741		Ryall, George	742
Rue, William	741		Ryall, Isaac	742
Ruecastle, John	37, 54, 55, 92		Ryan, John	278
			Ryan, Patrick	(2) 278
Ruff, John	741		Ryan, Timothy	278, 742
Ruhell, Azariah	277		Ryder, Barnardus	742
Rulass, Robert	741		Ryder, Garret	742
Ruker, Jacob	277		Ryder, John	742
Ruker, John	278		Ryder, William	742
Rulass, Robert	741		Ryerson, George	339, 372
Runals, James	278		Ryerson, John	372
Runk, Jacob	446		Ryerson, John G.	742
Runk, William	741		Ryerson, Martin G.	742
Runnals, James	741		Ryerson, Richard G.	743
Runnolds, John	741		Ryerson, Ryor	743
Runyan, Absolam	854		Ryerson, Thomas	16, 17, 32, 102
Runyan, Asa	741			
Runyan, Conrad	278		Rykeman, John	743
Runyan, Coonrad	278		Ryker, Cornelius, Jr.	743
Runyan, Elias	866		Ryker, Isaac	278, 743
Runyan, Enoch	741		Ryker, Peter	743
Runyan, Hugh	741, 837		Ryley, Jacob	279
Runyan, Job	741		Ryley, Philip	279
Runyan, John	742		Rynearson, Isaac	279
Runyan, Richard	(3) 742		Rynierson, Isaac	743
Runyan, Samuel	742, 866		Rynierson, John	743
Runyan, Vincen	742		Rynierson, Rynier B.	743
Runyan, William	867		Ryno, Esek	279, 743

Ryno, William	407	Saunders, John	(2) 279, 744
Ryon, John	279, 743		
Ryon, Walter	743	Saunders, Timothy	279, 744
		Savacool, William	744
		Sawings, Joseph	744
Sackville, Peter	743	Sawlex, Caleb	744
Saffin, Thomas	(2) 37, 72, 374, 837	Sawyer, see also Sayre	
		Sawyer, Michael	744
Sage, Miles	743	Sawyer, Samuel	279
St. Clair, Arthur	66	Saxon, Jesse	279
St. Clair, George	289, 766	Saxton, Charles	744
Salard, Benjamin	743	Saxton, Isaac	744
Salmon, John	743	Say, John	279
Salmon, Ludlam	372	Sayers, David	845
Salmon, Nathaniel	34, 106	Sayger, Philip	867
Salmon, Peter	407	Sayre, Annanias	279
Salmon (or Sammonds), Reuben	743	Sayre, Ezekiel	431
		Sayre, Jeremiah	407
Salmon, William	407	Sayre, Nathaniel	279
Salnave, Peter	279	Sayre, Rance	431
Salsbury, John	279, (2) 743	Sayre, Richard	858
		Sayre, William	280
Salter, Benjamin	743	Sayres, see also, Sears	
Salter, Henry	743		
Salter, James	867	Sayres, Abbot	744
Salter, John, Jr.	743	Sayres, Anthony	744
Salter, John, Sr.	743	Sayres, Benjamin	744
Salter, John P., Jr.	279	Sayres, Daniel	744
Salter, John P., Sr.	279	Sayres, David	(2) 744
Salter, Joseph	344, 360	Sayres, Ebenezer	744
Sammonds, see Salmon		Sayres, Ephraim	744
Sampson, Moses	743	Sayres, James	745
Sanborn, John	743	Sayres, John	745
Sanders, Daniel	743	Sayres, Joseph	745
Sanders, Israel	743	Sayres, Matthias	854
Sanders, John	279, 743	Sayres, Moses	745
Sanders, Peter	744	Sayres, Nathan	745
Sanders, Thomas	279, 744	Sayres, Nathaniel	745
Sanderson, James	744	Sayres, Pierson	745
Sanderson, John	744	Sayres, Richard	123, 470
Sanderson, Peter	874	Sayres, Samuel	745
Sandford, Elijah	446	Sayres, Stephen	745
Sandford, John	56, 87	Sayres, Uzal	745
Sandford, Peter	439	Sayres, William	745
Sandford, William	470, 744	Scantlin, Patrick	745
Sands, Joseph	744	Scantling, Patrick	280
Sanford, John	279, 744	Schaifer, Lambert	280
Sanford, William	(2) 744	Schamp, David	408
Sarge, James	279	Schamp, George	745
Sarvis, David	744	Schanck, Abraham	745
Satterly, Samuel	279, 744	Schanck, Abram	745
Saums, John	744	Schanck, Cornelius	745
Saunders, Isaac	279	Schanck, Garret	431

Schanck, J	871	Scott, Noah	280
Schanck, John	342, 372, 408, 745	Scott, Samuel	746
		Scott, Thomas	280, (3) 746, 854
Schanck, William	408	Scott, William	746
Schaner, Rulief	745	Scouten, Jacob	746
Schenck, Abraham T.	833	Scroggy, Thomas	280
Schenck, Crincyonce	745	Scudder, ...	408
Schenck, Curtenius	14, 29, 98	Scudder, Abijah	280
		Scudder, Amos	456
Schenck, Cyrenus	745	Scudder, Benjamin	746
Schenck, Garret	(4) 745	Scudder, David	280
Schenck, Henry	833	Scudder, Ephraim	746
Schenck, Henry H.	378, 408	Scudder, Jedeiah	747
Schenck, Jacob	745, 854	Scudder, Job	747
Schenck, John	(3) 408	Scudder, John	280, 327, 344, 378, 408, 849
Schenck, John G.	456		
Schenck, John H.	470	Scudder, Major	747
Schenck, Joseph	431, 745	Scudder, Matthias	747
Schenck, Koert	746	Sdudder, Nathaniel	344, 355
Schenck, Peter	408, 746	Scudder, Philip	280
Schenck, Peter F.	746	Scudder, Richard	747
Schenck, Roeloff	746	Scudder, Thomas	747
Schenck, William	746	Scudder, William	123, 344, 360
Schenk, Rulef	280		
Schillenger, James	746	Scull, Abel	747
Schofeeld, Joseph	746	Scull, Daniel	280, 747
Schofield, David	746	Scull, David	280, 747
Schooley, Asa	746	Scull, John	446
Schooley, John	280, 746	Scull, Joseph	747
Schooley, Samuel	38, 40, 102, 439	Scull, Peter	747
		Seaborn, see also Sebring	
Schull, Daniel	746	Seaborn, Frederick	280
Schureman, Abram	746	Seabrook, James	747
Schureman, James	446	Seabrook, Stephen	747
Schureman, John	746	Seabrook, Thomas	324, 344, 361
Schuyler, Abram	408		
Schuyler, General	18	Sealey, David	747
Schuyler, Philip	66	Sealey, Joshua	747
Scilman, Thomas	746	Seals, Joseph	280
Scobey, James	37, 107	Seaman, James	280
Scoby, Timothy	746	Seaman, Willets	747
Scoonover, Benjamin	746	Seaman, William	849
Scott, Andrew	280	Seaport, John	747
Scott, Charles	42	Searah, William	747
Scott, Israel	746	Search, James	280, 747
Scott, James	746	Search, Lott	(2) 747
Scott, John	746	Searing, James	833
Scott, John B.	(2) 17, 87, 347, 369	Searles, George S.	280
		Sears, Isaac	138
Scott, Martin	746, 839, 867	Sears, Nathaniel	280
		Sears, Peter	431
Scott, Micah	280, 746	Sears, Robert	747
Scott, Moses	74, 344, 378	Sears (or Sayres), Samuel	280, 281, 346, 369, (2) 747

Seawort, John	747		Service, Joseph	749
Sebring, Abram	748		Service, William	749
Sebring, Cornelius	748		Serviss, Philip	431
Sebring, David	748		Severn, Edward	749
Sebring, George	748		Severn, Jesse	281, 749
Sebring, Henry	748		Seward, Daniel	749
Sebring, Jacob	408, 748		Seward, John	281, 347, 355
Sebring, John	408		Seward, Obadiah	408
Seabring (or Seaborn), Richard	281		Seward, Samuel	281, 749
Sebring, Rodif	748		Sexton, Charles	749
Sebring, Ruliff	408		Sexton, Daniel	749
Sebring, Thomas	748		Sexton, Jared	281
Sedam, Charles	748		Sexton, Jesse	281
Sedam, Cornelius	456		Sexton, Jonathan	372
Sedam, Cornelius R.	748		Sexton, Samuel	431
Sedam, James	748		Sexton, Timothy	281
Sedam, John	281		Sexton, William	749
Sedam, Peter	748		Seymore, Jacob	281, 749
Sedam, Rick	748		Shackelton, Richard	749
Sedam, Ryke	748		Shackelton, William	749
Seday, Jacob	748		Shadrack, William	867
Seddons, Jacob	748		Sharwick, Levi	281
Seeds, Benjamin	281, 748		Shafer, Jacob	282
Seegers, William	281, 748		Shafer, John	282
Seeley, Enos	340, 355		Shafer, Joseph	282
Seeley, John	(2) 281, (2) 748		Shafer, Peter	749
			Shafer, Theophilus	282
Seeley, Josiah	(2) 21, 98, 340, 374		Shafer, William	282, 749
			Shafey, William	282, 749
			Shaler, Timothy	408
Seeley, Samuel	30, 50, 51, 92		Shamer, Thomas	282
			Shady, Jacob	749
Seeley, Sylvanus	345, 355		Shane, John	749
Seeley, Joshua	748		Shank, ...	369
Seers, David	748		Shankler, Andrew	749
Seors, Isaac	281		Shanks, ...	456
Seigler, Thomas	408		Shannon, Daniel	749
Seiler, William	748		Shannon, John	282
Seithen, John	281		Sharer, Joseph	845
Selleler, William	748		Sharp, Amos	749
Seloff, Daniel	748		Sharp, Anthony	21, 87, 325, 346, 369
Selover, Isaac	748			
Selvey, John	748			
Senker, William	748		Sharp, Henry	749
Sennet, Richard	281		Sharp, Jonathan	(2) 749
Sergeant, Andrew	281		Sharp, Matthias	457
Sergeant, David	281, 748		Sharp, Peter	282
Sergeant, James	281		Sharp, Robert	749
Sergeant, Joseph	749		Sharpey, Alexander	840
Sergeant, Samuel	749		Shatfer, Peter Barton	749
Sering, Jacob	749		Shatterton, see also Chatterton	
Sering, John	749			
Server, John	867		Shatterton, John	282
Service, John	749		Shaver, Isaac	849

Shaver, Jacob	282	Sheppard, Moses	328, 409
Shaver, Joseph	282	Sheppard, Nathan	328, 409, 431, 470
Shaver, Peter, B.	409		
Shaw, ...	409	Sheppard, Nathaniel	283
Shaw, Archibald	17, 32, 87	Sheppard, Peter	283
		Sheppard, Philip	283
Shaw, Cornelius	282	Sheppard, Reed	283
Shaw, David	282, 749, 750	Sheppard, Samuel	431
		Sheppard, Silas	478
Shaw, Isaiah	858	Sheppard, William	283
Shaw, John	(2) 282, 431, 750	Sheridan, John	283, 751
		Sheridan, Thomas	283
Shaw, Jonathan	282	Sherman, John	283, 751
Shaw, Joshua	(2) 282, 750	Sherod, Daniel	751
		Sherod, Stratton	751
Shaw, Joshua, Jr.	282	Sherrard, James	283
Shaw, Nathan	431	Sherrard, John	409, 837
Shaw, Oliver	282	Sherrard, Joseph	283
Shaw, Reuben	750	Sherred, Samuel	283, 751
Shaw, Richard	750	Sherwood, Moses	751
Shaw, Thomas	750	Shewbard, John	751
Shay, David	750	Shibley, John	751
Shay, James	123, 283, 750	Shidor, Joseph	751
		Shields, David	283
Shearer, ...	409	Shildol, Godfrey	751
Sherlock, John W.	283	Shill, Elisha	283
Shearman, John	283	Shimer, Abraham	409
Shearman, Josiah	750	Shimer, James	751
Shearma, Nathan	750	Shinfelt, Frederick	751
Sheff, David	750	Shinn, Buddle	(2) 16, 36, 102
Shegang, James	750		
Sheldon, Elisha	58	Shinn, Vincent	854
Sheldon, Ephraim	750	Shipman, Aaron	751
Sheldon, Joseph	283	Shipman, Abram	751
Shelly, Samuel	750	Shipman, Christian	751
Shenard, Benjamin	750	Shipman, David	751
Shennard, Benjamin	283	Shipman, Isaac	751
Shepherd, Daniel	750	Shipman, Jacob, Sr.	849
Shepherd, Furman	457	Shipman, John	751
Shepherd, Jacob	750	Shipman, Jonathan	751
Shepherd, James	750	Shipman, Joseph	61, 283, 751
Shepherd, Job	409		
Shepherd, Jonidab	409	Shipman, Matthias	347, 361
Shepherd, Joseph	409	Shipman, Paul	751
Shepherd, Lawrence	750	Shipman, Samuel	751
Shepherd, Nathaniel	750	Shippard, Elisha	471
Shepherd, Owen	750	Shippard, Samuel	20, 35, 53, (2) 54, 70
Shepherd, Thomas	750		
Shepherd, William	750		
Sheppard, Benjamin	283	Shippey, John	751
Sheppard, Charlton	409	Shippey, William	751
Sheppard, Elisha	409	Shiras, Richard	137
Sheppard, John	750	Shird, Hugh	751
Sheppard, Joseph	750	Shirts, Matthias	132

Shirtz, Peter	751	Shute, William	(2) 16, 17, (2) 31, 32, 53, 72, 346, 355, 841
Shiver, Joseph	283, 751		
Shockalear, Albertus	751		
Shoemaker, Hendry	867		
Shoemaker, William	284		
Sholster, Christian	471		
Shores, James	751	Siberry, William	752
Shores, Jonathan	751	Sicheverat, George	284
Shores, Peleg	284, 751	Sickels, James	471
Short, Garret	858	Sickle (or VanSickle), David	284, 752
Shotwell, Isaac	751		
Shotwell, Jacob	751	Sickle, Jacob	284
Shotwell, Jasper	752	Sickles, Jacob	132
Shotwell, John	752	Sickles, James	752
Shotwell, Joseph	752	Sickles, Samuel	284
Shotwell, Manning	752	Sickles, Thomas	14, 29, 102
Shoulder, Andrew	752		
Showers, Adam	284	Sickles, Zachariah	752
Showers, Joseph	284, 752	Siddle, Robert	123
Shoy, Jonathan	284	Siddon, Edward	471
Shreve, Benjamin	409	Sidnell, John	284
Shreve, Caleb	752	Sight, Henry	284, 752
Shreve, Israel	16, 31, 51, 64, 341, 355	Sigler, Henry	284, 752
		Silcoat, Isaac	752
		Silcocks, Gabriel	284, 752
Shreve, John	17, 31, 33, 34, (2) 52, 53, 93, 752	Silcocks, Henry	845
		Silcocks, Joseph	753
		Silcocks, Valentine	284, 753
		Sill, John	753
		Silsbury, David	753
Shreve, Joshua	752	Silver, John	753
Shreve, Richard	409	Silvery, John	753
Shreve, Samuel	341, 361	Simers, Daniel	753
Shreve, William	339, 355, 752, 833	Simerson, John	753
		Simkins, Benjamin	284
Shrope, Andrew (or Stroup)	867	Simkins, Ephraim	753
		Simkins, George	753
Shroppear, Edward	752	Simkins, James	753
Shroud, Stephen	752	Simkins, Seeley	284
Shubart, James	752	Simmons, ...	854
Shubart, John	752	Simmons, Benjamin	753
Shubert, John	284	Simmons, James	285, 753
Shuler, Jacob	346, 369	Simmons, Stephen	(2) 753
Shuley, John	752	Simmons, Reuben	285
Shupe, Henry	874	Simons (or Simonsons), 410	
Shurts, John	854	Simons, Henry	753
Shurts, Michael	752	Simonson, Abraham	753
Shusts, Matthias	284, 752	Simonson, Abram	753
Shute, Enoch	752	Simonson, John	753
Shute, Henry	(2) 409	Simonson, Samuel	285, 753
Shute, Samuel	17, 32, 33, 34, 52, 53, 93, 284, 752	Simonson, Simeon	(2) 753
		Simonson, Simon	410, 753
		Simonsons, see Simons	
		Simpson, Abraham	753
		Simpson, Alexander	753

Name	Page
Simpson, Allen	753
Simpson, David	753
Simpson, George	842
Simpson, Henry	753
Simpson, James	(2) 753, 874
Simpson, John	133, (2) 754, 867
Simpson, Stephen	754
Simpson, William	754
Sims, Cuthbert	754
Sims, John	285
Sims, Timothy	754
Sinclair, George	285
Sinclair, Peter	754
Siner, Jesse	754
Sinickson, Andrew	376, 410
Sinickson, John	446
Sinickson, Thomas	410
Sinker, William	754
Sinoff, Peter	285
Siolley, John	754
Sipphen Darrick	478
Sipple, Nathaniel	457
Siro, George	754
Sisco, Abraham	754
Sisco, Anthony	754
Sisco, Jacob	754
Sisco, Nathaniel	754
Sisco, Peter	754
Sisco, Peter J.	754
Sisco, Samuel	754
Sisco, Solomon	285, 754
Sisco, Tan	754
Sitcher, William	57, 93
Sites, Peter	285, 754
Sithens, David	432
Sithens, John	754
Sithin, John	138
Skellenger, Daniel	754
Skellenger, Elisha P.	754
Skelton, Joseph	38, 40, 98, 439
Skelton, Thomas	754
Skeoff, David	754
Skilling, Daniel	754
Skillman, ...	432
Skillman, Abraham	(2) 754
Skillman, Benjamin	754
Skillman, George	867
Skillman, Gerardus	754
Skillman, Jacob	754, 854, 867
Skillman, John J.	754
Skillman, John T.	755
Skillman, Thomas	123, (2) 755
Skinner, Amos	755
Skinner, Benjamin	755
Skinner, Daniel	755
Skinner, John	755, 858
Skinner, Jonathan	471
Skinner, Richard	410, 755
Skinner, William	755
Skirm, Joseph	845
Skitton, Thomas	755
Slack, Daniel	755
Slack, John	867
Slack, Thomas	755, 867
Slack, Uriah	755
Slackt, David	755
Slackt, John	755
Slader, Thomas	755
Slaight, ...	410
Slaughter, Isaac	755
Slaughter, John	285
Slawter, John	755
Slayback, Abel	755
Slayback, William	(2) 755
Sleight, Cornelius	755
Slesman, Gaspar	755
Slick, William	755
Slide, Philip	755
Slife, John	285, 755
Sligle, Frederick	755
Slineman, John	285
Slingerland, Peter	410
Slingsland, Henry	285, 755
Sloan, James	285, 755
Sloat, William	756
Slover, Daniel	756
Slover, Isaac	756
Slover, Jacob	756
Slover, James	756
Slover, John	756, 873
Sly, Isaac	285
Sly, Samuel	123
Small, William	285, 756
Smallery, Isaac	833
Smalley, David	410
Smalley, Isaac	756
Smalley, James	756
Smalley, John	756
Smalley, Jonas	756
Smallwood, James	756
Smallwood, John	285, 756
Smell, Robard	756
Smick, John	285, 756, 854

Smick, William	756	Smith, Jesse	(2) 758
Smiley, John	867	Smith, John	(2) 133,
Smiley, Robert	285		(6) 286,
Smilie, Robert	756		346, 369,
Smith, ...	760		372, (12)
Smith, Abraham	285		758, 867
Smith, Abram	867	Smith, John N.	758
Smith, Absalom	756, 867	Smith, Jonathan	410, 480
Smith, Adam	756, 867	Smith, Jonathan, Jr.	758
Smith, Amos	478, 481	Smith, Jonathan, Sr.	758
Smith, Andrew	(2) 756	Smith, Joseph	(2) 286,
Smith, Anthony	285, 756		(2) 758,
Smith, Asher	756		(5) 759,
Smith, Benjamin	(4) 756,		833, 854
	833	Smith, Joshua	759
Smith, Burrowes	756	Smith, Josiah	759, 867
Smith, Charles	(2) 756	Smith, Martin	480
Smith, Christian	757	Smith, Mathew	286
Smith, Daniel	285	Smith, Matthias	480
Smith, David	757, 854	Smith, Micha	759
Smith, Ebenezer	858	Smith, Michael	286
Smith, Elias	432, 757	Smith, Moses	759
Smith, Eliazer	757	Smith, Nathan	759
Smith, Elijah	(2) 757	Smith, Nathaniel	286
Smith, Elijah, Jr.	757	Smith, Nicholas A.	846
Smith, Eliphalet	285, 757	Smith, Noah	759
Smith, Elnathan	285, 757	Smith, Obediah	759
Smith, Ethan	757	Smith, Patrick	286, 759
Smith, Felix	757	Smith, Peter	(2) 287,
Smith, Garret	757		(2) 759
Smith, George	285, 757	Smith, Philip	759
Smith, Gideon	(3) 757	Smith, Samuel	287, 461,
Smith, Gilbert	446, 845		481, (3)
Smith, Henry	757		759
Smith, Hezekiah	757	Smith, Samuel B.	287
Smith, Hiram	93 457	Smith, Simeon	759
Smith, Hugh	286, 757	Smith, Staats	759
Smith, Isaac	342, 355,	Smith, Stadus	759
	410, (2)	Smith, States	287
	757	Smith, Stephen	759
Smith, Israel	72, 838	Smith, Terrence	287, 759
Smith, Jacob	(2) 286,	Smith, Thaddeus	759
	(3) 757	Smith, Thomas	32, 107,
Smith, James	(2) 286,		133, (2)
	446, (5)		287, (2)
	757		410, (3)
Smith, Jasper	757, 758		760, 835
Smith, Jel	286	Smith, Timothy	839, 867
Smith, Jeremiah	16, 32,	Smith, William	56, 67,
	33, 98,		(5) 287,
	341, 342,		342, 376,
	361, 369,		(2) 410,
	(2) 758		480, (8)
Smith, Jeremy	758		760, 854

- 115 -

Smith, William B.	854	Snyder, John	854
Smith, Zenas	287	Snyder, Peter	288
Smith, Zenos	760	Snyder, William	761
Smock, Abram	760	Sockwell, Jonadab	761
Smock, Barnes	410	Soden, John	761
Smock, Barnes J.	411	Soden, Joshua	288
Smock, Cornelius	760	Soden, Thomas	761
Smock, George	760	Soey, Joseph	761
Smock, Hendrick	411, 760	Soey, Nicholas	761
Smock, Henry	432	Soey, Samuel	761
Smock, John	344, 355, 760, 833	Sofield, Joseph	761
		Solen (or Solm), John	288, 761
Smock, Josiah	287, 760		
Smock, Matthias	760	Solley, Nathan	288, 761
Smock, Robert	760	Solm, see Solen	
Smock, Rynear	411	Solomon, John	288
Smyley, Robert	760	Solomon, John	(3) 762
Smyth, Eleazer	440	Solomon, Ludley	762
Smythe, Elias	446	Solomon, Nathaniel	432
Smyth, John	287, 760	Solovan, Joshua	483
Smyth, Joseph	760	Solsbury, John	288
Snailbaker, Daniel	760	Solter, Thomas	762
Snailbaker, Philip	760	Somers, see Summers	
Snalbacker, Daniel	288	Somers, James	411
Snap, George	761	Somers, John	411
Snedeker, Cornelius	761	Somers, Richard	342, 355
Snedeker, Garret	761	Sommers, David	762
Sndedker, Isaac	761	Sommers, Enoch	762
Snedeker, Jacob	761	Sommers, Isaac	762
Snedeker, James	(2) 761	Sommers, John	288, 762
Snedeker, John	761	Sommers, Richard	762
Sneethen, Stephen	288	Sommers, Thomas	762
Sneider, Chris	761	Soper, Benjamin	762
Sneider, Christian	288	Soper, Jonathan	762
Sneider, John	761	Soper, Joseph	762
Sneider, Martin	288	Soper, Reuben	762
Snelbacker, George	288, 761	Soper, Richard	288, 762
Snell, David	761	Soper, Thomas	288, 762
Snell, Henry	481	Sork, Michael	(2) 288
Snell, Robert	411, 871	Sorter, Peter	762
Snell, Samuel	411, 872	Sorton, Jacob	762
Snelly, Robert	761	Sortore, Henry	762
Snider, Henry	288, 761	Sortore, Jacob	762
Snook, Henry	761	Sortore, Thomas	471
Snook, Philip	411	Soulard, Benjamin	762
Snook, William	411	South, Benjamin	762, 867
Snooks, Peter	460	South, Elijah	762, 867
Snowden, John	761	South, Isaac	762
Snowden, Jonathan	30, 50, (2) 51, 58, 93	South, Michael	762
		South, Samuel	762
		South, William	762, 867
Snowden, William	411, 761	Southard, Abraham	288
Snyder, Henry	(2) 761	Southard, Henry	484, 854, 867
Snyder, Jacob	761		

Southard, Isaac	854, 868	Spence, Henry	289, 763
Southard, Richard	762	Spencer, Elihu	76
Southard, Zachariah	762	Spencer, Jacob	471
Southerland, Daniel	763	Spencer, Joseph	764
Southward, Benjamin	763	Spencer, Nathan	764
Southwell, William	763	Spencer, Oliver	(2) 56, 64, (2) 323, 341, 355
Southwick, Samuel	288		
Southwick, William	288		
Sowers, John	763		
Space, John	288	Spencer, Robert	72
Spader, Benjamin	763	Spicer, John	(2) 289, 764
Spader, Bergen	763		
Spader, Brogan	763	Spier, Abraham	764
Spader, Jonathan	763	Spier, John	329, 764
Spader, William	763	Spinage, Ebenezer	764
Sparklin, John	288	Spining, Benjamin	764
Sparks, Gabriel	763	Spining, Isaac	289, (2) 764
Sparks, George	471, 854		
Sparks, Henry	411	Spining, John	764
Sparks, Henry, Jr.	346, 369	Spining, Nathan	764
Sparks, James	763	Spire, John	764
Sparks, John	16, 17, 31, 33, 34, 87, 763	Springer, Jacob	289, 764
		Springer, Samuel	440
		Springer, Thomas	764
		Springstein, John	764
Sparks, Joseph	763	Sprinks, Rowley	846
Sparks, Robert	411, 763	Sprong, Jeremiah	764
Sparle, William	289, 763	Sprong, John	764
Sparling, Abram	763	Sprouls, Samuel	764
Sparling, George	289	Sprout, John	764
Sparling, Isaac	763	Sprowls, James	38, 40, 107
Sparling, James	763		
Sparling, John	763	Sprowls, Moses	53, 107
Sparling, Joseph	763	Squier, Ellis	764
Sparling, Peter	763	Squier, James	764
Speagle, Jacob	133	Squier, William	471
Spear, see also, Speer		Squire, Daniel	764
		Squire, Eleazer	764
Spear (or Speer), Abraham	763	Squire, Elijah	412
		Squire, Henry	412
Spear, Francis	763	Squire, John	764
Spear, Henry	763	Squire, Jonathan	478
Spear, Herman	432	Squire, Joseph	137
Spear, William	763	Squire, Samuel	(2) 764
Speen, James	289, 763	Squire, Simeon	(2) 764
Speer, see also, Spear		Staats, John	471, 834
		Staats, Peter	764, 838
Speer (or Spear), Abraham	289, 411	Staats, Rynear	412, 765
		Staatser, Isaac	765
Speer, Cornelius	411	Stack, Aaron, Jr.	854
Speer, Garret	432	Stackers, Amos	289
Speer, Henry	411	Stackhouse, Amos	289
Speer, James	447	Stackhouse, Francis	854
Speer, John	289, (2) 432	Stackhouse, Henry	289
		Stackhouse, John	289, 765

Stacks, Daniel	289, 765	Steelman, David	766
Stafford, James B.	872	Steelman, Ebenezer	766
Stager, Henry	765	Steelman, Frederick	766
Stagg, Albert	(2) 765	Steelman, George	766
Stagg, Cornelius	765	Steelman, James	766
Stagg, Isaac	412	Steelman, James, Sr.	766
Stagg, James	765	Steelman, Jonas	766
Stagg, John	(3) 765	Steelman, Jonathan, Jr.	767
Stagg, Paulus	123		
Stagg, Powles	765	Steelman, Jonathan, Sr.	766
Stagg, Thomas	765		
Stalm, Isaac	765	Steelman, Richard	767, 874
Staly, Christian	765	Steelman, Zephaniah	412
Staly, Jacob	765	Steenbrak, Egbert	767
Stanberry, Joseph	854	Steeples, Thomas	289
Stanberry, Recompence	471	Steelle, Abel	767
Stanbury, Jacob	765	Stelle, Isaac	767
Stanbury, Joshua	765	Stelle, Jacob	(2) 767
Stanbury, Peter	765	Stelle, Jonah	767
Stanbury, Samuel	765	Stelle, Joseph	767
Standley, Isaac	765	Stelle, Samuel	767
Stanley, Isaac	765	Stelle, Thompson	376, 412
Stanley, Thomas	289	Stenabock, William	767
Stansbury, Moses	765	Stenson, Stephen	289
Stanton, ...	412	Stephens, Adam	41, 71
Stanton, Jonathan	765	Stephens, Charles	290, 767
Stapleton, Richard	765	Stephens, David	767
Starke, Amos	457, 765	Stephens, General	41
Starke, Isaac	765	Stephens, Isaac	290
Starke, J.	854	Stephens, John	767
Starke, Jacob	765	Stephens, Joseph	767
Starke, John	345, 361	Stephens, Nicholas	290
Starker, Aaron	765	Stephens, Peter	290, 767
Starkey, John	766	Stephens, Prince	767
Starkey, William	289, (2) 766	Stephens, Robert	290
Starks, Ebenezer	766	Stephenson, James	290, 767
Starts, Henry	289, 766	Stephenson, John	767
States, Isaac	766	Stephenson, William	290, 767
Statsors, John	412	Sterges, Benjamin	290
Stear, Abram	766	Sterling, James	339, 369
Stearnes, Dudley	766	Steuben, General	65
Steason, James	766	Stevens, ...	849, 872
Steath, Robert	766	Stevens, Adam	842
Stedman, Richard	766	Stevens, Benjamin	767
Steel, Alexander	766	Stevens, Charles	290, 767
Steel, James	374	Stevens, Cornelius	767
Steel, Jonathan, Jr.	766	Stevens, David	874
Steele, John	766	Stevens, Henry	412
Steele, John, Jr.	766	Stevens, Isaac	290
Steele, Joseph	766	Stevens, John	767
Steele, Josiah	123, 766	Stevens, John, Jr.	343, 369
Steele, Rudolph	837	Stevens, Joseph	767
Steelman, ...	873	Stevens, Peter	767
Steelman, Andrew	766	Stevens, Robert	290, 767
Steelman, Daniel	766	Stevens, Stephen	290, 767

Stevens, William	290, 767, 837	Still, Ruel	291
		Still, Samuel	291
Stevenson, Augustus	768	Stillenger, Thomas	291
Stevenson, Cornelius	290	Stillinger, John	138
Stevenson, William	290	Stillwagon, Jacob	769
Stevins, William	868	Stillwagon, Peter	769
Steward, Charles	768	Stillwell, Azariah	769
Steward, David	768	Stillwell, Daniel	769
Steward, Ezekiel	768	Stillwell, David	457, 769
Steward, Hugh	290	Stillwell, Enoch	340, 361, 471
Steward, John	290, (2) 768	Stillwell, Ezeriah	769
Steward, Joseph	768	Stillwell, Garret	(2) 769
Stewart, ...	40, 107	Stillwell, Gershom	769
Stewart, Alexander	(2) 290, (3) 768	Stillwell, Jeremiah	769
		Stillwell, John	(3) 769
Stewart, Charles	333, 339, 356, 841	Stillwell, Joseph	412
		Stillwell, Nicholas	340, 356
Stewart, David	290, (2) 768	Stillwell, Obediah	769
		Stillwell, Samuel	769
Stewart, James	291, 412	Stillwell, Sias	769
Stewart, Joel	768	Stillwell, Thomas	769
Stewart, John	291, 412, 471	Stilson, Ebenezer	769
		Stilwell, Enoch	872
Stewart, John, Jr.	291, 768	Stilwell, Ezekiel	291
Stewart, John, Sr.	768	Stilwell, Jasper	291
Stewart, Jonathan	291	Stilwell, John	344, 374
Stewart, Robert	(2) 291, 768, 873	Stilwell, Nicholas	325
		Stilwell, Richard	412
Stewart, Stephen	768	Stilwell, William	291
Stewart, William	291, (2) 768, 854	Stimas, Christian	769
		Stimuts, Christian	769
Stibbins, Ebenezer	768	Stinbrook, Anthony	769
Stift, John	768	Stine, Martin	769
Stiger, Adam	768	Stinebaugh, Philip	769
Stiger, Baltus	768	Stiner, Matthew	769
Stiles, Aaron	(2) 291	Stinson, James	769
Stiles, Benjamin	768	Stinton, Joseph	770
Stiles, Daniel	768	Stirling, Lord, see also, Slexander, William	
Stiles, David	768		
Stiles, Elijah	291, 768		
Stiles, James	768	Stirling, Lord	41, 65, 67, 71
Stiles, Joab, see Stiles, Job			
		Stirwlwell, Ezekiel	291, 770
Stiles, Job (or Joab)	133	Stirr, Peter	770
Stiles, John	376, 842	Stites, Abner	770
Stiles, Jonathan	376, 833, 838	Stites, Henry	770
		Stites, Hezekiah	471
Stiles, Joseph	768	Stites, Humphrey	329, 412
Stiles, Moses H.	769	Stites, Joel	291
Stiles, Samuel	769	Stites, Richard	412
Stiles, Silas	769	Stites, Thomas	412
Stiles, Timothy	769	Stivers, Abram	770
Still, Elisha	769	Stivers, Daniel	770
Still, John	839, 868	Stivers, John	291, 770

Stivers, Simeon	770	Stotehoff, John	771
Stivers, Simon	770	Stotehoff, Peter	771
Stives, Samuel	291	Stoten, Samuel	771
Stives, William	291	Stotesbury, John	413
Stockbridge, John	770	Stothem, Thomas	771
Stockholm, George	770	Stout, Abel	771
Stockman, Benjamin	292	Stout, Abraham	22, 33, 52, 53, 93
Stockman, John	770		
Stockman, William	770		
Stockton, Benjamin	335, 378	Stout, Adam	771
Stockton, Ebenezer	75	Stout, Andrew	771
Stockton, James	440	Stout, Benjamin	(2) 771
Stockton, John	770	Stout, Caleb	292
Stockton, Robert	837	Stout, Cornelius	342, 343, 369
Stockton, Thomas	77		
Stoddard, ...	413	Stout, Daniel	771
Stoddard, Abel	770	Stout, Elijah	292, 771
Stoddard, Samuel	770	Stout, Elisha	123, 292
Stoddard, William	770	Stout, James	292, 413, (3) 771
Stoddart, Ichabod	292		
Stokes, John	413	Stout, Jediah	471
Stoll, see also, Stull		Stout, Jeremiah	771
		Stout, Jesse	292
Stoll, Jacob	413	Stout, John	(2) 292, (3) 771 (2) 772, 873
Stoll, Joseph	292, 770		
Stone, David	292, 770		
Stone, Jeremiah	292, 471		
Stone, Samuel	770	Stout, Jonathan	772
Stone, William	770	Stout, Joseph	17, 32, 33, 34, 87, 133, 413, (2) 772
Stonebank, Joseph	457		
Stonebank, Thomas	292, 770		
Stonebanks, Richard	413		
Stoneker, John	770		
Stoniker, John	858	Stout, Moses	457
Stookey, Benjamin	292	Stout, Nathan	413
Stoots, George	292, 770	Stout, Nathaniel	772
Storan, John	770	Stout, Rulif	772
Stord, Joel	770	Stout, Samuel	292, (2) 413
Storer, John	770, 872		
Storey, Daniel	770	Stout, Sin	772
Storey, John	771, 872	Stout, Thomas	772, 845
Storey, Joseph	771	Stout, Timothy	772
Storey, Luke	771	Stout, Wessel T.	37, 40, (2) 55, 94
Storey, Seth	771		
Storey, William	771		
Storkey, Jacob	771	Stout, William	772
Storms, Abraham	292	Stout, Wilson	481
Storms, David	771	Stout, Zephaniah	772
Storms, John	292, 478, 771	Stouten, Jacob	772
		Stouten, John	772
Story, J.	834	Stratton, Amariah	292
Story, William	292	Stratton, Annanias	292
Stotehoff, Albert	771	Stratton, Fithian	340, 372
Stotehoff, Cornelius	771, 833	Stratton, Lott	772

Stratton, Sherwood	292	Stults, Jacob	773
Stratton, Thomas	292	Stults, Peter	773
Stretch, Aaron	457	Stump, Jacob	773
Stretch, Peter	772	Stump, Sarah	77
Stricker, Adam	772	Sturge, Daniel	773
Stricker, Cornelius	772	Sturge, Nathan	773
Stricker, Henry	471	Sturges, Benjamin	773
Stricket, Robert	292	Sturges, Jedediah	773
Strickland, Joseph	772	Sturges, Joseph	774
Strickland, Samuel	772	Stute, Henry	774
Stricklin, Henry	772	Stutman, John	774
Striker, Bernard	478	Stutton, Philip	774
Strimple, John	133	Stymits, John	774
Strong, Charles P.	293	Stymits, Peter	774
Strong, James B.	293	Sudam, John	774
Strong, William	293	Sufley, William	293
Strope, George	293, 772	Sullivan, Daniel	(2) 293, (2) 774
Stroup, see Shrope			
Strowbridge, Joseph	293	Sullivan, David	293, 774
Strowder, Matthias	440	Sullivan, General	15, 65, 79
Strumble, John	293, 772		
Strung, John	772	Sullivan, James	774
Stryker, Abraham	772	Sullivan, John	23, 42
Stryker, Abram	293, 772	Sullivan, Joshua	139, 293
Stryker, Barnet	773	Sullivan, Patrick	293, 774
Stryker, Domincus	773	Sullivan, Samuel H.	837
Stryker, Henry	432	Sullivan, Thomas	868
Stryker, Isaac	773	Sullivan, Timothy	293, 854
Stryker, James	773, 833	Sullivan, William	774
Stryker, John	293, 413, (2) 773, 850	Sullivant, William	774
		Summers, George	457
		Summers, (or Somers), James	293, 774
Stryker, John D.	773		
Stryker, Peter	483, (2) 773	Sunderland, Edward	868
		Sunderland, John	(2) 868
Stryker, Peter, Sr.	773	Sunderland, Peter	868
Stryker, Peter T.	457	Sunderland, Thomas	774
Stryker, Rano	773	Sunderlin, John	774
Stryker, Simeon	773	Sunderlin, Peter	774
Stryker, Simon	773	Surdan, John	293
Stuart, James	773	Surl, William	774
Stuart, John	138, (2) 773	Sutcliff, William	774
		Sutfin, David	774
Stuart, Thomas	293, 773	Sutfin, Job	774
Studson, Joshua	326, 432, 872	Sutfin, John	774
		Sutfin, Joseph	774
Stuky, Jacob	773	Sutfin, Roeloff	413
Stull, see also, Stoll		Sutherland, William	774
		Sutliff, William	293
Stull, Gideon	773	Sutphen, Aaron	774
Stull, Henry	440	Sutphen, Abram	774
Stull, Jacob	413	Sutphen, Arthur	774
Stull, Joseph	773	Sutphen, Court	775
Stults, Henry	773	Sutphen, Derrick	471, (2) 775

Sutphen, Gilbert	775	Swallow, Jacob	777	
Sutphen, Gilles	478	Swan, Jedediah	413	
Sutton, Guisbert	775	Swan, Jesse	777	
Sutphen, James	(3) 775, 868	Swan, Joseph	294, 777	
		Swan, Nathaniel	777	
Sutphen, John	(3) 775	Swan, Peter	294	
Sutphen, Joseph	775	Swanby, Isaac	294	
Sutphen, Peter	(2) 775	Swandler, Isaac	777	
Sutphen, Richard	775	Swangler, Jacobus	777	
Sutphen, Ruliff	775	Swart, Baltus	777	
Sutphen, Samuel	775	Swart, Stephen	777	
Sutphen, William	471	Swartwood, Daniel	777	
Sutton, Amos	(3) 775	Swartwood, John	432	
Sutton, Benjamin	775	Swartwood, Peter	777	
Sutton, Daniel	775	Swartwout, Jacobus	472	
Sutton, Elijah	293	Sway, Timothy	294	
Sutton, Ephraim	293	Swaysee, Daniel	777	
Sutton, Henry	(2) 775	Sweating, Richard	294	
Sutton, Jeany	775	Sweazy, David	777	
Sutton, Jesse	775	Sweden, Richard	294, 777	
Sutton, John	294, 775, (3) 776	Sweeney, Daniel	294	
		Sweeney, Henry	294	
Sutton, Jonas	294, 776	Sweeney, James	294	
Sutton, Joseph	(2) 471, (3) 776, 868	Sweeney, Timothy	777	
		Sweeny, Timothy	294	
		Sweeny, Valentine	777	
Sutton, Nehemiah	776	Sweetman, Michael	413	
Sutton, Peter	294, (3) 776, 868	Sweetwood, ...	413	
		Swem, Jesse	294, 777	
Sutton, Robert	776	Swesey, Caleb	868	
Sutton, Uriah	294, 413	Swick, Bergum	294, 777	
Sutton, William	294, 776	Swift, Henry	294	
Sutton, Zachariah	776	Swift, James	123	
Sutton, Zebulon	776	Swim, Isaac	777	
Suydam, Charles	776	Swiney, Timothy	777	
Suydam, Cornelius	471, 776	Swing, Valentine	777	
Suydam, Cornelius R.	51, 107	Swisher, Abram	413	
Suydam, Hendrick	133, (2) 457	Syckle, Jonathan	777	
		Syckle, Samuel	777	
Suydam, Jacob	776	Syckle, Zachariah	777	
Suydam, Peter	776	Sylvester, Abram	294	
Suydam, Richard	776	Sylvester, Isaac	294, 778	
Suydam, Simeon	776	Sylvester, Obadiah	778	
Swachamer, Samuel	776	Sylvester, Peter	295, (2) 778	
Swaim, Isaac	776			
Swaim, John	776	Symmes, John Cleves	26, 348, 356	
Swain, Abraham	776			
Swain, Anthony	776	Symmes, Timothy	374	
Swain, Isaac	777	Sympeen, Cornelius	778	
Swain, Jacob	777	Symson, Abram	778	
Swain, James	294	Syron, John	295	
Swain, John	432			
Swain, Judeth	777			
Swain, Richard	777	Taggert, Jacob	837	
Swain, Samuel	294	Tallman, James	295, 414	

Tallman, Peter	414	Taylor, Israel	779
Tallman, William	295, 778	Taylor, Jacob	(2) 779
Tallyou, Peter	778	Taylor, James	295, (2) 779
Talmage, Daniel	778		
Talmage, Dayton	778	Taylor, John	295, 324, 325, 343, 344, 356, 361, 472, (4) 779, 780
Talmage, Noah	778		
Talmage, Thomas	123, 778		
Talyou, Peter	295, 778		
Tamtom, Francis	778		
Tanair, Michael	295		
Tant, Thomas	778	Taylor, John A.	295, 780
Tapin, John	295	Taylor, John V. R.	780
Tappan, Abram	778	Taylor, Joseph	295, 480, 780
Tappan, David	778		
Tappan, Harris	778	Taylor, Joseph B.	780
Tappan, Isaac	778	Taylor, Lawrence	440
Tappan, James	778	Taylor, Lewis	780
Tappan, John	778	Taylor, Nathan	780
Tappan, Moses	778	Taylor, Peter	295
Tapscott, James	778	Taylor, Robert	341, 356, 414, 432, 780
Tarball, David	778		
Tarbill, Nathan	295		
Tare, James	778	Taylor, Samuel	133, 296, 780
Target, John	778		
Tarney, David	295	Taylor, Thomas	(4) 780
Tarret, Cornelius	778	Taylor, Tragift	780
Tarrybury, John	295	Taylor, Willet	780
Tarsey, David	295	Taylor, William	296, (2) 780, 854
Taspin, Thomas	295, 778		
Tate, John	295	Teal, Samuel	780
Tatem, Charles	778	Teals, Peter	296
Tattler, John	779	Tedrick, George	296, 780
Tattuner, Benjamin	779	Teed, John	478
Taulman, Peter	57, 94	Teeple, George	780
Tauny, Lodwick	779	Teeple, John	780
Taver, Henry	295	Teeple, Luke	780
Taylor, ...	414, 872	Teeple, Peter	780
Taylor, Abner	779	Teets, Peter	296
Taylor, Benjamin	472, 858	Teir, Daniel	845
Taylor, Christian	133, 295, 779	Telford, John	780
		Temment, John Peter	296
Taylor, Christopher	295	Temple, Nathaniel	447
Taylor, Cyrus	779	Ten Brook, Henry	780
Taylor, Daniel	779	Ten Brook, Jasper	780
Taylor, David	295, 779	Tenbrook, John	343, 361
Taylor, Edward	779	Tenbrook William	21, 22, 107, 780
Tau;pr, Elisha	779		
Taylor, Gilbert	(2) 779	Ten Eick, Abraham	346, 356
Taylor, George	(2) 337, 344, 356, 472	Ten Eyck, Abram	781
		Ten Eyck, Andreas	483, 781
		Ten Eyck, Andrew	457
Taylor, Henry	(2) 779	Ten Eyck, Andrew J.	781
Taylor, Henry, Jr.	779	Ten Eyck, Andries	781
Taylor, Isaac	(3) 779	Ten Eyck, Conrad	472, 833

Ten Eyck, Coonrad	414	Tharpe, Benjamin	782
Ten Eyck, Cornelius	781	Tharpe, Peter	296
Ten Eyck, Frederick	833	Tharss, Thomas	296
Ten Eyck, Jacob	414, 432, 483, 781	Thatcher, Amos	782
		Thatcher, Elijah	782
Ten Eyck, Jacob, Jr.	457	Thatcher, Jeremiah	782
Ten Eyck, Jeremiah	414	Thatcher, Joseph	414
Ten Eyck, John	432, 781	Thaxton, John	782
Ten Eyck, Matthaias	781	Theilar, Jacob	414
Ten Eyck, Peter	483, 781	Theut, Stephen	782
Ten Eyck, Withen	781	Thier, John	296
Tennent, William	(2) 296, 781	Thimbal, Walter	782
		Thimpel, John	782
Teple, Hendrick	472	Thomas, Alexander	782
Terhune, Abraham	440	Thomas, Asa	296, 782
Terhune, Cornelius	296, 781	Thomas, David	782, 868
Terhune, Garret	781	Thomas, Edmund	19
Terhune, Jacob	414	Thomas, Edmund D.	22, 35, 37, 54, 98
Terhune, John	458		
Terhune, John D.	781		
Terhune, Nicausa	414	Thomas, Edward	333, 336, 341, 356, 414
Terhune, Stephen	781		
Terney, Henry	296		
Terell, Amos	781	Thomas, Heber	782
Terell, Enoch	(2) 781	Thomas, James	(2) 782
Terrell, Isaac	781	Thomas, John	123, 133, 296, (2) 297, 782, (2) 783
Terrell, John	781		
Terrepin, Isaac	781		
Terrepin, Uriah	781		
Terrill, Adam	447	Thomas, Luke	297
Terrel, John	296	Thomas, Martin	783
Terry, Abraham	781	Thomas, Matthew	297
Terry, Jonah	296, 781	Thomas, Matthias	783
Terry, Jonathan	(2) 781	Thomas, Moses	297
Terry, Joshua	782	Thomas, Richard	(2) 783
Terry, Josiah	782, 873	Thomas, Robert	(2) 783
Terry, Nathaniel	414	Thomas, Thomas	783
Terry, Richard	782	Thomas, Valentine	297
Terry, Thomas	782	Thomas, William	297, 783
Test, Francis	782	Thompson, Aaron	139, 297, 783
Test, John	782		
Teumey, John	782	Thompson, Abner	297
Teuny, John	782	Thompson, Abraham	297
Thackham, Thomas	854	Thompson, Alexander	297, 458, 854
Thackry, John	782		
Tharp, Asher	472	Thompson, Amos	297, 783
Tharp, Baker	782	Thompson, Andrew	57, 107, 297, 783
Tharp, Benjamin	(2) 296, 782		
Tharp, David	296, 782	Thompson, Benajah	414
Tharp, Jacob	782	Thompson, Benjamin	472, (2) 783
Tharp, James	782		
Tharp, John	433	Thompson, Caleb	783
Tharp, Jonathan	782	Thompson, Daniel	783
Tharp, Oliver	782	Thompson, David	783
Tharp, Solomon	296	Thompson, George	297, 783

Thompson, Hambleton	783	Throckmorton, James	298, 784
Thompson, Hezekiah	783, 854	Throckmorton, Job	298
Thompson, Jabez	783	Throckmorton, John	478
Thompson, Jacob	783	Throckmorton, Joseph	785
Thompson, James	297, 339, 472, 783, 847	Throckmorton, Samuel	472
		Thurston, Benjamin	298
		Thurston, David	298
Thompson, John	(3) 297, 447, (2) 783	Tibbet, Edward	785
		Tice, Elias	433
		Tice, Elijah	298
Thompson, Joseph	854	Tice, Jacob	440
Thompson, Joshua	297, (2) 783	Tice, John	785
		Tice, Peter	785
Thompson, Lewis	298, 784	Tice, Richard	785
Thompson, Mark	334, 336, 347, 357	Tice, William	785
		Tichener, Daniel	433
Thompson, Milage	784	Tichener, David	433
Thompson, Moses	123	Tichenor, Caleb	472, (2) 785
Thompson, Newcomb	414		
Thompson, Patrick	784	Tichenor, Elijah	785
Thompson, Price	134	Tichenor, Isaac	(2) 785
Thompson, Robert	298	Tichenor, Jabez	785
Thompson, Samuel	784	Tichenor, John	298, 785
Thompson, Thomas	414, 784	Tichenor, Jonathan	785
Thompson, William	(2) 298, (2) 784	Tichenor, Joseph	785
		Tichenor, Josiah	785
Thompson, William, Sr.	784	Tichenor, Martin	458
Thomson, Charles	784	Tichenor, Moses	785
Thomson, Cornelius	784	Tichenor, Samuel	785
Thomson, David	784	Tichenor, Walter	785
Thomson, Enoch	480	Tichenor, Zenas	298
Thomson, Hugh	784	Tichenor, Zenus	785
Thomson, James	298, 784	Tichenor, Zopher	785
Thomson, John	784	Tichnal, Peter	785
Thomson, Robert	298	Tidd, John	785
Thomson, Thomas	433, 784	Tidd, William	785
Thomson, William	784	Tides, George	299
Thorn, Lorain	784	Tighe, William	299, 785
Thorn, Richard	784	Till, John	415
Thorne, Joseph	414	Till, Peter	299, (2) 785
Thorne, Richard	298		
Thornell, Benjamin	298, 784	Tilley, James	785
Thornell, Israel	784	Tillny, Peter	786
Thornton, Gilbert	298, 784	Tilman, Philip	786
Thornton, Joseph	298, 784	Tilt, Martin	786
Thorp, Abel	298	Tilton, Abram	786
Thorp, Benjamin	298, 784	Tilton, Benjamin	786
Thorp, Elisha	298	Tilton, Benjamin, Jr.	786
Thorp, Johathan	784	Tilton, Daniel	786
Thorp, Reuben	784	Tilton, Edward	786
Thorp, Solomon	784	Tilton, John	458, 786
Thorpe, John	298	Tilton, Joseph	124, 786
Thorpe, Levi	298	Tilyer, John	472
Thorpe, Oliver	784	Tilyore, Peter, V.	786
Throckmorton, Holmes	298	Timberman, Jacob	786

Timett, John P.	786	Tomlin, William	787	
Tims, William	868	Tomlinson, James	440	
Tindall, John T.	786	Tomlinson, Samuel	787	
Tindall, Joseph	472	Tompkins, Amos	(2) 300, 788	
Tindall, Joshua	786			
Tindall, Richard	299, 786	Tompkins, Enos	788	
Tindall, Samuel	299, 854	Tompkins, Ichabod	788	
Tindall, William	(2) 299, (2) 786, 843	Tompkins, Isaac	788	
		Tompkins, John	788	
		Tompkins, Jonas	(2) 300	
Tindley, John	299	Tompkins, Joseph	300, 788	
Tindley, Robert	299	Tompkins, Stephen	788	
Tingley, Ebenezer	(2) 786	Tompkins, Uzal	788	
Tingley, Jeremiah	786	Tompson, George	440	
Tingley, Lemuel	786	Tompson, John	440, 788	
Tingley, Nathan	786	Tompson, Joseph	788	
Tingley, Samuel	299, 786	Toms, John	440	
Tinis, Absalom	299	Toms, Joseph	788	
Tinkey, Conrad	786	Toms, Michael	478	
Tinley, William	299	Tone, John	(2) 788	
Tinney, John	299, 786	Tone, William	788	
Tipper, Christopher	299	Toner, James	788	
Tippett, David	299	Tonkin, Samuel	341, 361	
Tisco, John	786	Tonson, Isaac	788	
Titton, John	786	Tonson, Lewis	788	
Titus, Asa	787	Tool, Patrick	300	
Titus, Benjamin	787	Toomy, Henry	300	
Titus, Jesse	787	Toomy, John	300	
Titus, John	787	Toomy, Samuel	300	
Titus, John H.	299, 787	Toppin, John	300	
Titus, Johnson	472	Totler, John	788	
Titus, Joseph	787	Totten, David	788	
Titus, Peter	299	Totten, John	788	
Titus, Samuel	787	Totten, Samuel	(2) 788	
Titus, Shadrack	299	Totten, Thomas	300, 788	
Titus, Solomon	787	Tourain (or Tournier), Redack	788	
Titus, Timothy	415			
Titus, Uriah	787	Tourattee, Peter	788	
Tobin, Isaac	299	Tower, Nathaniel	472	
Tobin, Peter	787	Towler, James	788	
Tobin, Thomas	433	Towlin, John	300	
Todd, David	787	Towne, John	788	
Todd, George	472	Townley, Charles	789, 854	
Todd, James	787	Townley, Edward	789	
Todd, John	299, 433	Townley, Effingham	789	
Todd, William	299, (2) 787	Townley, Evits	789	
		Townley, James	789	
Toland, John	787	Townley, James S.	789	
Toles, James	787	Townley, John	789	
Tomblin, James	472	Townley, Joshua	124, 789	
Tombs, Lewis	787	Townley, Steeds	789	
Tome, Andrew	299	Townley, Walter	789	
Tomlin, Elijah	787	Townly, Joshua	134	
Tomlin, Jacob	787	Townsend, Daniel	789	
Tomlin, Jonathan	787	Townsend, Elijah	447	

Townsend, Henry Y.	415		Tumey, Samuel	790
Townsend, James	789		Tummey, Henry	301
Townsend, John	789		Tummey, John	301
Townsend, Reddick	300, 789		Tummey, Samuel	301
Towser, Jeremiah	789		Tummy, Henry	301
Toy, John	300, 789		Tunison, Cornelius	415, 790
Traill, Robert	838		Tunison, Dennis	301
Trance, John	789		Tunison, Derrick	790
Traner, Simon	300, 789		Tunison, Fulkert	790
Treazey, John	789		Tunison, Garret	58, 74
Treen, William	872		Tunison, Henry	790
Trembler, Jonathan	789		Tunison, James	790
Tremley, Alexander	789		Tunison, John	790
Trenchard, George	415		Tunison, Richard	790
Tribit, John	789		Turk, John	790
Trigel, see Fegil			Turley, Robert	301
Trilligan, John	300		Turner, Alexander	847
Trimble, Jacob	789		Turner, Daniel	790
Trimley, Alexander	858		Turner, John B.	790
Tripp, Henry D.	77		Turner, Nathan	301, 790, 791
Triston, Samuel	868			
Troop, William	300		Turner, Robert	868
Trout, Jacob	300, (2) 789		Turner, Samuel	301
			Turner, William	124, 301, 472
Trout, William	789, 868			
Trow, Matthias	300, 789		Turneur, Woodhull	791
Trowbridge, Absalom	300		Turney, Joseph	791
Trowbridge, Job	854		Turse, Daniel	791
Trowbridge, Ralph	789		Turse, Jacob	791
Trowbridge, Shubel	789		Turse, John	791
Troy, John	300		Tussey, John	301
Troy, Samuel	789		Tustin, Jonathan	301, 791
Truax, Abraham	789		Tustin, Samuel	791
Truax, Jacob	789		Tuthill, Samuel	361
Truax, Samuel	(2) 790		Tuthill, Theodorus	791
Truesdall, Stephen	300, 790		Tuttle, Benjamin	874
Truesdall, Thomas	790		Tuttle, Caleb	301, 791
Truex, John	300		Tuttle, Caleb, Jr.	791
Trumey, Daniel	790		Tuttle, Chatfield	791
Tubbs, John	790		Tuttle, Daniel	301, 791
Tubbs, Samuel	790		Tuttle, David	21, 22, 98, 302, 791
Tucker, Abraham	301, 790			
Tucker, Charles	790			
Tucker, Absalom	301		Tuttle, Ebenezer	791
Tucker, Ezekiel	790		Tuttle, Isaiah	(2) 302
Tucker, James	868		Tuttle, Israel	791
Tucker, Joseph	790		Tuttle, John	(3) 302, (2) 791
Tucker, Moses	790			
Tucker, Samuel	12, 20, 790		Tuttle, Joseph, Jr.	791
			Tuttle, Josiah	302
Tucker, William	415		Tuttle, Nathan	791
Tudor, John	301		Tuttle, Phineas	791
Tuers, Jacob	790		Tuttle, Silvenus	791
Tullis, Moses	301		Tuttle, Simeon	791
Tullis, William	301		Tuttle, Timothy	415

Tuttle, William	51, 107, 302	Van Antwerp, Jacobus	792
		Van Arsdale, John	303, 792
Tuvey, Daniel	791	Vanarsdale, Lawrence	303
Tway, John	302	Van Arsdalen, Abraham	472, 478
Tway, Timothy	302, 791	Van Arsdalen, Abram	792
Twiner, Nathan	302	Van Arsdalen Caleb	793
Twining, John	868	Van Arsdalen, Capture	793
Tye, William	302	Van Arsdalen, Christian	793
Tyler, James	791		
Tyre, John	302, 791	Van Arsdalen, Christopher	793
Tyson, John	791		
		Van Arsdalen, Cornelius	793
Ubdike, Lowerance	791	Van Arsdalen, Donald	793
Ubdike, Rolif	791	Van Arsdalen, Garret	793
Ulph, Jacob	792	Van Arsdalen, Harmon	793
Underdunk, Isaac	792	Van Arsdalen, Hendrick, Jr.	793
Underwood, John	792		
Underwood, Shadrack	792	Van Arsdalen, Henry	793
Updike, Albert	415	Van Arsdalen, Isaac	447
Updike, Robert	302	Van Arsdalen, James	793
Updike, William	302	Van Arsdalen (or Van Norsdall, John	303, 472, (3) 793
Updyke, Brogan	792		
Updyke, Clement	792	Van Arsdalen, Mindart	481
Updyke, William	(2) 792		
Upson, Jesse	792	Van Arsdalen, Noah	793
Uptehouse, Henry	792	Van Arsdalen, Philip	415, 478
Upthegrove, Isaac	302, 792	Van Arsdalen, Philip, Jr.	793
Uriancy, John	447		
Uselton, John	792	Van Arsdalen, Richard	793
Utt, John	792	Van Arsdalen, Stuffe	(1) 793
Utter, Benjamin	792	Van Arsdalen, Wilhelmus	793
Utter, David	302		
Utter, Solomon	302	Van Arsdall, Cornelius C.	793
		Van Arsdall, Urias	793
Vail, Henry	458	Van Artsdalen, Jacob C.	793
Valentine, Benjamin	792		
Valentine, Borne	792	Van Asdalen, Jacob	793
Valentine, Jacob	134, (2) 792	Van Asdol, Hermanus	794
		Van Asdol, Isaac	794
Valentine, John	868	Vanatta, John	433, 794
Valentine, Jonas	792	Van Auddler, Abram	794
Valentine, Obadiah	792	Van Ausdaul, Jacob	794
Valentine, Thomas	302, 792	Van Bassum, David	415
Valentine, William	792	Van Beuren, Abram	794
Vallean, David	792	Van Beuren, John	794
Vallence, William	302	Van Beuren, William	794
Vanakin, Joseph	792	Vanblack, Arthur	303, 794
Vanakin, Nathan	792	Van Blarcom, Henry	415
Van Allen, Derrick	302, 792	Van Blarigan, Anthony	794
Vanamon, John	792	Van Blarigan, Henry	794
Van Anglen, John	14, 15, 29, 30, 87	Van Blarigan, Martin	794
		Van Blarkin, David	794
		Van Blercom, Albert	303

Van Blest, Garret	794		Vanderbeck, Jacob	795
Van Boskerck, George	303		Vanderbeck, Powles	795
Van Boskirk, Abraham	339,	378	Vanderbeck, Samuel	795
Van Bosom, Philip	794		Vanderbelt, Hendrick	472
Van Brackley, Stephen	794		Vanderbelt, Jacob	433, 854
Van Bracret, John	794		Vanderbelt, John	433
Van Brockle, John	794		Van Derbergh, Peter	303, 479
Van Brunt, Hendrick	345,	369	Vanderbilt, Cornelius	(2) 795
Van Brunt, Hendrick, Jr.	433		Vanderbilt, Jacob	(2) 795
Van Brunt, Nicholas	415,	794	Vanderbilt, Peter	795
Van Buffee, John	794		Vanderdunk, Henry	795
Van Buskirk, George	794		Vanderhall, Abraham	303, 795
Van Busse, David	433		Vanderhoof, Cornelius	303, (2) 795
Van Bussen, Philip	794			
Van Bussers, John	794		Vanderhoof, Cornelius P.	796
Van Camp, Gideon	794		Vanderhoof, Henry	796
Van Campen, John	481		Vanderhoof, John	(2) 796
Vance, Edward	794		Vanderhoof, Peter	458
Vance, James	794		Vanderhoven, James	796
Vance, Kennedy	794		Vanderhull, Gershom	796
Vance, Samuel	794, 833		Vanderipe, William	796
Vance, Thomas	303, 794		Vanderpool, Jacob	139
Van Clafe, Puryas	794		Vanderull, Abram	796
Van Cleaf, see also Van Cleve	794		Vanderull, Henry	796
			Vanderveer, Abram	796
Van Cleaf, Garret	794		Vanderveer, Cornelius	796, 833
Van Cleaf, Isaac	794		Vanderveer, Hendrick	433
Van Cleaf, John	415		Vanderveer, Hercules	796
Van Cleaf, Joseph	794		Vanderveer, James	796
Van Cleaf, Michael	794		Vanderveer, John	(2) 796
Van Cleaf, Peter	303		Vanderveer, Joseph	796
Van Cleaf, William	94, 415, 795		Vanderveer, Mathew	796
			Vanderveer, Peter	796
Van Cleave, John	795		Vanderveer, Tunis	472
Van Cleave, Joseph	795		Vanderventer, Abram	796
Van Cleave, Peter	795		Vanderventer, Christian	796
Van Clefe, Isaac	478			
Van Cleve (or Cleaf), Benjamin	342, 370, 415		Vanderventer, Christopher	796
Van Cleve, Isha	795		Vanderventer, Isaac	796
Van Cleve, William	36, 107, 415		Vanderventer, Jacob	796
			Vanderventer, James	796
Van Corte, John	795		Vanderventer, Jeremiah	796
Van Cortland, Philip	334, 341, 357		Vanderventer, John	483
			Vanderventer, Peter	796
Van Court, John	795, 833		Vandervoort, Cornelius	796
Van Court, Michael	795, 835		Vandervoort, Gabriel	796
Van Dabecke, Peter	795		Vandervoort, Peter C.	796
Van Dalsen, Henry	795		Van Deusen, William	796
Van Dalsen, William	795		Vandeventer, Jacob	416
Vanderbeak, Andrew	795		Vandeventer, Peter	29, 108, 447
Vanderbeak, Benjamin	795			
Vanderbeck, Abraham	795		Vandervort, Charles	797
Vanderbeck, Abram	795		Vandevort, John	797
Vanderbeck, Barent	795		Vandewater, Abram	797

Vandike, Hendrick	347, 357,	Vaneman, William	798
(or Henry)	797	Van Emburgh, John	344, 370, 798
Vandike, Henry, see also, Vandike, Hendrick	325	Vaness, Simon	433
		Vanest, Peter	441
Vandike, Henry	325	Van Etten, Benjamin	798
Vandike, Isaac	797	Vanetten, Daniel	441
Vandike, Jacob	(2) 797, 833	Van Etten, Gideon	798
		Vanetten, Jacob	447
Vandike, John	134, 320, (3) 797, 833	Van Etten, Peter	798
		Vanfleet, Abraham	303, 798
		Van Fleet, Cornelius	798
Vandike, Joseph	416	Van Fleet, William	798
Vandine, Denise	797	Van Gardner, Moses	798
Vandine, Francis	797	Van Gelden, Evourt	798
Vandine, John	797	Van Gieson, Henry	798
Vandoren, Abram	797	Van Gieson, John	798
Vandoren, Benjamin	797	Van Gilder, Abraham	799
Van Doren, Burgam	797	Van Gilder, Isaac	799
Van Doren, Christian	797	Van Gilder, Jeremiah	799
Vandoren, Isaac	797	Van Gilder, Peter, Jr.	799
Van Doren, Jacob	797	Van Gorden, ...	799
Van Doren, Peter	797	Van Gorden, Abram	799
Van Doren, William	797	Van Gorden, Henry	799
Van Dorn, Abraham	473	Van Gorden, John	799
Van Dorn, Benjamin	479	Van Gorden, William	799
Van Dorn, Chrystoyan	797	Van Gorder, Abraham	799
Van Dorn, Cornelius	(2) 797	Van Gordon, see also, Vreedenburgh	
Van Dorn, Esek	303		
Vandorn, Hezekiah	303	Van Harglen, Rynear	799
Van Dorn, Isaac	797	Van Harler, Edward	799
Van Dorn, Jacob	798	Van Harling, John	799
Van Dorn, John	798	Van Harr, Barney	868
Van Dorn, Nicholas	798	Van Harton, see Van Norton	
Van Duryke, John	798		
Van Duyck, Cornelius	798	Vanhater, John	303
Van Duyne, William	833	Van Hess, Garret	799
Van Dyck, Frederick	798	Van Hess, John	799
Van Dyck, John	798	Van Hook, Lawrence	416, 799
Van Dyck, William	798	Van Horn, Abram	845
Van Dyke, Cornelius	473	Van Horn, Cornelius	799
Van Dyke, Hendrick	798	Van Horn, Daniel	473
Van Dyke, John	420	Van Horn, James	799
VanDyke, Joseph	416	Van Horn, Peter, Jr.	458
Van Dyke, Lambert	868	Van Horn, William	(2) 303
Van Dyke, Mathew	798	Van Horne, Cornelius	447
Van Dyne, Abram	798	Van Horne, James	433
Van Dyne, Cornelius	798	Van Horne, Simon	303
Van Dyne, John	798	Van Houten, Abraham	799
Van Dyne, Martin	798	Van Houten, Adrian	799
Van Dyne, Matthew	473	Van Houten, Carinus	799
Van Dyne, William	798	Van Houten, Claus	479
Vaneman, Abraham	303, 798	Van Houten, Coriner	416
Vaneman, Amos	839	Van Houten, Cornelius	416
Vaneman, Richard	303, 798	Van Houten, Garret	799

Van Houten, Hendrick	799		Van Muler, Cornelius	801
Van Houten, Jacob	799		Van Nark, Jacob	304
Van Houten, John	799		Van Nartar, Joseph	801
Van Houten, John H.	799		Van Nartar, Nathaniel	801
Van Houten, Paulus	124		Van Natter, John	304
Van Houten, Powles	799		Van Nest, Abraham	416
Van Houten, Ralph	799		Van Nest, Abram	801
Van Houten, Roelif	799		Van Nest, Bernard	801
Van Houten, Tunis	479		Van Nest, Cornelius	801
Van Huysen, Hermanis	416		Van Nest, George	479, (2) 801
Vankirk, Arthur	799			
Van Kirk, Benjamin	479		Van Nest, Henry	304, 801
Vankirk, David	799		Van Nest, Jacobus	801
Vankirk, Jemison	799, 800		Van Nest, Jeromus	801
Van Kirk, John	374, (2) 800		Van Nest, Peter	416, 801
			Van Nest, Ruliff	801
Vankirk, Peter	868		Van Nest, Tunis	801
Vankirk, Samuel	303, 800		Van Neste, John	433, 447
Vankirk, William	(3) 800		Vannet, John	304
Van Koyor, Cort	473		VanNetten, John	304
Van Lant, (or Zant) John	800		VanNetter, John	801
			VanNeulen, James	801
Van Lew, Cornelius	800		VanNice, John	801
Van Lew, Denice	800		Vannoller, Cornelius	801
Van Lew, Dennis	800		VanNorden, Daniel	801
Van Lew, Frederick	303, (2) 800		VanNorden, David	(2) 801
			VanNorden, John	802
Van Lew, Hendrick	800		VanNorden, Michael	802
Van Lew, Jeremiah	800		VanNorden, Peter	802
Van Lew, John	800		VanNorden, Tobias	802
Van Lew, Peter	800		VanNorman, James	304, 802
Van Lew, Richard	800		VanNorsdalen, Philip	802
Van Liew, Frederick	845		VanNorsdall, see VanArsdalen	
Van Luven, Abram	800			
Van Marter, John	304		VanNorton (or VanHarton)	304
Van Marter, William	304			
Van Mater, Benjamin	800		VanNortwick, Hendrick	802
Van Mater, Cornelius	416		VanNortwick, Henry C.	802
Van Mater, Crynionce	800		VanNortwick, John	473
Van Mater, Cyrinus	800		VanNortwick, Martin	802
Van Mater, Gilbert	800		VanNortwick, Simon	802
Van Mater, Guisbert	800		VanNostrand, Crisparius	802
Van Mater, John	124		VanNostrand, George	304, 802
Van Meter, Joseph	800		VanNostrand, Jacob	802
Van Mickler, John	800		VanNote, Joseph	802
Van Middleswart, Tunis, Jr.	801		VanNowdent, Michael	802
			Vannoy, Anderson	802
Van Middleswart, Tunis, Sr.	800		Vannoy, John	802
			Vannoy, Joseph	802
Van Middlesworth, Andrew	473		Vannuys, Jacobus	(2) 802
			VanOrde, David	802
Van Middlesworth, John	801		VanOrden, Andrias	802
Van Middlesworth, Thomas	801		VanOrden, Archibald	845
			VanOrden, John	802
Van Middlesworth, Tunis	801		VanOrder, Peter S.	433
			VanOrman, Jonah	868

VanOrman, Josiah	869	VanSickle, Garret	804
VanOrmand, Amos	869	VanSickle, John	(2) 804
VanOrsdol, Cornelius	802	VanSickle, Stephen	804
VanOrsdol, Isaac	802	VanSickle, Thomas	804
VanOrsdol, Jacob	802	VanSickle, William	804
VanOrsdol, John	(2) 802	VanSickle, Zachariah	804
VanOstrand, Jacob	802	VanSkiock, Benjamin	804
VanOstrand, John	(2) 802	VanSkiock, Jonah	804
VanOstrand, Mathew	803	Vanskiver, John	304
VanPelt, ...	433	VanSyckle, Abram	804
VanPelt, Abram	(2) 803	VanSyckle, Cornelius	804
VanPelt, Alexander	803	Vantassel, John	804
VanPelt, Christian	803	Vantilburgh, Henry	804
VanPelt, Christopher	(2) 803	Vantilburgh, John	804
VanPelt, Garret	803	Vantilburgh, William	805
VanPelt, Hendrick	803	Vantine, Abraham	805
VanPelt, Isaac	803	Vantine, Ephraim	805
VanPelt, Jacob	304, (2) 803	Vantine, Isaac	805
		Vantine, Jacob	805
VanPelt, Johannes	803	Vantine, Rynear	805
VanPelt, John	(2) 803	Vantwicke, John	304, 805
VanPelt, Joseph	803, 869	Vantwicke, Joseph	304, 805
VanPelt, Kurlif	803	Vantyle, Abraham	458
VanPelt, Peter	803	VanTyle, Abram	(3) 805
VanPelt, Rulif	803	Vantyle, Isaac	458
VanPelt, Teras	803	VanTyle, John	(2) 805
VanPelt, Tunis	(2) 803	VanTyle, Orto	805
VanPelt, Walter	803	VanVark, James	304
VanPelt, William	473, 803, 804	VanVarrick, James	304
		VanVaughn, William	304
VanReid, Cornelius	304, 804	VanFleet, Garret	805
VanRiper, Caleb	804	VanVleet, John	47, 347, 370
VanRiper, Cornelius	804		
VanRiper, Garret	804	VanVliet, Abraham	304
VanRiper, Harmon	473	VanVoorhees, Abraham	473
VanRiper, John	804	VanVoorhees, Abram	305, 482
VanRiper, Richard	416	VanVoorhees, Jacobus	473
VanRiper, Thomas	804	VanVoorheese, Abram	805
VanSant, John	804	VanVoorheese, Abram, Jr.	805
VanSchaick, Court	804	VanVoorheese, Albert	805
VanSchoutz, Benjamin	804	VanVoorheese, Albert P.	805
VanSchoven, Albert	804	VanVoorheese, Court	805
VanSciver, Abram	804	VanVoorheese, John	805
VanSciver, Albert	304	VanVoorheese, Peter	805
VanSciver, Barnabas	804	VanVoorheese, William	805
VanSciver, Daniel	804	VanVoorst, Cornelius	339, 361
VanSciver, John	804	VanWagonen, C.	805
VanSciver, Walter	804	VanWagoner, Conrad	805
VanSeaman, ...	124	VanWickle, Henry	805
VanSickell, Andrew	473	VanWinkle, Elias	805
VanSickle, see also, Sickle		VanWinkle, Epson	124
		VanWinkle, Henry	805
VanSickle, Andrew	804	VanWinkle, Jacob	441
VanSickle, Ferdinand	804	VanWinkle, John	806

VanWinkle, Luke	806	Vliet, John	370
VanWinkle, Peter	806	Vliet, William	807
VanWinkle, Simeon	327, 416, 806	Voght, John	807
		Voorhees, Aaron	807
VanWinkle, Simon	806	Voorhees, Abraham	305, 473, 807
VanWinkle, Simson	806		
VanWinkle, Walling	458	Voorhees, Abram	482, 807, 854
VanWinkle, William	806		
VanWinkler, Evert	806	Voorhees, Albert	134, (2) 305, 807
VanZandt, Barnabas	806		
VanZandt, Jacob	806	Voorhees, Cornelius	372, 842
VanZandt, John	806	Voorhees, Court	(2) 807
VanZandt, Peter	(2) 806	Voorhees, Daniel	434
Vanzell, Henry	305	Voorhees, Folkard	807
VanZyle, Albert	806	Voorhees, Garret	(2) 305, 473, 807, 869
Varmon, Nehemiah	806		
Varrick, Abram	806		
Varrick, John	806	Voorhees, George	305, (2) 807
Vate, see Yates			
Vaugh, Jacob	806	Voorhees, Garardus	807
Vaughan, William	305	Voorhees, Gilbert	807
Vaughn, Daniel	441	Voorhees, Grades	807
Vaughn, George	850	Voorhees, Guisbert	807
Vaughn, John	305, 806	Voorhees, Henry	807
Vaughn, Samuel	806	Voorhees, Isaac	460, 479
Vaughn, William	305	Voorhees, Jacob	473
Vaught, Peter	806	Voorhees, James	305, 484, (2) 807
Veal, Noah	806		
Veal, William	305, 806	Voorhees, James J.	807
Veghte, Henry	806	Voorhees, James R.	807
Veghte, Rynear	416	Voorheese, Jaques	808
Venet, John	305	Voorhees, Jeremiah	808
Verbryck, Ralph	806	Voorhees, John	305, 416, 808, 845
Verbryck, Samuel	806		
Verbryck, Samuel G.	458	Voorhees, John, Jr.	416
Verbryck, William	347, 370, 376	Voorhees, John L.	447
		Voorhees, Lucas	(2) 808
Verbryke, Samuel	328, 458	Voorhees, Martin	484
Vermule, Eder	433	Voorhees, Martines	808
Vernalen, Abram	806	Voorhees, Minnah	808
Vernon, David	806	Voorhees, Minne	77, 837
Verrcler, Samuel	806	Voorhees, Nicholas	808
Vervelen, Abram	806	Voorhees, Obadiah	808
Vervelen, Daniel	806	Voorhees, Peter G.	808
Vervelen, John	806	Voorhees, Teunis	872
Vervelen, Samuel	806	Voorhees, Theunis	77
Vickars, Samuel	74	Voorhees, Tunis	808
Vincent, ...	416	Voorhees, William	473, (3) 808
Vincent, John	305, (2) 807		
		Voorheese, Abram	808
Vincent, Levi	305, 807	Voorheese, David	808
Vint, John	305, 807	Voorheese, Garret	(2) 808
Vliet, Daniel	807	Voorheese, Garret R.	808
Vliet, David	416, 807	Voorheese, Hendrick	808
Vliet, Jacob	807	Voorheese, Henry	305, (2) 808

Voorheese, Isaac	808			Vunck, Henry	479	
Voorheese, Jacob	(3) 808			Vunn, John	810	
Voorheese, Jacobus	808					
Voorheese, Jacques	808					
Voorheese, James	808			Waddell, Henry	417	
Voorheese, John	808, 809			Wade, see also, Ward		
Voorheese, Martines	809			Wade, Abner	810	
Voorheese, Obadiah	809			Wade, Calvin	810	
Voorheese, Paul	305, 809			Wade, Daniel	810	
Voorheese, Peter	(2) 809			Wade, Henry	134, 810	
Voorheese, Ram	809			Wade, Henry, Jr.	306	
Voorheese, Roeliff	809			Wade, Jonathan	473	
Voorhies, Daniel	809			Wade, Joseph	810, 854	
Voorhies, John R.	809			Wade, Matthias	810	
Voorhies, Peter V.	14, 15, 29, 30, (2) 50, 87			Wade, Nathan	810	
				Wade, Nathaniel	810	
				Wade, Nehe(h)iah	379	
				Wade, Nehemiah	341, 370	
Vorehase, Oake	458			Wade, Noadiah	39, 88	
Vorhiss, John	833			Wade, Obediah	810	
Vorious, Nicholas	809			Wade, Robert	434	
Vorious, Peter	809			Wade, Simon	810	
Vory, Isaiah	809			Wade, Thomas	810	
Vosseller, Jacob	809			Wade, Timothy	306, 810	
Vosseller, Jacob, Jr.	809			Wager, Charles	810	
Vosseller, Lucas	809			Wager, Ezra	810	
Vosseller, Luke	809			Wager, James	306, 810	
Vosseller, Peter	809			Waggoner, Adam	810	
Vought, see Fough				Waggoner, Christopher	810	
Vourhase, Abraham	479			Waggoner, George	124, 810	
Vredenburgh, ...	305			Waggoner, John	(2) 810	
Vredenburgh, Isaac	77			Waggoner, Michael	306	
Vredenburgh, James	305			Waglum, Benjamin	306	
Vredenburgh, John	77			Waglum, John	417	
Vreden, Jacobus	305			Wagoner, John	306	
Vredon, James	305			Wainright, Thomas	417	
Vreedenburgh (alias VanGordon) James	809			Wainright, John	810	
				Wainright, Vincent	810	
Vreeland, Abraham	306, (2) 809			Wake, John	810	
				Walbrook, William	124	
Vreeland, Abram	479			Walburn, Francis	139	
Vreeland, Cornelius	809			Waldie, John	855	
Vreeland, Daniel	306, 809			Waldron, Benjamin	811	
Vreeland, Garret	809			Waldron, Chris	811	
Vreeland, Garret, G.	473			Waldron, Cornelius	811	
Vreeland (or Freeland) John	306, 417			Waldron, Samuel	306, 811	
				Waldron, William	811	
Vreeland, Michael	809			Waldruff, George	811	
Vreeland, Peter	809			Walker, Aaron.F.	811	
Vroom, George	809			Walker, Aaron Forman	482	
Vroom, Hendrick P.	473			Walker, Abram	811	
Vroom, John	810			Walker, Asher	811	
Vroom, Peter	810			Walker, Benjamin	811	
Vroom, Peter D.	347, 362			Walker, Forman	811	

Walker, Francis	306, 811	Walton, William	473
Walker, George	52, 53, 94, (2) 811	Wambaugh, Henry	473
		Wanamager, Henry	812
		Wanamaker, Henry	459
Walker, Isaac	811	Wandall, David	307
Walker, James	811	Wandall, Jacob	307
Walker, John	124, 306, (3) 811	Wandle, Samuel	812
		Wanton, John	872
Walker, Masher	134	Ward, Abijah	812
Walker, Paddy	306	Ward, Amos	812
Walker, Ralph	855	Ward, Benjamin	307
Walker, Robert	441, 811, 833	Ward, Bethuel	812
		Ward, Caleb	134, 812
Walker, Samuel	811	Ward, Caleb, Jr.	812
Walker, Thomas	811	Ward (or Wade), Calvin	307
Walker, William	139	Ward, David	812
Wall, George	306, 811	Ward, Edward	812
Wall, James	306, 434, 447, 811	Ward, Enos	812
		Ward, George	812
Wall, John	458	Ward, Isaac	307
Wallace, John	811	Ward, Israel	417
Wallace, William	306, 811	Ward, Israel, Jr.	812
Wallen, John	811	Ward, Jabez	812
Wallen, Robert	306	Ward, Jacob	812
Wallen, William	811	Ward, James	(2) 812
Wallenger, Jacob	137	Ward, John	307, 812
Walles, John	812	Ward, John B.	307
Walling, Carhart	306, 812	Ward, Jonas	327, 417, 813
Walling, Daniel	812		
Walling, F ...	458	Ward, Jonathan	307, 417, 813, 869
Walling, James	306, 812		
Walling, John	(2) 812	Ward, Joseph	813
Walling, Joseph	306, 434	Ward, Josiah	813
Walling, Ladis	370	Ward, Matthias	341, 362
Walling, Louis	417	Ward, Nathaniel	813
Walling, Philip	812	Ward, Nehemiah	307
Walling, Thomas	417	Ward, Peter	47, 328, 417
Wallinger, Jacob	306		
Walmsley, Christopher	434	Ward, Samuel	813
Walsh, David	306	Ward, Samuel C.	813
Walsh, James	306	Ward, Stephen	813
Walsh, Michael	306	Ward, Timothy	(2) 813
Walter, Henry	482	Ward, Timothy C.	434
Walter, Jacob	(2) 812	Ward, William	307, (2) 813
Walter, John	812		
Walter, Richard	812	Ward, Zebina	813
Walters, Jacob	306	Ward, Zenus	813
Walters, John	(2) 307	Wardell, see also, Fowler	
Walters, John, Jr.	307		
Walton, Carhart	812	Wardell (alias Fowler), Robert	307
Walton, Elisha	344, 370		
Walton, Job	458	Warden, Paul	307
Walton, John	328, 329, 417, 441	Ware, James	869
		Ware, Thomas	813

Waring, Thomas	855	Webb, Henry	814, 845
Warman (or Warner) William	307, 813	Webb, Matthew	814
		Webb, Matthias	814
Warne, Elijah	813	Webber, John	814
Warner, see also Warman		Weblinger, Jacob	308, 814
		Webster, John	47, 343, 357
Warner, ...	872		
Warner, Benjamin	441	Webster, Roswell	814
Warner, Charles	307	Webster, Thomas	308, 814
Warner, George	813	Weeden, James	814
Warner, John	813	Weeks, Arthur	814
Warner, Joseph	813	Weeks (alias Green), James	815
Warner, Joshua	813		
Warren, Charles	307, 813	Weeks, Job	815
Warren, Elijah	813	Weeks, John	815
Warren, James	813	Weeks, Richard	815
Warrick, John	813	Weeks, Zephaniah	815
Wart, George	307	Wegton, Samuel	308, 815
Wartenby, William	814	Weis, Jacob	834
Warters, Silas	479	Welch, David	308
Wartnabe, William	814	Welch, George	815
Washburn, Nathaniel	814	Welch, Hugh	815
Washer, George	814	Welch, James	(2) 308, 815
Washington, ..	42		
Washington, General	(2) 41, 60, 64, 321, 336, 350, 352, 402, 445	Welch, John	815
		Welch, Peter	434
		Welch, William	417
		Welcher, John	815
		Welden, Alexander	815
Watere, Jacob	814	Welden, Seth	815
Waters, Henry	307, 814	Weldron, Thomas	815
Waters, Jacob	814, 869	Welet, Valentine	815
Waterson, Thomas	307, 814	Weller, Philip	815
Watkins, Thomas	307, 814	Weller, Thomas	815
Watson, David	308	Wellice, John	815
Watson, John	308, (3) 814	Welling, John	(2) 815
		Wells, Elisha	370
Watson, William	308, 417, (2) 814	Wells, Enos	61, 308
		Wells, Peter	815
Watts, Bowan	814	Welsh, David	308
Watts, Bowen	308	Welsh, John	869
Watts, Robert	134	Welsh, Michael	308, 815
Wayne, Anthony	42, 68	Welsh, Nathaniel	308, 815
Wayne, John	308	Welsh, Thomas	309
Weasel, Michael	869	Welstead, Edward	855
Weatherby, Benjamin	56, 88, 434, 814	Weltner, Lewis	61
		Wence, Jacob	815
Weatherby, David	417, 814	Wench, James	309, 815
Weatherby, George	814	Wench, John	309
Weatherby, William	814	Wendell, David	309
Weatherton, John	459	Wendell, Jacob	309
Weaver, Anthony	308, 814	Wendover, Hercules	815
Weaver, John	308, 814	Wendover, Hercules, Jr.	815
Weaver, Joseph	417	Wentzel, ...	418

Name	Page
Wentzel, Daniel	417, 418
Wentzel, David	418
Werts, William	815
Weser, Jacob	815
Wessels, Hendrick	815
Wessels, Jacob	816
Wessels, Joseph	309
Wessels, Wessel F.	816
Wessells, Nicholas	309
Wessell, Samuel	309
West, Frederick	816
West, George	858
West, Israel	816
West, Jacob	324, 347, 357, 838
West, John	309
West, Stephen	309, 816
West, Thomas	124, 816
West, Uriah	816
West, William	309
Westbrook, Aaron	816
Westbrook, Abram	816
Westbrook, Avan Ross	374
Westbrook, Cornelius	816
Westbrook, Henry	816
Westbrook, Housever	448
Westbrook, James	816
Westbrook, John	816
Westbrook, John J.	816
Westbrook, Onee	434
Westbrook, Peter	418
Westbrook, Samuel	326, 348, 370
Westbrook, Severyne	459
Westbrook, Wilhelmus	328, 459
Westcott, Arthur	441
Westcott, John	(2) 320, 418
Westcott, Richard	342, 370
Westcott, Samuel	418
Westervelt, ...	434
Westervelt, Albert	309, 816
Westervelt, Benjamin	816
Westervelt, Benjamin P.	816
Westervelt, Casparus	816
Westervelt, Cornelius	473
Westervelt, Cornelius P.	474
Westervelt, Jeremiah	816
Westervelt, Johannes	816
Westervelt, John	816
Westervelt, Uriah	816
Westfall, Benjamin	818
Westfall, Cornelius	816
Westfall, David	816
Westfall, Jacobus	816
Westfall, James	816
Westfall, Samuel	816
Westfall, Wilhelm	418
Weston, Paul	309
Weston, William	309
Wetchell, Jacob	309
Wetherhawk, Johannes	816
Wetherill, ...	(2) 418
Wetherill, John	343, 357
Wetherington, Benjamin	309, 817
Wetherington, David	817
Weverling, Peter	309
Wey, Stephen	817
Weyman, Abel	38, 39, 40, 52, 53, 88, 459
Whalen, James	434
Wahling, Richard	309
Wharr (or Whurr) John	309
Wharr (or Whurr) William	309
Wheatly, Joseph	309
Wheaton, Elijah	309
Wheaton, Isaac	448
Wheaton, J ...	418
Wheaton, Joseph	448
Wheaton, Peter	817
Wheaton, Robert	817, 869
Wheaton, Samuel	310
Wheaton, Silas	817
Wheaton, Uriah	817
Wheavour, Adolphus	817
Wheeler, Caleb	817
Wheeler, Charles	817
Wheeler, Ebenezer	817
Wheeler, Ezra	817
Wheeler, James	418
Wheeler, Joseph	418
Wheeler, Simon	817
Wherry, Robert	124
Whilden, Seth	418
Whilson, Peter	817
Whilsin, William	817
Whitacar, Joseph	817
Whitacre, Samuel	817
Whitaker, Elinathan	310, 817
Whitaker, John	310, 817
Whitaker, Jonathan, Jr.	474
Whitaker, Nathaniel	474
Whitaker, Stephen	434

Name	Pages	Name	Pages
White, Anthony Walton	20, 59, 64	Whitlock, John	434, 818
White, Caleb	310, 817	Whitlock, Lockhart	818
White, David	310	Whitlock, Robert	818
White, Denice	817	Whitlock, William	818
White, Denny	817	Whitmore, Amos	311
White, Henry	310, 817	Whitmore, Jonas	819
White, Jacob	(2) 310, 817	Whitnack, Abraham	819
White, James	817	Whitnack, Andries	819
White, Jennings	817	Whitnack, Benjamin	819
White, John	(3) 310, (2) 817, (2) 818	Whitney, Thomas	311
		Whitsey, James	311
		Whittall, Benjamin	320, 418
		Whitton, William	855
		Wholehan, Martin	311
White, Joseph	(2) 310	Whortman, John	819
White, Joshua	818	Whurr, see Wharr	
White, Lewis	818	Wible, Robert	311, 819
White, Peter	310	Wick, John	819
White, Samuel	310, 818	Wick, Morris	819
White, Thomas	(3) 310, 818	Wick, Moses	819
		Wick, William	819
White, William	818	Wicker, Samuel	311
Whiteal, Nathan	818	Wickes, Lambert	872
Whiteanack, Bleker	818	Wickoff, Cornelius	819
Whiteaneck, John	818	Wickoff, Garret	(3) 819
Whitecar, Benjamin	484	Wickoff, Jacob	(2) 819
Whitecar, Thomas	434	Wickoff, Joachan	819
Whitehead, Aaron	818	Wickoff, John	(2) 819
Whitehead, Abner	818	Wickoff, Peter	819
Whitehead, Daniel	818	Wickoff, Samuel	819
Whitehead, David	818	Wickoff, William	819
Whitehead, Jacob	818	Wickstroff, Peter	819
Whitehead, James	310	Widenor, Michael	819
Whitehead, John	818	Wiggins, Jonathan	855
Whitehead, Moses	818	Wiggins, Thomas	311, 819
Whitehead, Onis	818	Wiggon, James	311
Whitehead, Samuel	311, (2) 818	Wigon, James	819
		Wigton, Samuel	124, 474
Whitehill, Thomas	869	Wikoff, Auke	345, 357
Whitekar, Carrol	134	Wikoff, Jacob	869
Whitemore, Jonas	311	Wikoff, Peter	418
Whitenaught, Andreas	818	Wikoff, William	479
Whitenaught, John	818	Wilabee, William	311, 819
Whitenight, Abram	818	Wilber, John	819
Whitenight, John	818	Wilber, William	819
Whiterhock, John	311	Wilberson, Steron	820
Whiting, David	311	Wilbur, Richard	820
Whitlock, ...	818	Wilcocks, Daniel	311, 820
Whitlock, Ephraim	38, 39, 40, 50, 51, 70, 459	Wilcocks, Isaac	311, 820
		Wilcocks, James	311, 820
		Wilcocks, John	311, 820
		Wilcox, Daniel	820
Whitlock, James	311, 344, 371, (2) 818	Wilcox, Thomas	(2) 820
		Wild, John	820
		Wildrick, Michael	311

Name	Page
Wiles, Daniel	820
Wiley, James	820
Wiley, John	311, 820
Wilgus, James	855
Wilgus, William	(2) 820, 845
Wilhelm, Henry	311, 820
Wilkins, Jeptha	820
Wilkins, John	820
Wilkinson, J. Dunham	312, 820
Wilkinson, James	(2) 820
Wilkinson, John	419, 820
Wilkinson, Nathaniel	837
Wilkinson, Samuel	312, 820
Wilkinson, Thomas	820
Wilkinson, William	312, 820
Wilkison, Aaron	820
Wilkison, Nathan	35, 37, 54, 55, 94
Will (Negro)	869
Willer, Jacob	820
Willer, Peter	820
Willer, Philip	820
Willes, Isaac	125
Willet, John	474
Willet, Jonathan	474
Willets, Hope	872
Willets, James, Jr.	419
Willett, Amos	820
Willett, Cornelius	474
Willett, Hartshorn	821
Willett, Humphrey	821
Willett, Joseph	821
Willett, Peter	(2) 821
Willett, Samuel	(2) 821
Willett, Taylor	821
Williams, Aaron	821
Williams, Abner	821
Williams, Benjamin	821
Williams, Burnett	312
Williams, Caleb	821
Williams, Charles	821
Williams, Cornelius	327, 419, 821
Williams, Daniel	312, 821
Williams, David	312, 474, (2) 821
Williams, David, Jr.	821
Williams, Ebenezer	821
Williams, Edward	312, 821
Williams, Eleizer	821
Williams, Elijah	821
Williams, Enoch	821
Williams, Enos	821
Williams, George	821
Williams, Henry	474, 312
Williams, Isaac	312, (2) 821
Williams, James	(2) 312, (2) 821
Williams, Jarus	822
Williams, Jedediah	822
Williams, Joel	822
Williams, John	134, (4) 312, (5) 822, 855
Williams, Jonathan	822
Williams, Joseph	312, (2) 822, 855
Williams, Joshua	822
Williams, Matthias	822
Williams, Miles	822
Williams, Moses	312, 822
Williams, Nathan	312, 822
Williams, Noah	822
Williams, Owen	312, 822
Williams, Peter	312
Williams, Samuel	(3) 822
Williams, Silas	312
Williams, Simeon	822
Williams, Simon	822
Williams, Squier	822
Williams, Stephen	(2) 822
Williams, Thomas	313, 419
Williams, William	(2) 313, (2) 822
Williams, Zenus	822
Williamson, Abram	822
Williamson, Arthur	822
Williamson, Bar	822
Williamson, Benjamin	839
Williamson, Cornelius	823
Williamson, David	823
Williamson, Garret	313
Williamson, Henry	313, 823
Williamson, Isaac	474
Williamson, Jacob	313, (2) 823, 869
Williamson, James	823
Williamson, John	313, 434, (2) 823
Williamson, Joseph	823
Williamson, Matthias	323, 339, 350, 834
Williamson, Matthias, Jr.	837
Williamson, Nicholas	823
Williamson, Peter	483
Williamson, Richard	313

Williamson, William	419, (2) 823	Wilson, Robert	434
		Wilson, Robert, Sr.	825
Willin, Henry	313, 823	Wilson, Shinah	825
Willing, John	328, 372	Wilson, Stafford	825
Willing, M ...	459	Wilson, Thomas	(2) 825
Willion, Moses	313	Wilson, William	314, (3) 825
Willis, Abram	869		
Willis, Bethuel	823	Winans, Abraham	825
Willis, Henry	823	Winans, Benjamin	419
Willis, Isaac	823	Winans, Elias	434
Willis, John	419, 823	Winans, John	825
Willis (or Willys) Joseph	(2) 313, (3) 823	Winans, Kelsey	825
		Winans, Lewis	825
Willis, Russel	823	Winans, Matthias	825
Willis, (or Willy) Samuel	823, 869	Winans, Moses	825
		Winans, Samuel	825
Willis, William	(2) 823	Winans, William	825
Willock, William	(2) 823	Winants, William	336, 341, 378
Willson, John	125		
Willy, see Willis		Wincoop, Cornelius	825
Willys, see Willis		Windany, Jacob	855
Wilmot, Amos	869	Winds, Barney	825
Wilmot, Edward, Jr.	419	Winds, Brigadier General	365
Wilmouth, Lazaruse	823		
Wilrick, Michael	824	Winds, Lieutenant Colonel	15
Wilsey, John	824		
Wilson, Albert	474	Winds, Samuel	825
Wilson, Andrew	313, 824	Winds, William	(2) 13, 65, 345, 350
Wilson, Benjamin	824		
Wilson, Calvin	824	Winfield, David	825
Wilson, D ...	434	Winfield, Emanuel	825
Wilson, Daniel	(2) 824	Winfield, Henry	825
Wilson, Elijah	824	Winfield, Matthew	314, 825
Wilson, Francis	824	Winget, Benjamin	826, 869
Wilson, Garret	313, 824	Winget, Joshua	826
Wilson, Henry	313	Winings, Benjamin	826
Wilson, Isaac	(2) 824	Winings, Craton	826
Wilson, Israel	824	Winings, Philip	826
Wilson, Jacob	(2) 824	Winn, Henry	314
Wilson, James	(2) 313, (4) 824	Winn, John	314
		Winn, Josiah	826
Wilson, Jeremiah	313, 824	Winner, Abram.	846
Wilson, John	(2) 313, (2) 314, (6) 824, 850, 869	Winner, Jacob	826
		Winner, John	826
		Winser, Comfort	826
		Winter, Henry, Jr.	448
Wilson, Joseph	(2) 825	Winter, Isaac	419
Wilson, Kindert	825	Winter, Jacob	314, 419, 479, (2) 826
Wilson, Lawrence	825, 839		
Wilson, Lewis	74		
Wilson, Mindart	825	Winter, James	826
Wilson, Moses	314	Winter, John	459
Wilson, Nathaniel	825	Winter, Joseph	314, (2) 826
Wilson, Peter	825		

Winter, Peter	826	Wood, Timothy	855
Wintermute, George	826	Wood, William	(3) 315,
Wintermute, Peter	826		(3) 827
Winters, Henry	869	Wooden (or Wooten)	315
Winters, James	314	Morris	
Wintersteen, Henry	826	Woodes, John	315
Wintersteen, Jacob	826	Woodes, William	315, 827
Wintersteen, Jacobus	826	Woodeth, John	315
Wintersteen, James	484	Woodhouse, Mansfield	435
Wintersteen, Nicholas	826	Wooding, James	827
Winterstein, Philip	459	Woodman, Joseph	827
Witchel, Jacob	314, 826	Woodmancy, Asa	827
Witherspoon, James	69	Woodmancy, David	827
Witherspoon, John	74	Woodmancy, James	827
Witt, Francis	826	Woodruff, Aaron	827
Woan, Peter	826	Woodruff, Abram	827
Woglum, John	826	Woodruff, Amos	48, 419
Wolf, David	835	Woodruff, Benjamin	827
Wolf, Sebastian	855	Woodruff, Caleb	827
Wolfe, George	826	Woodruff, Daniel	315, 828
Wolfe, Henry	314	Woodruff, David	327, 435,
Wolfe, Peter	826		(2) 828
Wollea, Joseph	826	Woodruff, Ebenezer	(2) 315
Wood, ...	419	Woodruff, Eleazer	315, 828
Wood, Aaron	827	Woodruff, Elias	379
Wood, Abram	(2) 314	Woodruff, Enos	828
Wood, Asa	827	Woodruff, Enos, Jr.	459
Wood, Azariah	827	Woodruff, Ephraim	(2) 315,
Wood, Benjamin	314, (2)		435
	827	Woodruff, Ezekiel, Jr.	341, 371
Wood, Ceah	869	Woodruff, Gabriel	828
Wood, Christopher	827	Woodruff, Ichabod	315
Wood, Clement	39, 108	Woodruff, Isaac	315
Wood, Daniel	314, (2)	Woodruff, Jacob	828
	827	Woodruff, Jesse	828
Wood, Daniel S.	419	Woodruff, Job	315, 828
Wood, Ellis	314	Woodruff, John	(2) 316,
Wood, Ezekiah	827		(2) 828
Wood, Ezekiel	314	Woodruff, Jonathan	316, 828
Wood, George	(2) 827	Woodruff, Joseph	828
Wood, Isaac	314	Woodruff, Josiah	828
Wood, Jehu	419	Woodruff, Lewis	38, 102,
Wood, Jeremiah	827		448
Wood, Jesse	827	Woodruff, Nathaniel	828, 855,
Wood, John	315, 419,		869
	833, 855,	Woodruff, Pierson	828
	869	Woodruff, Robert	828
Wood, Jonas	474	Woodruff, Samuel	(3) 828,
Wood, Jonathan	419		842
Wood, Joseph	315, 827	Woodruff, Stephen	316, 828
Wood, Joseph, Sr.	827	Woodruff, Thomas	828, 843
Wood, Josiah	315	Woodruff, Timothy	828
Wood, Matthias	827	Woodruff, Uzal	316, 828
Wood, Michael	315, 827	Woodruff, Watts	828
Wood, Reuben	315, 827	Woodsides, Robert	316

Woodward, Asa	316		Wright, Joseph	317, 420, 829
Wool, Isaiah	88			
Wool, Jeremiah	828		Wright, Nathan	38, 40, 102, 833
Woolcocks, John	828			
Woolever, Benjamin	828		Wright, Nathaniel	835
Wooley, ...	419		Wright, Samuel	317
Wooley, Abraham	474		Wright, Smith	829
Wooley, Abram	828		Wright, Thomas	317, 829
Wooley, Jacob	869		Wright, William	317
Wooley, Samuel	828, 870		Wrose, Joseph	829
Wooley, Stephen	828		Wyckoff, Garret	830
Wooley, William	829		Wyckoff, George	474
Woolinger, Jacob	316		Wyckoff, Isaac	830
Woolley, Isaac	316, 829		Wyckoff, John	(2) 830
Woolley, Jacob	316, 829		Wyckoff, John B.	830
Woolsey, ..	419		Wyckoff, John C.	474
Woolsey, Ephraim	829		Wyckoff, Peter	420, 830
Woolsey, Isaac	316		Wye, N ...	870
Woolson, John	829		Wygant, James	317
Woolston, Joseph	419		Wyley, John	830
Woolverton, John	829		Wyllys, Joseph	830
Woolverton, Stephen	829		Wynn, Henry	830
Woolverton, Thomas	420			
Wooten, see Wooden				
Wordin, Samuel	125		Yard, Daniel	838
Workman, Morris	829		Yard, Elijah	830
Workman, Samuel	316		Yard, Furman	834
Worne, Benjamin	441		Yard, Isaiah	420
Worrall, William	316		Yard, John	317
Worrell, Nicholas	829		Yard, Josiah	435, 833
Worrick, Samuel	829		Yard, Samuel	830
Worth, George	316		Yard, Thomas	16, 32, 33, 88, 845
Worth, James	829, 837			
Worth, John	829			
Worth, William	316, 346, 379, 829		Yatee, John	317
			Yateman, John	830
Wortman, Abraham	829		Yates, Benjamin	830
Wortman, Andrew	829		Yates, Ephraim	830, 870
Wortman, David	829		Yates, Jacob	870
Wortman, John	479, 829, 850		Yates, James	317
			Yates, John	135, 317
Wortman, Samuel	61, 316		Yates, Joseph	125, 830
Wradley, William	829		Yates, (or Vate) Richard	448
Wrese, Joseph	479			
Wright, Charles	829		Yates, Thomas	870
Wright, David	(2) 316		Yates, William	317, 830
Wright, Edward	829		Yawger, Peter	830
Wright, George	125		Yeagley, Adam	830
Wright, Gilbert	855		Yeardon, William	317
Wright, Jacob	316, 829		Yearton, Peter	317
Wright, James	317, 420, 441, 829		Yeaters, John	317
			Yeates, John	459
Wright, John	125, (2) 317, (2) 829, 837		Yeates, Robert	830
			Yeatry, John	317
			Yeoman, see also, Youmans	

Yeoman (or Youmans) Isaac	830	Young, Jonas	831
		Young, Josiah	870
Yeomans, see also, Youmans		Young, Morgan	831, 855
		Young, Nathan	831
Yeomans, Moses	839	Young, Noah	831
Yetman, James	125	Young, Peter	479, 855
Yherts, John	317	Young, Philip	318, 479, (3) 831, 870
Yorke, Andrew	346, 374		
Yorty, Frederick	135		
Youmans, see also, Yeoman, Yeomans		Young, Powell	831
		Young, Robert	831
Youmans, (or Yeomans) Isaac	317	Young, Stephen	(2) 831
		Young, Sylvester	(2) 318
Young, A ...	850	Young, Thomas	318, 855
Young, Aaron	317, 830	Young, Uriah	(2) 831
Young, Amos	830	Young, William	831, 870
Young, Daniel	(2) 830	Younglove, ...	108
Young, David	317, 830	Youngs, David	474
Young, Ephraim	830	Yourson, Giles	318, 831
Young, George	830		
Young, Gilbert	830, 839		
Young, Grover	830		
Young, Hance	831	Zabriskie, John	339, 362
Young, Henry	317, 435, 459, 834	Zabriskie, Yost	435
		Zane, Elnathan	845
Young, Hezekiah	831	Zant, see Van Lant	
Young, James	474, (4) 831, 870	Zeak, Baltus	318
		Zeoliff, Daniel	831, 858
Young, John	135, 318, (3) 831, 870	Zimmerman, Jacob	831
		Zopus, Isaac	318

www.ingramcontent.com/pod-product-compliance
Lightning Source LLC
Chambersburg PA
CBHW070913160426
43193CB00011B/1444